Strategic Reputation Management

Strategic Reputation Management examines the ways in which organizations achieve "goodness" through reputation, reputation management, and reputation strategies. It presents a contemporary model of strategic reputation management, helping organizations and stakeholders to analyze the business environment as a communicative field of symbols and meanings in which the organization is built or destroyed. Authors Pekka Aula and Saku Mantere introduce the eight generic reputation strategies, through which organizations can organize their stakeholder relationships in various ways. They illustrate their arguments using real-world examples and studies, from the Finnish Ski Association to Philip Morris International.

This book will serve as required reading in advanced courses covering public-relations practice, advanced topics in PR, corporate communication, management, and marketing. Professionals working in PR, business, management, and marketing will also find much of interest in this volume.

Pekka Aula is Professor of Communication at Department of Communication, University of Helsinki, Finland. His research interests lie in the problematic of formation and reformation, construction and reconstruction of communicative processes in and between complex organizational networks. His has published and edited several books, and published articles in national and international journals. He is also adjunct Professor at the University of Jyvaskyla.

Saku Mantere is acting Professor of Management and Organization at Swedish School of Economics and Business Administration in Helsinki, Finland. His research is focused on understanding organizational strategy as a social phenomenon, e.g., its discourses, practices, and social positions. He has published in journals such as *Organization Science, Journal of Management Studies, Strategic Organization,* and *Journal of Organizational Change Management,* and *Business & Society* and *Scandinavian Journal of Management.*

LEA's Communication Series
Jennings Bryant/Dolf Zillman, General Editors

Selected titles in Public Relations (James Grunig, Advisory Editor) include:

Aula/Mantere—*Strategic Reputation Management: Towards a Company of Good*

Austin/Pinkleton—*Strategic Public Relations Management: Planning and Managing Effective Communication Programs*

Culbertson/Chen—*International Public Relations: A Comparative Analysis*

Fearn-Banks—*Crisis Communications: A Casebook Approach*, second edition

Grunig/Grunig/Dozier—*Excellent Public Relations and Effective Organizations: A Study of Communication Management in Three Countries*

Hearit—*Crisis Management by Apology: Corporate Response to Allegations of Wrongdoing*

Lamb/McKee—*Applied Public Relations: Cases in Stakeholder Management*

Ledingham/Bruning—*Public Relations as Relationship Management: A Relational Approach to the Study and Practice of Public Relations*

Lerbinger—*The Crisis Manager: Facing Risk and Responsibility*

Mickey—*Deconstructing Public Relations: Public Relations Criticism*

Millar/Heath—*Responding to Crisis: A Rhetorical Approach to Crisis Communication*

Spicer—*Organizational Public Relations: A Political Perspective*

Strategic Reputation Management

Towards a company of good

Pekka Aula and Saku Mantere

Routledge
Taylor & Francis Group

LONDON AND NEW YORK

First published by
Lawrence Erlbaum Associates
10 Industrial Avenue
Mahwah, New Jersey 07430

Reprinted 2009
by Routledge
270 Madison Ave, New York, NY 10016

Simultaneously published in the UK
by Routledge
2 Park Square, Milton Park, Abingdon, Oxon OX14 4RN

Routledge is an imprint of the Taylor & Francis Group, an informa business

© 2008 Taylor & Francis

Typeset in Sabon by The Running Head Limited, Cambridge
www.therunninghead.com
Printed by the MPG Books Group in the UK

Library of Congress Cataloging in Publication Data

Aula, Pekka.
  Strategic reputation management : towards a company of good / by Pekka Aula
and Saku Mantere.
    p. cm.
      Includes bibliographical references.
  1. Corporate image—Management. 2. Corporations—Public relations.
  3. Communication in management. 4. Strategic planning. I. Mantere, Saku. II. Title.
    HD59.2.A95 2008
    659.2—dc22   2007044930

ISBN 10: 0–8058–6425–3 (hbk)
ISBN 10: 0–8058–6426–1 (pbk)
ISBN 10: 1–4106–1859–5 (ebk)

ISBN 13: 978–0–8058–6425–0 (hbk)
ISBN 13: 978–0–8058–6426–7 (pbk)
ISBN 13: 978–1–4106–1859–7 (ebk)

Contents

Figures and tables

Figures

Tables

Preface

A good company is a paradox. Contemporary organizations have to be good, look good, and perform good deeds. Yet, at the same time, truly ethical business is unethical. An ethical company easily betrays its promise of profit-making to the shareholders, while ethical actions fail to be authentic if the only underlying objective is to make profit. Despite this, most companies and other organizations strive to be "good companies"—to be organizations with a good reputation.

The book is built around four main themes: good reputation, doing good, communicating the good, and making good relations. We argue that the three latter themes constitute the first—a good reputation is built on the foundation of doing, and communicating about, deeds that can stand the light of day. Good deeds do not constitute a reputation if nobody knows about them; that is, if they are not communicated. Furthermore, in a network society, it is central to have a strategy about whom one communicates with.

Strategic Reputation Management is a conceptual book combining both academic and professional genres. It builds on the authors' vast research and consulting experience, and draws on a comprehensive literature and research review on reputation management from communication and strategy perspectives. We build on data gathered from various research and organizational development projects. The book utilizes a database of 300 interviews on corporate strategy matters, dozens of interviews on reputation management, and content analysis of reputation media coverage.

The book is written for three audiences. First, we seek to address a gap in academic literature on reputation management. While many authors have addressed the topic, we understand very little of the interpretive processes in which reputation is enacted among organizations and their stakeholders. Second, we hope to cover all the relevant bases in literature so that the book will be a relevant introduction to students in reputation management. Third, we truly wish to communicate with practitioners puzzling over reputation management—be they communications or marketing people, executives, managers, reporters, activists, or concerned citizens.

We have tried to maintain a balance between international case examples and those nearer to us. We are both Finns and feel that our business context contains a number of illuminative cases. We consider their presence in the text to be a strength, as many readers will probably have little access to these discussions. However, we have taken care to avoid marginalizing our arguments, and have included an equal number of cases from across the world. It will be left to the reader to decide whether our choice has been warranted.

Acknowledgments

This book has been written for readers, intrigued by the notion of a good company. What makes us think a company is good, benevolent, capable, nice, friendly, responsible, caring? How do companies strive to be good? Companies devote an enormous amount of time and energy, as well as large sums of money, to make us think of them as good. We believe that good reputation is the key to the processes of becoming good and staying that way. We do not, however, offer an easy solution for building a good reputation. Instead, we aim to demonstrate that a good company's strategic reputation management is full of contradictions. Our aim is to help companies understand the processes of goodness while encouraging the reader to critically examine the notion of goodness in companies and their activities.

The book was created through dialogue between two scholars. "A company of good" represents a middle ground between Pekka's work in the fields of reputation management and organizational communications, and Saku's research on the practice of strategic management and corporate ethics. The preparation of this book was a process, structured by meetings where one of us bought donuts while the other made the coffee. We are quite pleased with each other as we had great fun writing the book.

During the process of writing this book, we have benefited from insights, critique and support by a number of friends and colleagues. Ron E. Rice gave us the push to develop a book for an international audience, and provided help and advice at a number of points along the way. He is, in a way, responsible for us embarking on this project and being able to finalize it. Jouni Heinonen and Tuomo Lähdesmäki read and commented on an earlier manuscript, offering many practical insights. Reijo Jylhä, head coach for cross-country skiing at the Finnish Ski Federation, provided unique insight by analyzing his own organization in the light of our reputation arenas. Reputation Management Consultancy Pohjoisranta provided us with access to reputation research material. Our students on our Reputation Management courses at the University of Helsinki during the fall semesters 2006 and 2007 offered many fine insights which helped propel our arguments forward.

Various colleagues have made a number of insightful suggestions about potential case examples which we have used to illustrate our points. These colleagues are, in alphabetical order: Petri Aaltonen, Antti Ainamo, Igor Blumberg, Frederick Büchner, Joep Cornelissen, Rudy Durand, Patrick Furu, Sudheera Gangireddy, David Ing, Aki-Mauri Huhtinen, Virpi Hämäläinen, Claus Jacobs, Gerry Johnson, Elisa Juholin, Päivi Karjalainen, Eero Korhonen, Wendelin Küpers, Juha-Antti Lamberg, Miia Martinsuo, Markku Maula, Roy Nyberg, Kalle Pajunen, Matleena Pankakoski, Patrick Regnér, Sampsa Samila, David Seidl, John Sillince, Petri Sipilä, Jouni Sipponen, Anders Stenbäck, Kimmo Suominen, Petri Takala, Eero Vaara, Jouni Virtaharju, Liisa Välikangas, Markus Wartiovaara, and Leif Åberg.

We are grateful to the editorial staff at LEA/Routledge, in particular Kerry Breen, Linda Bathgate, and Karin Bates for the fruitful collaboration that we have shared throughout the project. Carole Drummond at The Running Head Limited and Dr John Gaunt have been invaluable in the editing of the manuscript.

We would like to thank the Academy of Finland and the Finnish Work Environment Fund for funding the research work that provided the basis for this book. In addition, we would like to thank the WSOY Literature Foundation for helping us to write this book.

We dedicate the book to our families, Hanna-Mari, Aava, and Saana; and Outi, Tekla, and Iivari.

Pekka Aula and Saku Mantere
Helsinki, Finland
March 2008

Part I

The company of good

A contradiction in terms?

Chapter 1

The question concerning the good company
A good question

> This world is always chasing after clichés, always trying to function according to them regardless of what cliché it is that time—the information society, IT shares, the new economy . . . And these clichés de facto change the way we function.
> (Business area director of a major international corporation)

Routine morning. I wake up and fry some bacon using Flora margarine in a new Teflon-coated frying pan. It's a hot summer's day, so instead of coffee I enjoy some refreshing Nestea iced tea. There has been talk of buying a new car, so on the spur of the moment I reserve a Kia Sportage for a test drive. To get to work I drive a small Hyundai Getz. I feel good; I'm wearing a pair of boxers washed in Omo Color detergent. I'm still a little groggy, so I sip some Powerade sports drink. I save the Bonaqua mineral water I've bought for the anticipated afternoon heat wave. While driving I remember the fun holiday recently spent in Copenhagen at the Marriott Hotel. Nice place, although the Renaissance in Amsterdam was more stylish. In Copenhagen I was able to tank the car using my Finnish Neste credit card at Texaco gas stations. It's hard to focus on work. I'm looking forward to spending an evening watching movies. After careful consideration I've invested in a new Sanyo video projector. At the same time I exchanged my old Fisher receiver–amplifier for a new one. My day at work leaves me with a good feeling; the Wal-Mart example I use in my lecture on image-building was given a good reception. While watching the evening's movie I enjoy a delicious Magnum ice cream.

It's been a good day, yet all along I've been a co-conspirator in projects of varying degrees of malevolence—at least if one is to believe the findings of the Swedish national pension fund Sjunde AP concerning unethical business practices. According to the Sjunde AP's report, every product that I used during the course of the day, from Omo to Fisher and Sanyo to Magnum, casts a shadow of evil. Yet still there is increasing talk about how important it is for companies to be good.

Table 1.1 Companies and crimes: examples of unethical investment targets according to the Swedish national pension fund Sjunde AP. Source: *Helsingin Sanomat* newspaper, May 15, 2005.

Company	Brand	Crimes
Chevron Texaco	Texaco	American oil and gas giant. Guilty of human rights violations in Nigeria and environmental crimes in the Amazon.
Coca-Cola	Nestea, Powerade, Bonaqua	American refreshment drinks giant. Infringed on workers' rights and guilty of discrimination in the USA and Central and Latin America.
DuPont	Teflon	American chemical giant. The company's product has caused injury to people and damage to nature.
Hyundai/Kia	Kia Sportage, Hyundai Getz	Korean car manufacturer. Has restricted unions from operating, maintains poor working conditions in South Korea.
Marriott	Marriott Hotel in Copenhagen, Renaissance Hotel in Amsterdam	American hotel chain. Sexual harassment of minors in company offices in Costa Rica.
Sanyo Electric	Sanyo, Fisher	Japanese electronics manufacturer. Discrimination against women at its production plant in Mexico.
Unilever	Omo, Flora, Magnum	Dutch foodstuffs company. Subsidiary guilty of environmental crimes in India.
Wal-Mart	Wal-Mart	American shop chain. Discrimination against women in Guatemala, restricted unions from operating, infringed on workers' rights in USA.

An essential contradiction is inherent in all the good deeds performed by companies. Whenever a company does something good, its motives are questioned. A company can be up to no good while doing the right things. It is as if the "good side" of a company is always counterbalanced by an "evil side." And performing good deeds is just a way of covering up the evil side, or making it look good. When a multinational hamburger chain collects funds and builds houses for families of sick children, the outcomes of the deed itself are good as they improve the lives of those we sympathize with. But since the organization in question is not UNICEF, for example, we assume that there must be some evil motive behind the gesture. Even if we are unable to demonstrate where or what that evil motive is, it has to be there somewhere. If concrete examples of the twisted motives of good deeds cannot be found in our immediate neighborhood, they can certainly be found elsewhere, probably in the third world.

Today's business environment demands a lot of corporate responsibility and a robust ethical backbone. On the one hand, it is claimed that goodness improves the public perception of a company and builds a positive image. In this way good operations influence people's decision-making, which naturally has enormous importance for the success of the company. Even the "faceless markets" of the global economic system are ultimately influenced by decisions made by someone somewhere.

Goodness also attracts investments, also in a concrete way. The so-called ethical investment funds have become popular, even if their market share is in a minority among all funds. An example of an ethical fund is the SEB Lux Fund—Ethical Global:

> The fund invests globally in equities and equity-related securities. The ethical restrictions are based upon GES®, Global Ethical Standard, which origins from international norms concerning human rights, labor, environment, bribes, corruption, and weapons. The fund also excludes companies for which more than 5 percent of the business is derived from weapons, alcohol, tobacco, gambling, and pornography. The ethical review is performed by GES Investment Services. SEB donates 13.5 percent of the fund's management fee to the WWF every year.
>
> (www.seb.se, read June 7, 2005)

If investors are becoming seekers of goodness, consumers also want to buy things from a company of good. Many studies indicate that "ethics" and "responsibility" are still in fashion. This should mean that we as consumers make direct daily decisions that benefit companies and products that we know, or think, suit our own personal values. But something still seems wrong. It seems that even if customers have values, this does not automatically lead to good operations. It has been estimated that the market share of ethical funds in Finland is between 0.5 and 1.0 percent. According to a publication released by the Finnish Foundation for Share Promotion, a total of around €170 million was invested in funds adhering to certain principles of social responsibility at the end of 2004. At the same time the total capital of all funds was over €31 billion. Investors in the USA are more ethical. There the share of socially responsible funds is over 10 percent of all funds. Matters are made even more interesting by information that suggests that it pays to invest in "badness" or "vices," as reported by Finland's leading daily newspaper *Helsingin Sanomat* (May 15, 2005). The Vice Fund in the USA invests successfully in companies that are active in gaming, tobacco, alcohol, and aerospace and defense. Since its inception in 2002, the fund has averaged an annual return of 18 percent. As the Vice Fund Prospectus states:

> It is the Advisor's philosophy that although often considered politically incorrect, these and similar industries and products . . . will continue to experience significant capital appreciation during good and bad markets. The Advisor considers these industries to be nearly "recession-proof."
>
> (Vice Fund Prospectus, July 31, 2006, p. 2)

Of course, investment decisions are made by very few consumers on a regular basis. Selecting the food we buy is much more common. But even here our daily bread is seldom produced naturally; just a couple of years ago the market share of organically produced bread was less than 2 percent (The Ministry of Trade and Industry, 2002). At least organic eggs are doing better. According to a 2004 ACNielsen study, their market share in terms of total sales in that year was 4.8 percent.

Despite the contradiction between words and deeds, responsible business operations are still considered to be extremely important for achieving success. Companies invest enormous sums of money in good deeds, as well as in good presentations to promote the public image of being a responsible company. And the bigger the company, the bigger the deeds.

Many pharmaceuticals companies have invested large sums in various kinds of virtuous projects. A well-known example is provided by Merck & Company, which has played a major role in treating so-called "river blindness" caused by parasites in sub-Saharan Africa. River blindness is a painful ailment that often leads to permanent loss of vision. Merck & Company has distributed free of charge over 250 million treatments, each of which costs more than €1 (BBC News article, "River blindness drug revives village life," September 15, 2002, www.bbcworld.com).

The treatment was discovered by Dr William Campbell, a veterinary researcher at Merck & Company who was studying parasite-inflicted illnesses in animals. The company developed the treatment in cooperation with the World Health Organization. Sub-Saharan Africa was and still is a poor region. After failing to receive funding from the US government and several other bodies, Merck & Company decided to donate the treatment to everyone in need of it for as long as the disease prevailed. The company has maintained its commitment for over 20 years (www.merck.com).

Table 1.2 The "projects of good" of a pharmaceutical company in 2005. Source: *Novartis Annual Report*, Novartis Access to Medicine Projects 2005.

Project	Objective	Target region	Program value 2005 (US$ millions)	Patients reached 2005
Malaria/WHO	Provide Coartem at cost for public-sector use	Africa, Asia, Latin America	36[1]	5,600,000
Leprosy	Eliminate leprosy by providing free medications to all patients worldwide with WHO through 2010	Global	3[2]	407,000[3]
Tuberculosis	Donation of fixed-dose combinations[4]	Tanzania, Sri Lanka	3[5]	20,000
Novartis Institute for Tropical Diseases (NITD)	Discover novel treatments and prevention methods for major tropical diseases; NITD discoveries to be available in poor endemic countries without profit	Developing countries	10	
Novartis Foundation for Sustainable Development	Work at policy and field level to improve access to healthcare for the world's poorest people	Developing countries	7	58,000
Patient Assistance Programs (PAP); excl. Gleevec	Assistance to patients experiencing financial hardship, without third-party insurance coverage for their medicines	US	205	214,000
Gleevec US PAP	Within capability of Novartis, continue to ensure access for patients in the US who cannot afford the drug	US	85	4,840
Glivec Global PAP	Within capability of Novartis, continue to ensure access for patients outside the US who cannot afford the drug	Global (excluding US)	284[6]	10,635
Together Rx[7]	Prescription savings program for elderly low-income Medicare recipients, without other insurance	US	49	175,000

Table 1.2 (continued)

Together Rx Access	New discount program for the uninsured	US	0.3	10,000
Emergency Relief	Support major humanitarian organizations[8]	Global	14	–
		Total	**696**	**6,500,000**

Notes
1 Production: 33.6 million treatments. Shipments: 9.2 million treatments
2 Reduction reflects success of the program
3 In 2004
4 For 500,000 patients over five years through WHO
5 Shipments for 100,000 patients
6 Dosage increased, some additional stock
7 Ended because new Medicare drug benefit plan is now available
8 Emergency medical needs, relief programs.

Swiss pharmaceuticals giant Novartis has been similarly active, donating enormous amounts of medications to developing nations and the poor in 2004. The company invested a total of €440 million in socially responsible projects around the world. These projects had an effect on over four million people. Even small deeds count. Novartis Finland sponsors an annual "Community Partnership Day" with the Finnish Federation of the Visually Impaired. The Novartis Finland website describes the project as follows:

> The basic ideology of Community Partnership Day is that company employees donate one-day's labor for a community project of their choosing. Community Partnership Day is organized by Novartis worldwide and is part of the company's Corporate Citizenship. Last year over 10,000 Novartis employees in 45 countries participated in Community Partnership Day.
>
> (www.novartis.fi, read June 6, 2005)

Other pharmaceuticals companies also work hard to do good. For example, the amount of the donations made by British company Glaxo-SmithKline in 2003 equaled the funding earmarked by the Finnish State for aid to developing countries (*Helsingin Sanomat*, February 6, 2005). All in all, the major international pharmaceuticals companies are distributing treatments free of charge and contributing billions of euros annually to charity.

The importance of goodness is magnified when a company's operating environment is considered to be part of the "network society" (Castells, 1996). The network society is created by increasing the diversity of the interactions between individuals, organizations, and societies and by managing various kinds of immaterial property. The success of organizations is dependent on building strategic partnerships and operating within these. As Manuel Castells (1996) points out, society's core processes are organizing ever more clearly within networks. The same can be said to apply also to companies: internationalization, outsourcing, partnerships, subcontractor networks, investor relations, media relations, client relationships, relations with competitors, and so on. Operating within networks or remaining outside of them is essential for both a company's existence and its success. The focus of corporate management is indeed shifting from managing people, operations, and processes to managing networks.

In other words, goodness has a market value. It is connected to the networking that can be found throughout society in at least two ways. First of all, the network society emphasizes the meaning of meanings—consumers form their identity through their consumer behavior; we buy a good life by selecting products manufactured by good companies. Networked communications bring transparency to corporate activities. Managing the many different types of media in the network society is difficult. If a company's operations cannot survive the light of day, it is increasingly likely that someone will bite them in the neck. It is still possible for companies to do bad things, but the network society makes it much easier for them to get caught in the act. It used to be much easier to manage the flow of information and the creation of image.

Companies are part of the network society. Another reason why goodness is maintained for the sake of market value is the networking that takes place among companies. A company who enjoys the reputation of being a good partner is a safer choice when determining cooperation partnerships at a time when no one really has the time to focus on anything. The reputation of a good company is a resource, as the company—or a person working for that company—earns reliability points in networks on which future cooperation relationships are determined. Good companies, good entrepreneurship, and the good reputation of companies and their interest groups provoked our interest. The reputation of a good company is a key success factor.

Strategic reputation management: being good, doing good, looking good

> If a company performs well, the CEO's salary is increased; if the company performs poorly, workers are laid off, and the managing director's salary is increased.
>
> (Finnish philosopher Jukka Relander on
> Finnish radio, June 13, 2005)

Companies operating within the network society are also operating within a society marked by intense competition. Cooperation is often a plus when establishing networks. On the other hand, competition and cooperation are often incompatible bedmates. A company that tries to protect its reputation in the network society faces a major challenge: on the one hand it has to construct an image of itself as a good and reliable partner, yet on the other, cooperation in this game is ultimately compromised by the fact that each player is striving to win as much for himself as possible. It is easy to believe that the rules of this game are written on the terms of competition, that they are relatively Spartan and are known to all.

Because reputation is a resource for companies, they have to strive to manage their reputations specifically as a strategic resource. The question of strategic reputation management lies close to the core paradox of being a good company. The reputation of being a good company is a strategic goal, yet the reputation of being a good company also entails that the dominance of strategies be downgraded. This claim is based on the idea that strategic management contains within itself the germ of a psychopathic organization.

Old-school strategic management: a psychopathic organization?

> *Question*: Do you believe that the strategy of your organization will be realized?

> *Answer*: I guess it can be realized, as it has been around for decades. It just requires certain kinds of people. Those of us who think emotionally and have soft skin are not suitable.

> *Question*: What kinds of people are needed?

> *Answer*: In my opinion, tougher people are needed. They need to have a tough face, in principle to be two-faced, to be the kind of person who only looks after his own interests. The kind of person who thinks of others that they are not fit for the job, that they will be walked all over.
> (Salesperson in a shop's textile department)

The topic of the psychopathic behavior of companies surfaces at regular intervals in public discussion. The increased cynicism and social awakening after the Vietnam War was crystallized in the "science and technology studies" movement that, in addition to analyzing the social impact of technology, studied the behavior of companies utilizing technology. The misconduct that was revealed by the collapse of the giant Enron Corporation a few years ago is said to have changed everything. The operations of countless numbers of companies have been criticized, especially outside of their domestic markets, as methods are employed in foreign countries that are perhaps not available at home: from bribery to the maintenance of entire totalitarian states (Bakan, 2004). Many companies have been caught red-handed.

Although the psychotic behavior of corporations is repeatedly discussed, the connection between strategic management and psychopathic behavior has not been made. This is strange, as psychopathic behavior is specifically strategic behavior: calculating, using others as tools, maximizing one's own advantage. Psychopaths seek a "competitive advantage" just as a strategist does.

What exactly is a psychopath? Even though the concept of a "psychopathic personality" has a precise psychiatric definition, we are more interested in the popular conception of a psychopathic personality, since the reputation of a good company is based specifically on such common conceptions. "Psychopath" is thus considered here as a moral judgment and not as a diagnosis (see Hare, 1991).[1] By "psychopathic behavior" we refer to the generally understood definition; in other words, behavior in which an individual seeks his own goals with total disregard for the well-being of others. For example, the psychopaths depicted in movies are scary because their behavior is unpredictable and selfish. The psychopath breaks all the norms that instruct us to consider others.

Strategic reputation management can simply refer to a company's goal-oriented activities by which it strives to achieve a good reputation. However, the concept of "strategic reputation management" that we have adopted would seem to market a kind of double morality: companies are like the coldly calculating movie psychopaths who act like good neighbors and citizens until one day their true motives are revealed. A great example of this kind of character is the psychopath Max Cady, who torments a middle-class American family in the movie *Cape Fear* (1991) and is chillingly portrayed by Robert DeNiro. One particularly pertinent line is: "well, you can trust in me 'cause I'm the 'Do-Right Man.'"

In fact, the psychopathic germ is sown in companies by the law. By discharging shareholders from liability for the bad deeds performed by companies, companies themselves are defined as legal persons. The entire premise of this legal person is to achieve an instrumental, and usually financial, benefit for its owners. Finland's new Companies Act includes the following:

§2 Legal person and limited liability of shareholders

A limited liability company is a legal person that is separate from its shareholders and that is created by registering the company.

Shareholders are not personally responsible for the company's obligations. The articles of association can, however, define a shareholder's obligation for making various kinds of payments to the company.

§5 Purpose of operations

The purpose of the company's operations is to create a profit for its shareholders, unless otherwise defined in the articles of association.
(Ministry of Justice, www.om.fi, September 1, 2006; unofficial translation)

Companies are thus independent legal persons that are themselves responsible for their operations and whose basic aim can be defined as psychopathic: to achieve their own (or their shareholders') financial advantage before all other value goals. Joel Bakan, professor of law, has pointed out that one would be deceiving oneself if one imagined the most recent corporate scandals to be a case of just "a few rotten apples"—the point is that a psychopathic seed has been planted in the basic legislative definition of companies. According to Bakan (2004), historically a gaping hole was created in corporate ethics when shareholders were discharged from responsibility for all possible wrongdoings.

Bakan's claims can be countered by the fact that all people have goals, and many of these are financial. From a psychologically egoistic perspective it can even be claimed that all individual goals can be equated with personal advantage—if a millionaire builds hospitals in Africa, he is buying a good conscience with his money. Furthermore, it can be claimed that all organizations are created for a specific purpose. Surely it cannot mean that if a company's purpose has been defined by law, then that company is essentially a psychopath?

We consider Bakan's claim about the moral dubiousness of the juridical definition of companies to be credible. First of all we believe that individuals and companies can act altruistically and realize goals that do not achieve anything for themselves. In other words, we are not psychological egoists in our view of individual morality. If the reader feels that, ultimately, people are only out for their own good, then many of the concerns raised in this book probably seem trivial. Second, the problem of the definition of companies is not that their operations are goal-oriented, but that the law itself defines their role as looking after their own interests.

Strategic management is thus a company's reflected image. It can also be claimed that the popularity of strategic management is directly related to the nature of our times, which glorifies psychopathic behavior—"market discipline and managerial power," as communications researcher

Anu Kantola (2002) has insightfully described it. The highly competitive nature of today's markets is probably more the reason behind strategies than the result of them—we have adopted the masculine and bloody metaphor of strategies as the jewel in the crown of management because our times are as they are.

British organizational researchers David Knights and Glenn Morgan (1991) have studied the development of strategic management in parallel with the historical change of business directors. The researchers suggest poignantly that, in fact, directors do not make strategies, rather strategies make directors. According to Knights and Morgan, strategies turn directors into military leaders, justifying their violent worldview. Strategies transform directors by

- making decisions made in uncertain conditions rational,
- maintaining the right of directors to make decisions,
- creating a sense of personal security for directors,
- bolstering and maintaining the masculine identity of male directors in particular,
- demonstrating the rationality of directors for stakeholders,
- justifying the use of power, and
- categorizing the members of an organization into various instrumental classes.

Strategies thus have the tendency to make directors be like them, optimizers of the instrumental good. As a counter-argument we could propose that not all strategies are bad, nor all strategists psychopaths. These days hospitals and charity organizations make strategies just like arms dealers do. We do not deny, of course, that strategies represent practical management disciplines that can and should be applied in many different ways. We also do not claim, naturally, that directors or strategists are psychopaths. We do claim, however, that companies who take seriously the worldview of the economic strategy literature that dominates the markets face a real threat of acting psychopathically (see, for example, Ghoshal, 2005; Shrivastava, 1986). In particular, shortsighted strategic thinking can in the long term turn a company against itself as it loses the trust of its stakeholders. In other words, when reputation management is "strategic," a good company faces the risk of turning into a calculating psychopath.

We are therefore aware of the contradictory nature of the concept of strategic reputation management. One of the central aims of this book is to consider how strategic management should be viewed so that strategic reputation management will create a good company and not a psychopath.

Antonym to the old school: towards a good corporate life

> We were at some customer meeting and [our competitors] had been there before us; they had arrived in a white convertible BMW, whereas we pulled up in a Lada Niva [a soviet car brand]. We got the deal the moment we stepped through the door. In Finland you don't go to visit customers in Lamborghinis ...
>
> (Managing Director, IT startup company)

The public who wants to buy a good life through a company's products does not want to buy a psychopath's products. The same applies to a company's own employees—who wants to work for a psychopath? Cooperation within a corporate network also cannot succeed in the best possible way with a company that everyone knows will betray its partners as soon as it can profit from doing so. A good company should therefore be able to resist turning into an instrumentalizing psychopath. It should be able to combine the strategic goal-orientation of the instrumental good with socially sustainable, intrinsically good operations.

A company's good nature comes from within, from its own working community. The life of a company selling a good life through its products is easily cut short if its own employees are not leading a good life. This means mutual respect between employees and management, who are closer to the shareholders, as well as the goal of the actual working community to do good in the world around them.

Key concepts for this book

This book is concerned with communication, strategy, and reputation. We will argue that communicative action is a constitutive element in creating networks of meanings, both internal and external to an organization, in which organizational reputation resides.

Reputation

We are aware that in many cases the concept of corporate reputation has been used simply to substitute the earlier term "public image," which is nowadays often perceived negatively (as "spin"), especially among journalists. We, however, follow scholars who regard reputation as an opportunity for new beginning in corporate policies and communicative practices (social responsibility, socially sustainable development, business ethics, and dialogical communication). In addition, we believe that you cannot transmit, transplant, or project good reputation; you have to earn it by reliable and responsible activities, service, and/or products.

In other words, an organization cannot just "look good"; it has to "be good." Furthermore, the building of organizational reputation through communicative means is related to corporate social responsibility. While it can be argued that socially conscious behavior is economically worthwhile to an organization, financial reasons should only be one factor in motivating such an approach.

Reputation can be regarded as reflecting intangible organizational capital, which is founded on, and mediated by, the concepts of trust, respect, and social capital (see, for example, Carow, 1999; Coleman 1988; Petrick et al., 1999). Internal communication networks built on trust are related to external reputation-building. There is wide evidence that (external) organizational image and (internal) organizational identity are reciprocally interlinked—image is best built on core identity and image reflects back on identity (Dutton & Dukerich, 1991; Dutton, Dukerich, & Harquail, 1994; Gioia & Thomas, 1996; Gioia, Schultz, & Corley, 2000).

Strategy

While reputation places an emphasis on external stakeholders, organizational strategy can be regarded as a "pattern in a stream of action" for internal stakeholders (Mintzberg & Waters, 1985), providing purpose for work as well as a sense of belonging to the organizational community, energizing the community to collective action (e.g. Bartlett & Ghoshal, 1994; Weick, 2001). We recognize that this pattern may be prospective, i.e. a fictional narrative about the future (Barry & Elmes, 1997) or a planned course of action; or a retrospective, emergent pattern (Mintzberg, 1978), logic of action (Hamel & Prahalad, 1989) connecting recent actions that are discovered or made sense of ex post facto. Shared strategy maintains purpose for the work of individuals (Bartlett & Ghoshal, 1994; Weick, 2001), as do shared languages, routines, scripts, and narratives (Barry & Elmes, 1997), which are all components of organizational social capital (Nahapiet & Ghoshal, 1998). Shared strategy is in turn enhanced by social capital, because shared language and narratives enable the sharing of organizational goals and planned strategies (Beer & Eisenstat, 1996; Hart, 1992). Strategy can, however, also be a language game for the elite that marginalizes and impedes the participation of a large portion of organizational stakeholders (e.g. Knights & Morgan, 1991; Mantere & Vaara, forthcoming; Shrivastava, 1986).

Communication

Human communication, particularly so-called communicative action is one of the most important forms of social interaction (Habermas, 1985).

We comprehend communication not just as transmission of messages over space, but more in terms of the maintenance of a community in time. James Carey (1975) introduced the ritual view of communication, emphasizing the common roots of the terms "commonness," "communion," "community," and "communication." If the archetype of the transmission view is the extension of messages across geography with intent to control, the archetype of the ritual view is the sacred ceremony that draws individuals together in fellowship and commonality. John Dewey (1997) concluded: "Society not only continues to exist by transmission, by communication, but it may fairly be said to exist in transmission, in communication." The continuous process of communication is constitutive of society.

Thus we emphasize the constructivist ontology of the word "communication." In mainstream reputation writings corporate communication is considered to be a one- or two-way interaction in which reputation-enhancing messages are sent and received. For example, Grahame R. Dowling (2006) argues that the corporation should actively support reputational messages, and that "to enhance their virtue, companies need to develop programs to become better corporate citizens and to communicate these improvements to both their internal and external stakeholders" (p. 83). In addition, Haywood (2005) describes the importance of communication in reputation management: a solid marketing communications strategy, which presents the company in its true light and manages the various channels of communication accurately and effectively, results in higher shareholder value.

Even though we strongly agree that good reputation is valuable to an organization, our target audience has no specific organizational function. We are not writing solely for marketing people, corporate communications people, the top management, or the strategy people. From our perspective, and for our purposes, it is not essential to differentiate between different "types," "genres," or "functions" of communication in organizational contexts, such as corporate communications, management communications, and marketing communications (Cornelissen, 2004; Van Riel & Fombrun, 2007). These kinds of differentiations are useful when we want to address reputation regarding a certain organizational function (e.g. "management," "marketing," "communications") or on a particular intra- or inter-organizational level ("personnel," "stakeholders"). However, our focus is on interpretation processes and meaning-negotiations, and from our perspective different types of organizational communications serve different kinds of attempts to affect these interpretive processes. In general, we follow Jamieson and Campbell's (1997, p. 3) broad definition of communication, where "all communication is reciprocal, jointly created by the source and the audience . . . It is an interact (inter = between) or a transact (trans = through, across) that comes into being because the participants cooperate in creating meaning and sharing experience." In addition, and in more micro-level, we agree with Daniels et al. (1997, p. 92) who "regard communication as shared meaning created among two or more people through verbal and nonverbal transaction."

The organization is a form of life, the role of which is paramount in understanding Western civilization, if only because almost all individuals spend most of their days in organizations of some sort (work organizations, schools, homes for the elderly, etc.). The fact that organization studies concerned with the problematics of reputation has recognized the role of communication (Van Riel & Fombrun, 2007) as a potential source of value can have beneficial outcomes in management and strategy practices. This recognition, however, also poses the threat that managerialist hegemony is extended to cover an even larger area, with an official grand narrative crafted to account for intangible capital as a resource to be exploited in the creation of shareholder value. A polyphony of voices needs to be heard instead of the sole voice of, for example, the "heroic leader," representing the organization (Barry & Elmes, 1997; Boje, 1991, 1995; Boyce, 1995; Hazen, 1993).

Communicative activities that the organizational members engage in create or destroy reputational capital in the perceptions and experiences that stakeholders have of the organization. Perceptions and experiences create discourses that are transmitted among stakeholders in communication networks (Aula, 1999; Aula & Heinonen, 2002). On the other hand, communicative practices that facilitate the sharing of organizational strategy both enable the realization of organizational strategy (Johnson, Melin & Whittington, 2003; Mantere, 2005 forthcoming; Mintzberg & Waters, 1985) and make individual work purposeful (Bartlett & Ghoshal, 1994; Mantere, 2005). The understanding of communicative practices that form reputational capital is essential for the value-making processes in organizations.

Yet, on the other hand, a critical and reflexive approach is needed in order to avoid managerialist hegemony in the discussion of reputational capital, both in practice and in scientific discourse. The continuous risk of managerialism is shown in, for example, public organizations mimicking firms (DiMaggio & Powell, 1983), adopting outdated management practices—recent models of university funding being one example. Indeed, organizational reputation is a latently contested concept: on the one hand it is influenced by its critical sociological roots and on the other by the managerialist mainstream of organization studies.

Plan for this book

This book is based on a desire to understand why and how companies strive to present themselves as good companies. In fact, all the stakeholder activities carried out by companies and other organizations can be interpreted as attempts to demonstrate that the company is good, as well as to ensure that the company is seen, and considered, to be good.

The view of this book regarding these processes of good has been formed around the concepts of reputation, reputation management, and strategies. We try in this book to understand the reputation strategies of good companies. The battleground of good companies lies in the no-man's land between the instrumental, strategic good and a good, virtuous nature. They strive to succeed financially, instrumentally, but in the network society it is required that the instrumental good be partially overlooked or its psychopathic goal-orientation be covered up. A strong paradox thus lies at the heart of a good company's reputation, a paradox that we try to comprehend and shed light on. A good company lives off its reputation. Reputation has a value as an instrumental goal, but it cannot be achieved if the company itself does not seek a good reputation—or at least convince the general public and key stakeholders that goodness is itself a core value of the company.

Part II

Strategic reputation management

Charles J. Fombrun begins his book *Reputation*, which many consider the rallying call to managers regarding the importance of reputation, thus:

> Do you recall the last time you hired a contractor to make improvements to your house or apartment? Or the last time you called on a travel agent for assistance in planning a trip? . . . If you are like most people, you didn't just pick their names out of a phone book. You probably went to them because they were recommended to you by a family member, friend, or someone else you trust. If so, you hired them based on their reputation.
>
> (Fombrun, 1996, p. 1)

Let us build on Fombrun's compelling example and suppose, first, that you are a carpenter. You do your work conscientiously and your customers are satisfied with you. You do not advertise or make a big noise about yourself. Summer season begins and cottagers arrive at your locality. One wants to have a new yard building, the second to rebuild a dock, and the third perhaps needs a new patio. They are looking for the maker. The stories begin to spread. Your reputation reaches along the neighborhood. And suddenly you are the most wanted woodworker of the area.

The second story: your fine-functioning tiled stove breaks down in downtown Helsinki. What do you do? The finding of the tiled-stove expert in the middle of a stone jungle is not an easy task. You decide to phone the friend who had the same problem a few years ago. You get one telephone number for a repairman, and the couple of words of warning: he is a good man but a little bit lazy, the work will be of high quality, when eventually he gets the job done. Your friend gives a second hint: he found a tiled-stove repairer from the Web. He seems promising, the web-pages are appropriate, and the references are OK. In addition, your friend recommends him, but still gives a third tip-off about a relative who knows a lot about stoves. You might want to consult him about whom to pick. You ponder the options, make some calls, and listen to your friends. Eventually you end up with the second man on the basis of the estimates you have heard. And when you do so, the decision has been made on the basis of the third man's assessment of the second man—that is, the second man's reputation.

The stories about the carpenter and about the repairer of the tiled stove describe what reputation is all about. When people do not have personal experiences of the subject at hand, they most likely make their decisions based on other people's recommendations and stories; in other words, they make decisions on the basis of the subject's reputation. A friend's, acquaintance's, or otherwise reliable person's recommendation can be good or bad, favorable or unfavorable. Either way, a mention affects the decision-maker's behavior.

What is striking about the story is the absence of the carpenter and thje bricklayer from the focus of activity in these stories. Their reputations are carried forward by others. In such situations where key decisions are made, they can only have a distal effect on the focal activity.

The carpenter of good reputation must be worthy of his reputation, or he will have no work. Stories also create bad reputation. However, as noted earlier, the actor cannot dictate the stories. In a conventional business environment the most important medium of exchange is money, in the markets of meaning it is expressions, expectations, and experiences.

In the second part of the book we will explore reputation from two main angles: as capital and as interpretation. While we acknowledge the value of good reputation, we promote a view where the interpretive, extra-organizational nature of reputation is given serious consideration. To augment the capital view with the interpretive view, we argue for an arena model of reputation, where companies compete for their reputations in arenas, where organizations and audiences meet at marketplaces of meaning.

Chapter 2

The reputation of the good company

> Nokia is one of the most respected brands in the world, so a good reputation is vitally important for us: it helps us maintain the respect of our employees, investors, operators, consumers, governments, NGOs, and the media.
>
> (www.nokia.fi, February 15, 2005)

What do we mean by "reputation"? Webster's *New World Dictionary* offers the following definition: (1) the regard, favorable or not, shown for a person or thing by the public, community, and so forth; (2) such regard when favorable (for example, to lose one's reputation); (3) distinction. According to its etymology, the word "reputation" has its roots in the Latin word *reputare*, which means to "deliberate", or to "reckon."

Importantly, reputation is something that is spoken about and discussed. At its core is something that is talked about or mentioned. Reputation also involves assessment; that is, the target of reputation being labeled either good or bad ("the regard, favorable or not") and that which distinguishes something or someone from others ("distinction"). In other words, reputation is a question of good or bad, beautiful or ugly, or in principle any other value. In this way the reputation of a company is the way in which its stakeholders assess its goodness or badness.

Furthermore, reputation lies to a great extent elsewhere than in its actual subject ("among others"), i.e. among a company's audience, stakeholders, interest groups, and others, as was illustrated in our carpenter and stove-builder examples. To a great extent reputation does not exist within its subject but in the opinions and interpretations of those assessing the subject.

Early definitions of reputation were built on stakeholders' perceptions. Levitt (1965) defined reputation in terms of a number of attributes consisting in the extent to which the company is well-known, good or bad, reliable, trustworthy, reputable, and believable. Spence (1974) stated that reputation is the product of a competitive process in which companies point out their key characteristics to stakeholders to maximize social status (as cited in Bennett & Kottasz, 2000). Fombrun (1996) takes words such as goodwill, prestige, esteem, standing, name, and status as synonyms and/or metaphors of the reputation of an organization. Based on the *American Heritage Dictionary*'s description of the word, Fombrun (1996, p. 37) defines corporate reputation as "the overall estimation in which a company is held by its constituents. A corporate reputation represents the 'net' affective or emotional reaction—good or bad, weak or strong—of customers, investors, employees, and the general public to the company's name." In addition, Fombrun (1996, p. 72) describes reputation as "a perceptual representation of a company's past actions and future prospects that describes the organization's overall appeal to all of its key constituents when compared with other leading rivals."

Who gets to define reputation?

The competition over conceptual ownership of reputation is intense. Many different parties are doing their best to achieve the authority to define reputation: what is reputation, what is it good for, what use is it, how should it be managed? This struggle is being fought by business executives, consultants, researchers, institutions, the media, and representatives of state authority. The simplest explanation for this competition over the right to define reputation is very basic: money. Reputation is rapidly turning into business for a variety of parties ranging from PR consultants to insurance agents. And he or she who controls the content of the concept of reputation controls the business of reputation. It is a question of the power to define, and defining is always about silencing the definitions of others.

When pondering the importance of reputation, one may come across something like the following claim made by a Finnish advertising company (www.dynamo.fi, read May 31, 2005): "It [a good reputation] creates positive interest among people and makes the holder look and feel better than reality." This claim is powerful, yet difficult. Why?

This seemingly harmless sentence suggests that a company managing its reputation tries to appear to its stakeholders in a naively positive light by emphasizing its good aspects, hiding its bad characteristics, and leaving the rest untold. In other words, a company tries to appear like something that in reality it is not. Only a thin red line separates reputation management from deception or lying.

The most important stakeholders, especially for publicly listed companies, are investors, who demand efficiency and productivity from companies. Investors do not, however, act on the basis of economic variables alone, but instead rely on current views about the company's condition and future. One of the bases of forming these views is the company's reputation. According to research carried out by Wirthlin

Worldwide in 2002, 82 percent of companies' business stakeholders claim that credibility is a critical factor for a company's reputation (Aula & Heinonen, 2002). Credibility in turn is based on trust and openness— and the truth. The aforementioned claim about "looking better than reality" is not a solid way of building or maintaining credibility, and in the longer term a company without credibility is a joke that is not funny in the minds of investors.

A good reputation helps companies acquire capital and facilitates financing. By contrast, a bad reputation makes it harder to get financing and increases the risk factors for its shares, factors that are reflected, for example, in the share price recommendations made by analysts. Reputation influences whether an investment is considered stable and reliable, and thus low-risk.

According to the same Wirthlin study, investors are three times more ready to pay more for the shares of companies considered to have a good reputation, and also three times more ready to recommend these shares to others. Reputation is important when a company is establishing an interactive relationship with investors. It determines whether a good and trustworthy relationship is established between the company and investors or whether investors shift their money elsewhere. Reputation is not easily earned; it requires continuous good business practices. This is why building reputation is not possible through cosmetic magic tricks, and why it is not worth trying to look "better than reality" in front of investors. A good example of this is the "angel financing" of the IT bubble at the end of the twentieth century, which demonstrated how short this road was.

Various trends have developed around how people view reputation, trends that sometimes fight among each other and sometimes reinforce each other. However, no one seriously claims that the role of reputation is to make some look or feel better than they really are. If, for example, the purpose of investor communications were to make something look like something it is not, the very foundation of investor relations collapses. And if reputation is lost in the eyes of investors, the company will eventually be left with nothing—not even respect.

In addition to directors, investors, and consultants, the academic world is also pondering reputation. Science recognizes no single "theory of reputation." Rather it is a question of views and models that have come to be shared by various parties. We can outline several schools of thought regarding reputation whose views are for the most part the same but which also feature certain clear differences. Certain basic assumptions can also be presented for each school of thought regarding what reputation is, where it comes from and what its value is. Reputation has relevance for economics, strategic research, marketing research, organizational research, sociology, and accounting (Fombrun & Van Riel, 1997;

Van Riel & Fombrun, 2007). The management and corporate communications trends are also strong. Despite many differences, these schools of thought have at least one common presumption or premise: in terms of the past, present, and future of organizations, reputation has its own important role to play. Organizations benefit from their historical reputations, and their current reputations improve their operating circumstances today and tomorrow.

The language of reputation serves both to unite views and schools of thought and to separate them from other schools of thought. This can be seen, for example, in the linguistic symbols—metaphors—used when talking about reputation, many of which have already established their place in business jargon. Imbuing the reputational concept with various forms of significance is an example of how the power of definition is wielded. This game of defining reputation is harsh. When reputation is discussed in a certain way, this naturally emphasizes one mode of expression at the expense of others.

Reputation as past, present, and future

According to Cornelissen and Thorpe (2002, p. 173) "the reputation construct is, through its undifferentiated use, so general in scope, and so ambiguous in meaning, that it is almost unbounded in its potential range of applications, and therefore virtually impossible to refute." However, from various definitions it becomes evident that reputation is a dynamic concept, which on the one hand changes over time, and on the other bridges together different temporal perspectives. Through reputation the firm's past record, current observations, and future prospects are linked together.

1   **Past actions.** Reputation is related to a company's history in the sense that reputation is a set of attributes "ascribed to a firm, inferred from the firm's past actions" (Weigelt & Camerer, 1988, p. 443), and it mirrors the narrative of the firm's past actions (Yoon, Guffey & Kijewsky, 1993). Reputation is a "subjective, collective assessment of an organization's trustworthiness and reliability" based on past performance (Fombrun & Van Riel, 1997, p. 10), and qualities that "build up over a period" (Balmer, 1998, p. 971). In addition, reputation represents "the estimation of the consistency over time of an attribute of an entity based on its willingness and ability to perform an activity repeatedly in a similar fashion" (Herbig & Milewicz, 1995, p. 24). So in this respect reputation has an important retrospective component.

2   **Current state.** In addition to its historical nature, reputation is defined with regard to a perceived current state of a company. Reputation is

built upon the way stakeholders observe a firm's present affairs, behavior, and communications. This means that reputation is formed on the basis of direct and indirect experiences and information received (Fombrun & Shanley, 1990).

3   **Future prospects.** In addition to reputation's retrospective and "up-to-date" nature, reputation is also often defined in relation to the future of the company. This means that a company's current reputation is affected by expectations regarding its future. The financial value of many stock exchange companies' reputation is at least in part based on expectations, on their prospects. This future-oriented aspect of reputation is highly important to new startup companies who have to survive without a history of their own. This might also be the most risky part of reputation. Cases like Enron, WorldCom, and BP show us what can happen if the expectations are not based on a realistic or truthful impression.

Old and rich organizations have other starting points for the building of reputation than those of new growth companies. They have different strengths to be used in reputation stories. Strong traditions and a long history are a fruitful source of legitimating narratives, which make, for example, consumers interested in the products and services of the organization. But new growth companies have to legitimize their being without history. Their success story is founded on a promise that they represent tomorrow. While lack of history may mean less legitimacy, there is the advantage of being relieved of the burden of history.

In some cases, a firm's survival is dependent on how well the organization tells its story. This is especially true with startups. Successful growth entrepreneurs may be good businessmen or businesswomen, but first and foremost they must be good storytellers. But the stories alone are not enough. They must always meet a reality. Otherwise the good story can turn into a lie. The so-called "IT bubble" of the end of the 1990s is an excellent example of successful story narration—good and bad. The problem was that many of the future-creating stories were based on building the image ("looking good") of the company, and not on reputation ("being good").

The genesis of reputation in management

When and why did reputation find its way into management discourse? Why do we need it? It is hard to pinpoint the birth of reputation's business dimension in history. Depending on perspective, reputation has either always been present, or it has entered the business world only recently—depending on how rigid we are in our interpretation of what we count as reputation.

Balmer (1998) relates the development of reputation theory to the three-pronged evolution of the theory relating to corporate identity management. In the 1950s development focused on company image, "giving way in the 1970s and 1980s to an emphasis on corporate identity and corporate communications, and then in the 1990s to a mounting interest in corporate brand management and thence reputation" (Bennett & Kottasz, 2000, p. 224).

In the 1980s the focus of reputation-related literature shifted in order to view reputation from within organizations. The key words were company identity, culture, and personality. Following this trend company reputation was combined with marketing to form more comprehensive concepts that are thought to be behind all the successes or failures of a company. These days many management research branches have their own, often contradictory, words to denote what reputation is or how it should be managed.

The pursuit to trace the origin of reputation in management is further complicated by the existence of a number of overlapping terms. There exists a body of literature on themes related to corporate image, either from a marketing perspective or from a psychological perspective. The literature on image is focused on an effort to understand and verify the effects of the impressions people form about companies on the concrete experiences of these same companies and the related behavior of consumers and other stakeholders. Company names and visual images were an essential part of what we today refer to as company reputation. This connection between corporate image and reputation can be found in the modern reputation literature. For example, one of the most cited reputation books is Charles Fombrun's 1996 *Reputation: Realizing Value from the Corporate Image*.

Key to understanding the relationship between the concepts of image and reputation is an appreciation of the difference between vision and speech. The concept of image can be seen already in the 1930s within marketing discourse, but it became more popular in the 1950s in the USA. One of the key factors of the popularity of the visionary concept of image was the mushrooming of television, which, employed by the markets, emphasized the use of visualization in communication. Because of this, marketing people started to emphasize the visual significances relating to products. In Finland, our native country, the concept of image landed only about 20 years later when marketing thinking got more room and the prevalence of television sets approached that encountered in the USA. After this technological development, image soon became a trend and its use also became common outside the business world as well. Nowadays, the concept of image is so befuddled that sometimes one hears it proposed that the use of the word should totally be given up.

In a nutshell, image refers to a company's publicity. A company wants to be perceived in a specific way in the media. The concept is very visual and image-building efforts are often intended to have effect through the methods of visual communication. From this point of view, corporate image is a picture of the organization.

Critical journalists seem to dislike image and image professionals. In a journalistic discourse image has been stigmatized to mean a kind of false picture, created to embellish the organization, blatantly galvanized from reality. This is a critical, pessimistic approach to image and it reflects the main thoughts from Daniel Boorstin's classic 1960s book *The Image* (1962). To Boorstin, image is a personality profile for the individual, institution, company, product, or service, built up by professionals. Furthermore, image is a synthetic, artificial picture of a complex reality that has been simplified. That is why image professionals should be perceived as spin doctors.

Not all agree with this pessimistic view of image, that image is only a cleaned picture of a dirty subject. Many believe that the image represents reality and that it is based on an organization's real character and actions. In fact, some argue that in image-building image should be based on reality. This more optimistic view of image has its own classic as well. In 1956 Kenneth Boulding published *The Image* (yes, the same main title), where image is described in terms of efficient and pithy communication through which one can tell how the organization serves the customers' needs.

Dolphin (2004) found that between academics and practitioners alike there remains much confusion over the terms "reputation" and "image"; are the two one and the same? From our perspective, corporate reputation is not the same as corporate image, even though the concept of reputation is deeply connected to image. We argue that in a way similar to image, reputation is a public conception of the organization, held by external stakeholders. For example, Dutton and Dukerich (1991) used the concept of organizational image to refer to what organizational insiders believe outsiders think is distinctive, central, and enduring about the organization. However, we argue that reputation differs from image in at least the following aspects:

- Reputation consists of symbolic meanings, for example stories, anecdotes, and slogans, whereas image is more oriented to how things appear. Reputation and image represent different but somewhat overlapping aspects of organization.
- Reputation is dynamic, as meanings are constantly enacted in stakeholder sensemaking (e.g. Weick, 1995). Image can also be regarded as dynamic, yet to a considerably lesser extent.
- Reputation is non-centralized as it is held and constantly re-enacted by a variety of stakeholders. It is more fragmented than image. As

such, reputation can be influenced by various parties but it is much harder to "manage" or "control" than image is.

- Reputation involves a stronger emphasis on authenticity than image. Reputation is a concept deeply rooted in popular moral language. It is a very old word, often used to assess the moral character of a person. For instance, Abraham Lincoln stated "Character is a tree and reputation like its shadow. The shadow is what we think of it; the tree is the real thing" (quoted in Eccles, Newquist, & Schatz, 2007, p. 108).

Reputation and image relate differently to time. As Bennett and Kottasz noted:

> Because reputations evolve over time they cannot be fashioned as quickly as images. Moreover, an organization might have a good reputation (e.g. for providing excellent products) yet possess a low-impact, old-fashioned, or otherwise inappropriate image. The reverse could also be true: a strong image crafted via a powerful organizational identity program, advertising, public relations, and integrated marketing communications might not be matched by a cogent reputation.
>
> (Bennett & Kottasz, 2000, p. 224)

Another important conceptual sibling to reputation is brand or brand equity. Indeed, brand equity is highly salient in recent reputation discussions. We argue that reputation is related to a person or an organization. Originally "the brand" meant the burned mark on a cow's skin by which the buyer, or the thief, identified the ranch from which the cattle came. Also villains could be branded for their sins—through the mark on their skin they were distinguished from others forever. Indeed, one of the brand's main functions today is to make a difference, to differentiate a product from its rivals.

Brand is the essence of a product and consists of name, signs, symbols, and brand identifies its target and, above all, distinguishes it from other similar targets. So behind a good brand there is a good product, but the brand is said to be more than just a product. The brand is what the user thinks, knows, and feels about the product. When buying the product, the consumer justifies the decision with seemingly logical reasons: quality, permanence, resale value, or long maintenance interval. However, the true reasons for the acquisition are typically different, and are deeply rooted in emotions. Logical thinking interacts with emotional drives, invoked by the status, design, success, or appreciation offered by the brand. In strategic terms, the physical product itself can be copied but the "brand spirit" cannot.

We follow the distinction made by Fombrun and Van Riel, where the similarities between the concepts of reputation and brand are recognized but

> brand and reputation are not synonymous—and they differ in important ways. On one hand, a brand describes the set of associations that customers have with the company's products. Reputation, on the other hand, involves the assessments that multiple stakeholders make about the company's ability to fulfill their expectations. A company may have strong product brands or even a strong corporate brand—but still have a weak or poor reputation.
>
> (Fombrun & Van Riel, 2004, p. 4)

The authors specify (2004, p. 4) the hierarchical relationship between brand and reputation in a punchy way: "Succinctly put, branding affects the likelihood of a favorable purchase decision by customers. Reputation, however, affects the likelihood of supportive behavior from all of the brand's stakeholders. Branding is therefore a subset of reputation management."

In other words, a brand is mainly related to a product and, in a sense, marketing communications. Brand is a marketing value of the name (Doorley & Carcia, 2007) of a product. Brands are created by organizations for their products and are controlled by the managers. Reputations are related to organizations. They are more fragmented, more dynamic, and less controllable than brands. Furthermore, we argue that discussion of brand equity is strongly related to the economic debate around the value of corporate intangibles, while our account is concerned with the social and cognitive processes of reputation-building. We consider brand equity to be the economic value of a brand. As with brand equity, any terms we use will be clearly defined and used only to the extent that they further our conceptual framework.

Evaluating reputation

Despite the seeming heterogeneity of the reputation concept, we can nevertheless point out two factors on which most reputation researchers seem to agree. First of all, reputation has intangible value as a strategic resource— reputation and its management are considered to be a strategic resource for companies. Reputation is related to the legitimation and purpose of a company (Hatch & Schultz, 2000; Rao, 1994). Reputation builds a company's (intangible) capital and does not just impact on the opinions and assessments about the company made by stakeholders. In this way reputation, like any other resource, is a success factor for companies.

Good companies create reputation through actions, through the expectations based on these actions, and through the fulfillment of these expectations, and they live for their reputation. Doing good, doing well, and taking good care are at the heart of reputation. Taken to its extreme, this chain of thought would imply that a good company's business strategy should be subordinate to its reputation strategy, and not the reverse. The idea that reputation is something permanent should be avoided, however. As investment guru and currently the world's second-richest person Warren Buffett has been quoted as saying, "It takes 20 years to build a reputation and five minutes to ruin it. If you think about that, you'll do things differently" (www.quotedb.com, read June 13, 2007).

On the one hand, reputation is based on continuity, stability, and permanent operations. Reputation defines the interpretations created about a subject and thus constructs the images about a company. This side of reputation that emphasizes that continuity is conservative in its development; reputation is built and developed over a long period of evolution.

Yet, on the other hand, a good reputation also has to reflect a company's continuous ability to change. Reputation reflects the direction, strategies, and goals of a company's development. At the same time a good reputation is a mark of the movement that for its own part drives a company towards its goals and better operations. Often this change is surprising. Reputation is developed within revolutions, by leaps. For good reputations this revolution is not a problem. However, if the reputation is in bad shape, sudden changes may cause a reputation crisis.

In addition to the absolute recognition that reputation has value, there is common agreement about another aspect. It is generally believed that the most important key to good reputation is how well a company takes care of its relations with the society around it, with various audiences, and above all with a variety of stakeholders. By stakeholders we mean in this connection any individual or group whatsoever that can have an effect on the achieving of an organization's goals or that can be affected by the realization of an organization's goals (Freeman, 1984).

Reputation management is thus first and foremost taking care of stakeholder relations, which involves taking care of your own employees, but also, for example, taking care of clients, investors, subcontractors, analysts, government regulators, or the media. Professor James Grunig of the University of Maryland particularly emphasizes the importance of relations in reputation management. According to Grunig (2002), reputation cannot be managed directly, but can be influenced, for example, by how the company's directors behave in relation to stakeholders. Reputation is thus a direct consequence of company–public relations and their success. In fact, through reputation a company can classify individuals outside of traditional stakeholder groups according to how these individuals think of the company. The reputation formed among individuals, and thus stakeholders, is based on direct experiences with the company and its activities, the behavior of, for example, its employees, or observations about the company made in the media (Aula & Heinonen, 2002; Fombrun, 1996; Fombrun & Van Riel, 2004). Stories and fragments of information that move within social networks are also central.

A company's reputation is thus always formed in relation to the company's stakeholders. From this perspective the concept of reputation is also defined in terms of stakeholders. Charles Fombrun (1996) relates stakeholders to reputation when he defines reputation as a representation of an organization's operations to date and future plans that describes the organization's general attractiveness in the eyes of all key parties compared to competitors. D. B. Bromley (1993), having studied reputation from a psychological perspective, defines reputation as a collection of subjective beliefs about a subject, distributed or shared within a social group, that also includes an assessment of the subject's nature or value. Similarly, for example, Caruana, Pitt, and Berthon (1995) suggest that reputation involves the process of forming opinions by people using information. These definitions are remarkably close to the dictionary definition presented earlier (a common conception or opinion about something or someone (among others); "name"), which explains the ease with which reputation is understood.

Different stakeholders make different assessments, and not all stakeholders share the same view of what a good reputation is. For some companies the views of investors are more important than those of government regulators; for others, the views of subcontractors are more important than those of suppliers. Furthermore, the values of these groups differ over time. What was important yesterday may not necessarily mean as much tomorrow. For a good reputation, however, two groups of stakeholders are nevertheless above all others: employees and customers. Depending on the company the order of these two groups varies, but together they represent the dynamic duo of reputation-building. This observation is supported by a number of studies and reports. For example, a reputation study carried out in seven European countries and the USA in 2000–2001 demonstrates how these two groups rank at the top of stakeholders who influence reputation (table 2.1).

As reputation is a relationship, a particularly good reputation means that both employees and customers feel that they are getting something special or are part of something unique by being in a relationship with the company. Reputation determines whether this relationship becomes good and reliable or whether, for example, a group turns to the competition.

The importance of a good reputation is often described using the concept of attractiveness. A company's reputation affects how attractive the company is considered to be. The more attractive the company, the better chances it has of achieving financial success. A good or bad reputation affects the behavior of stakeholders, including their consuming,

Table 2.1 Corporate reputation influencers. Source: *Corporate Reputation Review*, 6(2) 2003.

Ranking	Mean	Standard deviation
1 Customers	4.58	0.17
2 Employees	3.92	0.29
3 Reputation of managing director	3.70	0.27
4 Print media	3.24	0.11
5 Shareholders	3.05	0.38
6 Internet	2.90	0.18
7 Industry analysts	2.78	0.43
8 Financial analysts	2.64	0.22
9 Government regulators	2.64	0.37
10 Electronic media	2.40	0.36

n = 1,019, scale from 1 to 5: 5 = "significantly influences," 1 = "does not influence at all."

buying, and investment decisions. Fombrun puts it straightforwardly: the better the reputation, the better the result.

Many companies want to be the "first choice." Fombrun (1996) emphasizes how companies become the first choice of their stakeholders precisely through their good reputation. A company with a good reputation is the first choice for its employees, which helps the organization both recruit the best employees and maintain the best possible expertise within the company. Good reputation stimulates productivity and increases profitability. With a good reputation companies can also become the first choice among customers. Good reputation attracts new customers and reinforces existing market shares. In addition, companies with good reputations are also the first choice for investors, which facilitates financing and encourages a good price for share capital.

Reputation is not only significant in an organization's relationships with its external environment. Reputation is also relevant within the organization; that is, among its personnel. The advantages of having a good reputation from the viewpoint of personnel can be bundled into a few main arguments (Alvesson, 1999; Garbett, 1998; Morley, 1998).

Good reputation increases the job satisfaction of workers as the good external reputation of the company is reflected in the internal world. This stems from the tendency of workers to identify more strongly with a well-reputed employer. Strong identification leads to such positive organizational outcomes as enhanced customer connections. Correspondingly, weak reputation nurtures a low work ethic among the personnel.

It feels good to work in a good company. In the company of good reputation the member feels proud and experiences the sense of community and togetherness. In the company of good reputation the workers' commitment to the company is strong, which leads to higher productivity and to better stakeholder connections.

For the same basic reasons as above, a company of good is more likely to be able to attract valuable personnel because people want to work in an appreciated company. According to the US study by the Cherenson Group, new applicants have been ready to work for a smaller salary in companies of good reputation (cited in Aula & Heinonen, 2002).

Every person, company, and organization has a reputation, whether they want it or not. The question, therefore, is not whether we have a reputation, or even what the use of a reputation is. Thinking about reputation in terms of stakeholders involves assessing reputations. Reputation is based on experiences and ideas that stakeholders use to evaluate organizations, and this evaluation is made through various factors. These factors allow reputation to be measured.

What, then, is a good reputation made up of? If reputation is an immaterial resource that produces value for companies, how can this abstract concept be assessed and studied? Building a reputation always involves an assessment that stakeholders make, based on various criteria about a company. These criteria form the dimensions of good reputation.

Cornelissen and Thorpe (2002) have pointed out the tendency to ignore the dynamism and variation that may occur in the process of reputation-formation. They have arrived at the insight by looking at the two approaches you can take into reputation. Reputation can be seen as a coin that has two sides. On the one side, reputation appears as an intangible asset of an organization. According to this organizational perspective, reputation, due to its effect on market behavior is seen as a valuable resource that can give institutions sustainable competitive advantage (Cornelissen & Thorpe, 2002). On the other side, the psychological view portrays reputation as an external perception. Reputation is a product of perceptions and evaluative assessments of institutions by third parties who receive signals and messages about them (see Cornelissen & Thorpe, 2002).

The two perspectives are not opposite, but they do include different assumptions. Most importantly, stressing one perspective over another may have a significant effect on how to measure reputation. Existing methods seem to be building on the organizational perspective, and thus they are most of all practical tools to measure reputations and establish rankings. However, taking the psychological perspective more strongly into account increases the validity of the method, and with that we can get closer to what reputation is all about—people's perceptions about an organization.

According to Cornelissen and Thorpe (2002), one of the main ideas in the organizational perspective is that perceptions of stakeholders in

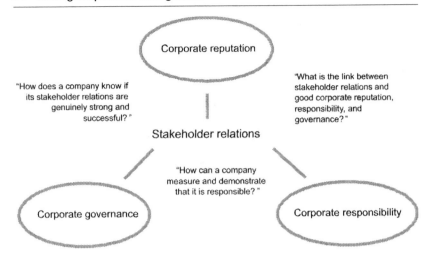

Figure 2.1 The three dimensions of stakeholder relations. Source: www. henleymc.ac.uk, read March 31, 2005.

the aggregate are relatively stable, and thus market value can be treated as a company's intangible asset (e.g. brand equity and reputation). Due to the certain stability in the process of reputation-formation, it has been presumed that the aspects of the process (organizational assets, perceptions, market behavior) are closely linked and need not be set apart, nor, for that matter, need the construct of reputation be refined to one of these aspects, perceptions in particular (Cornelissen & Thorpe, 2002).

We extend Cornelissen and Thorpe's notion of stakeholder perceptions by identifying three aspects of what the nature of these reputation-forming perceptions may be. Following the idea of the multifaceted nature of reputation definition, we discern three main views, all of which are focused on specific phenomena among stakeholders. These three can be labeled the relations view, the emotions view, and the interpretations view. In addition, we propose a thought about a fourth definition stream—a culture-sensitive view.

According to the approach to measuring reputation that emphasizes stakeholder relations, reputation is built within the stakeholder networks that surround companies. Henley Management College has sought to measure reputation by analyzing the interactive relations between companies and their stakeholders, seeking to account for the past, present, and future. The central research questions in this project were: how does a company know if its stakeholder relations are genuinely strong and successful? How is reputation related to corporate governance and corporate responsibility? And how can a company measure and demonstrate the importance of corporate responsibility (see figure 2.1)?

Table 2.2 The seven dimensions of corporate personality. Source: http://www.
mbs.ac.uk/research/corporatereputation/reputation-chain.aspx, read
June 26, 2007.

Corporate personality	Agreeableness
	Enterprise
	Competence
	Chic
	Ruthlessness
	Machismo
	Informality

The second approach to measuring reputation that emphasizes stakeholder emotions considers the emotional ties of stakeholders to companies
by analyzing the "personality" of companies. The Corporate Reputation
Institute at the Manchester Business School has developed a method in
which companies are considered as humans with personalities (table 2.2).
In this method personality tests are made for these metaphorical companies in the same way as they are for real people. Seen from this perspective
reputation is based on corporate identity ("who we are") and the image
among stakeholders ("how they see us"). Between these two is an emotional bond ("I hate you"). This test is founded on the basic concept
of being a good company mentioned earlier: a company's goodness is
often assessed according to its good-naturedness, as an overall view of its
personality.

According to the view of reputation that emphasizes stakeholder attributions, the essential elements are the observations and attributions made
by stakeholders about corporate activities. Reputation research in this
field focuses on clarifying how certain groups attribute various factors
to companies. According to this perspective, reputation is based on the
different dimensions of corporate activities, based on which stakeholders
form their opinions about companies. Analyses that mirror these stakeholder concepts are also popular among the press; they are often made in
order to rank companies on Top 10 lists—and lists sell magazines.

For over 20 years *Fortune* magazine has published its list of America's
Most Admired Companies. *Fortune* analyzes the reputation of American companies according to eight factors: management ability, quality
of products and services, social responsibility, employee expertise, innovativeness, financial stability, corporate value as a long-term investment,
and the efficiency of utilizing corporate assets. *Fortune* magazine's assessment method is very straightforward. A select group of executives, directors, and analysts analyzes the reputation of companies within their own
industry on a scale of one to ten.

Fortune magazine also publishes a list of Global Most Admired Companies that employs the same method as the American survey. In the most

Table 2.3 Most admired companies 2005 and 2007.

Global most admired companies 2005. Source: www.fortune.com, read March 30, 2005.

Rank	Company	Country
1	General Electric electronics	US
2	Wal-Mart Stores retail	US
3	Dell	US
4	Microsoft	US
5	Toyota Motor	Japan
6	Procter & Gamble	US
7	Johnson & Johnson	US
8	FedEx	US
9	Intl. Business Machines	US
10	Berkshire Hathaway	US

World's most admired companies 2007. Source: money.cnn.com, read April 2, 2007.

Rank	Company	Country
1	General Electric	US
2	Toyota Motor	Japan
3	Procter & Gamble	US
4	Johnson & Johnson	US
5	Apple	US
6	Berkshire Hathaway	US
7	FedEx	US
8	Microsoft	US
9	BMW	Germany
10	PepsiCo	US

recent listing from 2007, only two non-US companies make the Top 10 (Toyota Motor, BMW). In 2005 the first European company could be found in position 11 (BMW). Nokia is ranked 26th (table 2.3).

Fortune magazine's corporate reputation surveys have more or less influenced all others. Business papers and magazines have become obsessed with reputation surveys. *Asian Business*, the *Financial Times*, *Management Today*, the *Far Eastern Economic Review*, and many local

Table 2.4 The dimensions of the Reputation Quotient and their attributes (see, for example, Fombrun & Van Riel, 2004).

Emotional appeal	A good feeling about a company, respect, trust
Products and services	High quality, innovativeness, price/quality
Vision and leadership	Leadership excellence, clear vision of the future
Workplace environment	Justice in rewarding, a good place to work, good employees
Financial performance	Better than the competition, known for profitability, not liable to risks, growth expectations
Social responsibility	Supports good issues, environmental responsibility, treats people well

business magazines throughout the world publish similar surveys. Many surveys that rank corporate reputation according to various assessment criteria are based on specific reputation dimensions and factors that have become more or less standard. The analysis has been limited to a couple of indexes and various factors listed in terms of their importance. These annually published listings are a great focus of discussion and media attention. Albeit acknowledged and important, the *Fortune* listing has been under heavy criticism. For example, Fryxell and Wang (1994) point out that the *Fortune* index is mainly about measuring financial perform-ance, not overall reputation. Bias in the respondents has been noted also. They are mainly senior executives and therefore biased to justify corpo-rate reputation based on financial factors.

In addition to *Fortune* magazine's surveys, the Harris-Fombrun Rep-utation Quotient (RQ) by Harris Interactive is also well known. RQ measures corporate reputation according to 20 factors that are grouped under six dimensions (table 2.4). In 2005 the Reputation Institute launched an updated version of the RQ instrument named RepTrack, "designed to track and analyze corporate reputations" (Van Riel & Fombrun, 2007, p. 253).

Towards a culture-sensitive view?

A fish discovers its need for water only when it is no longer in it. Our own culture is like water to a fish. It sustains us. We live and breathe through it. What one culture may regard as essential, a certain level of material wealth for example, may not be so vital to other cultures.

(Trompenaars & Hampden-Turner, 1998, p. 20)

Assessment methods based on stakeholder concepts, discussed above, are often well founded, sensible, and credible. However, one thing they do not take into consideration is cultural factors influencing reputation. If assessment methods are based on factors that are not relevant in certain conditions, there is a great risk that they may measure reputation accurately, but with wrongly contextualized attributes.

The reputations of organizations are most often studied through the concepts of the quality of management, quality of products and services, innovativeness, long-term investment value, financial soundness, employee talent, social responsibility, use of corporate assets. So being, two notions are relevant from the reputation's culture-sensitive point of view: (1) does an organization mean these above-mentioned things to everyone, no matter what culture they represent, and (2) what does each of these dimensions mean in different cultures (e.g. what is "good quality" of the products or the services, or what is "responsibility")?

The culture-related reputational problem is similar to what Trompenaars and Hampden-Turner describe in their 1998 book *Riding the Waves of Culture*:

> However objective and uniform we try to make organizations, they will not have the same meaning for individuals from different cultures. The meanings perceived depend on certain cultural preferences. . . Likewise the meaning that people give to the organization, their concept of its structure, practices, and policies, is culturally defined. Culture is a shared system of meanings. It dictates what we pay attention to, how we act and what we value.
>
> (Trompenaars & Hampden-Turner, 1998, p. 13)

In addition, Dowling (2001) argues that "it is important to note, that values are culture dependent" (p. 22).

Thus it could be argued that the members of one culture do not construct an organization's reputation on the basis of the same evaluations and interpretations as do those of another. According to Trompenaars and Hampden-Turner (1998, p. 3) it is not important to consider where organizations are found physically, but what they mean to people in different cultures. This, in turn, means that any local culture will accept some reputational messages sent by an organization, while rejecting others almost entirely. Reputation is a global, universal phenomenon, but—very importantly—locally constructed, with "local" here standing for both geographical and lifestyle conceptions of space. The configuration and composition of an organization's reputation is thus "space-dependent"; that is, highly dependent on the organization's cultural context.

In fact, this was the case in three reputation studies conducted in Finland in 2001–2003 to find out the attributes that form the corporate

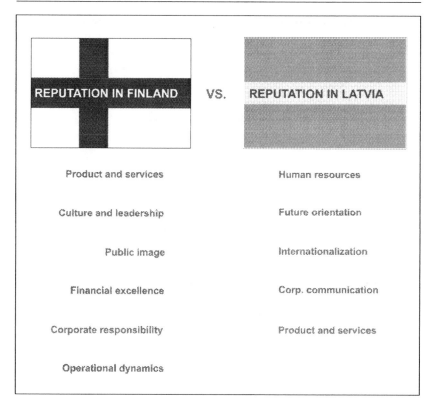

Figure 2.2 Differences in reputation structures in Finnish (*left*) and Latvian (*right*) contexts

reputations of leading Finnish firms. Three studies of organizational reputations were carried out (years 2001, 2002, and 2003) where the key dimensions of reputation were used to measure the reputation of the hundred largest Finnish public companies, according to which the dimension of social responsibility is one of the key issues of reputation.

The study was repeated in Latvia in 2003–2004 to find out the attributes that form the corporate reputations of esteemed Latvian firms, as well as the variance and influence of culturally bounded factors. Findings in the Latvian study (figure 2.2) confirmed that even though the meaning of social responsibility was measured both in Finland and in Latvia, the concept of social responsibility was not the same across the two countries:

1   Corporate social responsibility has a significant role in relation to a company's overall reputation in a Finnish context, but it plays a much lesser role in Latvia.

2   There is a strong correlation between the images of how the company is internally led and managed and the stakeholders' notions around the dimension of social responsibility.

3   There are cultural differences how important CSR is considered to be in relation to corporate success.

4   There are cultural differences about what attributes are most important in relation to overall corporate reputation.

5   Corporate actions around social responsibility do not match demands for social responsibility among the local stakeholders.

The two studies led to an improved specification of what kind of cultural aspects lead to reputation formation, enhancement, and change. Even though it is possible to give reputation an applicable universal definition, it is not self-evident that the operationalization of reputation is identical the world over. For example, when examining reputation in a peripheral location it is not necessarily valid to directly apply the drivers eligible in the United States or Britain, or at the global core of the financial, political, and social environments.

The two country cases support the idea that the reasons for the lack of organizational actions to improve upon reputation (Fombrun, 1996, pp. 5–6) have to do with the social embeddedness (Granovetter, 1985) and culturally bounded nature of interpretations and meanings, as well as realities perceived by individuals (Ainamo & Tienari, 2002).

Summary: the reputation of a good company

Reputation is based on many different attributes that stakeholders use to assess companies. Reputation management is a demanding discipline. All stakeholders must be looked after, yet at the same time it is important to be able to prioritize who should be looked after better and when. The same perception should be applied to the contents of reputation: What reputational factor is essential at what time and for whom? Cees van Riel, who has written extensively about reputation, compares reputation management to a juggler. All balls "have to be kept in the air at all times. If too much attention is paid to financial performance, for example, other areas will be neglected" (interview in *Kauppalehti* business newspaper, February 15, 2001).

From our point of view, reputation consists of a company's operational and communicational dimensions. Reputation management is a strategic issue for companies that can be used to direct operations in order to influence the kinds of experiences felt by important stakeholders and the views and opinions formed about companies. Reputation management is founded on the interaction between a company's actual activities and the experiences and views of its public. Stakeholders play the leading role in this interaction. Taking good care of stakeholder relations is essential to reputation management.

If reputation is anything like we claim it to be and important for good companies and their success, it is necessary to further define what we mean by reputation.

Chapter 3

Is reputation capital or interpretation?

It is easy to agree that the way stakeholders relate to companies is a crucial aspect of reputation. The concept of achieving a good reputation becomes more problematic when we consider the processes in which reputations are built.

The previous discussion should demonstrate that a large portion of the extant literature on reputation has focused on ways of assessing reputation. Our knowledge on how reputation is built—the dynamics of reputation, if you will—is much more limited. In this respect we agree with Rindova, Petkova, and Kotha (2007), who note, that "while strategy and organizational researchers increasingly recognize that observers' perceptions and beliefs about firms have a substantive effect on firms' access to resources and performance, the processes through which these perceptions form are not well understood" (p. 31). To understand these reputation-formation processes, we need to delve deeper into what we mean by the concept of reputation. Indeed, as we will demonstrate through an analysis of the extant reputation literature, the definition of reputation is contested terrain. The main contestants can be seen to represent opposite aspects of the contradiction in terms that is the company of good that we discussed earlier. Authors who conceive of reputation as an asset—that is, in economic terms—support the instrumentalist notion of good. Authors assuming an interpretive stance see eye to eye with the notion of goodness residing in organizational "character."

In this chapter, we will first outline the debate on the definition of reputation between the economic and interpretive schools. We will then propose a way to reconcile the two discourses by laying the foundation for what we call the arena model of organizational reputation. The arena model will characterize our view on reputation throughout the rest of the book.

We will next outline what we take to be the two main contestants in the struggle of defining what reputation is and what is involved in its building. We shall call these the capital view and the interpretive view.

Reputation as capital

> Corporate reputations have bottom-line effects.
>
> (Fombrun, 1996, p. 81)

According to contemporary thinking, reputation creates economic benefits for companies. Albert Caruana (1998, pp. 109–118) concluded his analysis of reputation's advantages by reporting various studies, according to which reputation increases sales (Yoon, Guffey, & Kijewsky, 1993), by for instance, positively moderating the relationships between buyers and sales staff in a buying situation (Brown, 1995); enhancing perceived product quality (Weigelt & Camerer, 1988); contributing to performance differences between firms (Rao, 1994); attracting investors, lowering the cost of capital, and enhancing the competitive ability of firms (Fombrun and Shanley, 1990); and enabling strong organization identification by employees and "inter-organizational co-operation or citizenship behavior" (Dutton, Dukerich, & Harquail, 1994).

Reputation as capital is rooted in "true" facts like "reputation is money" or "reputation is a company's immaterial capital." An economic view seeks to provide various phenomena with measurable values. It is such a central part of all business activities that it is sometimes hard to see the wood for the trees. Value is given to things with no value, and at the same time, in almost a banal way, attempts are made to estimate the value of all things. Society places a value on knowledge, skills, and human life. Economic variables have become a prerequisite for efficiency and a measuring stick for success. Operations are not valuable if they cannot be converted into numbers, indices, percentages, averages, and dollars. Economics demands that a value be placed on reputation—preferably in dollars. This financial discourse is in evidence when we study a short sample of the names of the reputation bestsellers. For example, what many consider the *locus classicus* of corporate reputation literature, Charles Fombrun's 1996 book, is named *Reputation: Realizing Value from the Corporate Image*, and his newer (2004) book, *Fame and Fortune: How Successful Companies Build Winning Reputations*, with Cees van Riel, implicates this financial reputational value. In addition, Grahame Dowling wrote (in 2001) *Creating Corporate Reputations: Identity, Image, and Performance*, and Ronald J. Alsop published in 2004 *The 18 Immutable Laws of Corporate Reputation: Creating, Protecting, and Repairing Your Most Valuable Asset*.

The reputation-as-capital view is motivated by the argument that reputation is positively related to the competitive advantage of a firm (Fombrun, 1996; Fombrun & Van Riel, 2004; Podolny, 1993; Rindova, Petkova, & Kotha, 2007). Through an excellent reputation, in comparison to other organizations, an organization becomes the first choice of its public, including its employees, customers, and investors. Good reputation helps the company to recruit the best employees and to retain them, to win new customers and to reinforce the loyalty of existing ones, as well as enabling low-cost finance and a good price for its products, services, and share capital (Rindova, Pollock & Hayward, 2006).

Besides making the organization the first choice of its many interest groups, superior reputation safeguards the organization by forming a "protective shield" (Kambara, 2000) against the various impacts of crises, thus mitigating their negative impact (Fombrun & Van Riel, 2004). In particular, a good reputation plays a significant role in the organization's interaction with the media; information coming from an organization with a superior reputation is trusted (Aula, 2000) and it is actively consulted (Aula & Heinonen, 2002).

Thus an excellent reputation enhances an organization's scope for action while serving to restrain the actions of competitors against the organization. According to Fombrun (1996), reputation's significance is thus clear: the better the reputation, the higher the financial profit. Weigelt and Camerer (1998) make reputation the single most important driver in the organization's financial success. In this view, reputation is by definition intangible capital.

Aula and Heinonen (2002) propose that companies will have reputation capital when their market value is bigger than the book value. The same thought can be presented as a formula: net worth + reputation = market value. They propose the concept of ROR (Return On Reputation, indicating the business success effect of reputation investments) for estimating the yield of reputation. Investments in reputation refer to the inputs that have been made into different factors of the reputation, such as to enterprise culture, to communication, or to social responsibility. Economic success refers, for example, to the increase in turnover or to the growth of profitability. In other words, ROR shows how much economic surplus value reputation investments bring to the company.

Dowling's studies of reputation's financial significance follow similar lines of thought:

> In short, firms with an above-average *Fortune* reputation score exhibit either (a) a greater ability to sustain an above-average return on assets (ROA), or (b) a greater ability to attain an above-average ROA. These findings support the competitive advantage theory of corporate strategy, which says that firms can gain a sustainable competitive advantage by developing their intangible and inimitable assets—such as their corporate reputations.
>
> (Dowling, 2001, pp. 1–2)

In their *Fortune*'s Most Admired-based study Peter Roberts and Graham Dowling found support for the following relationships: "(1) Good corporate reputations increase the length of time that firms spend earning superior financial returns (a carry-over effect), and (2) Good corporate reputations may reduce the length of time that firms spend earning below-average financial returns (a lead-indicator effect)" (Dowling, 2001, pp. 15–16).

Reputation as capital emphasizes the significance of "invisible money." Whenever an organization does good deeds, the reputational cash register goes "ka-ching!" When the right situation arises, therefore, reputation can be capitalized on. For instance, in the 1985 book *Competitive Advantage*, which many consider to be the *locus classicus* of modern strategic management, Michael Porter suggests that being first in a specific market can lead to a pioneer reputation which in turn creates a unique competitive advantage. A particularly compelling case is the watchmaker Breguet, which created the first wristwatch for Queen Caroline of Naples. The following account can be found on their website:

> The first true wristwatch (that is, conceived from the outset to be worn on the wrist) was created in the Breguet workshops in response to a commission from the Queen of Naples dated June 8th 1810. Breguet watch no. 2639 took two years and a half to complete. It was of revolutionary construction and unprecedented sophistication, consisting of a repeating watch with additional refinements, oblong and exceptionally slender, with a wristlet made of hair intertwined with gold thread. Only towards the end of the 19th century did it begin to achieve popularity. Women adopted it first, and then soldiers, attracted by its practical aspects. In the early years of the 20th century it was further promoted by the daring pioneers of aviation and the automobile industry, and began to supplant the pocket watch. Today, it is difficult to imagine everyday life without this most convenient of Breguet's innovations.
>
> (www.breguet.com, read June 27, 2007)

The company prides itself on its products being referenced in fine European literature, from Jules Verne to Leo Tolstoy to Alexandre Dumas père. Among more recent references, not openly endorsed by Breguet, is the character Patrick Bateman in Bret Easton Ellis's controversial novel *American Psycho*. Even the master of movie dialogue, Quentin Tarantino, includes an apparent Breguet reference in his script to the movie *Pulp Fiction*. The wristwatch, which has been passed from generation to generation in the family of a professional boxer, portrayed by Bruce Willis, plays a fateful role in the unraveling of events in the film, which has turned out to be one of the cornerstones of Western cinema. In the scene where the watch is introduced, a Vietnam veteran, portrayed by Christopher Walken, visits the son of a fellow prisoner of war to deliver the deceased father's watch to the son. This is the part of the story he tells to the son about the watch:

> This watch I got here was first purchased by your great-granddaddy. It was bought during the First World War in a little general store in Knoxville, Tennessee. It was bought by private Doughboy Erine Coolidge the day he set sail for Paris. It was your great-granddaddy's war watch, made by the first company to ever make wrist watches. You see, up until then, people just carried pocket watches.
>
> (Tarantino, 1994, p. 67)

While Breguet does not openly pride itself in the presence of its products in the more prosaic contexts of modern-day films and novels, it seems clear that its unique reputation capital endures almost 200 years after the invention of the first wristwatch. Indeed, it has managed to capitalize its being first on the scene. It also seems clear that the current owner of Breguet, the Swatch corporation, only receives a passing reference in the margins of the Breguet website.

In this era of market determinism, the symbols attached to property may be the only arguments that are listened to and applied as a basis for operations. In this market economy that is directed by selfish pursuit of benefits and compulsive greed, and in which everyone seems to be in a perpetual hurry, interest is only aroused if the speaker presents the opportunity to succeed or make more money. Good reputation increases a company's so-called goodwill value, when goodwill is defined as the price that is created when the buyer deducts tangible assets from the price paid for the company and this difference is recorded as goodwill in the balance. Especially in conversations about immaterial capital concerning listed companies, the goodwill concept is often used in certain parts as a synonym for reputation, and it is largely dependent on images connected with companies (for example concerning a company's future).

In financial discourse, in other words, reputation is conceptualized as an organization's "capital." It is something that an organization can own, sell, exchange, lend, or steal. But it is also something for which a value can be calculated, just as with any other form of capital. Reputation is a unit of wealth in the same way that machinery, equipment, cash, or even people are. Reputation is an organization's capital but, unlike tangible resources, it is intangible by nature. Reputation is an organization's intangible capital. And just as with brands, for example, people want to put a dollar sum on reputation, an economic value: what percentage of a company's value is reputational value, how big a share of its assets is so-called reputational capital, how can it be recorded, and

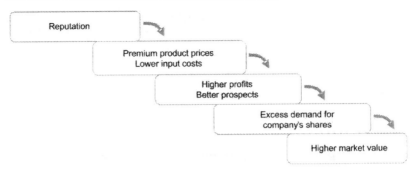

Figure 3.1 An example of a reputational value chain. See Fombrun & Van Riel (2004, p. 27).

how can it be charted? Brand capital has been approached from at least three different perspectives: how much has been invested in the brand, how much has been paid for the brand in acquisitions, for example, and how much can the brand produce in the future (Kapferer, 1997)? In the same way, a process can be applied to reputation that shows how it produces wealth (figure 3.1).

Fombrun and Van Riel's use of Porter's (1985) value-chain concept places reputation alongside other valuable and coveted assets positioned early in the value chain, such as knowledge or innovations. As capital, reputation becomes something that is in the control of its owner. Analysts fond of creating charts develop quantitative variables for valuing reputation in dollars, euros, or yen. Investing in reputation is an investment whose impact on economic success can be forecast. The valuation is directed by a view that is simultaneously both an assumption of established quality and the result of research and analysis: reputation correlates with a company's financial indicators. For example, companies with good reputations have a higher market value and better profitability than those with bad reputations.

Jeffries-Fox Associates carried out research for the Council of Public Relations Firms to find out why reputation has a value for organizations. On the basis of a comprehensive report utilizing business, PR, and marketing literature, Jeffries-Fox came up with 11 advantages of good reputation for companies (see Grunig & Hung, 2002). Good reputation can increase a company's market share, reduce the marketing costs of products and services, reduce distribution costs of products and services, enable "premium" pricing of products and services, protect a company in times of crisis, increase the loyalty and productivity of employees, help attract and maintain the best possible employees, help attract investors and financiers, help enter new markets, and help achieve positive publicity. In addition to indirect benefits, good reputation creates a strategic and financial advantage, as reputation is considered to prevent the mobility of competing companies in markets by making it harder to launch competing products and services. Good reputation provides stakeholders with a strong signal of the good quality of products and services. It also attracts better job applicants, thus ensuring the quality of operations, helps entry into capital markets, and makes companies more attractive to investors (Dowling, 2001).

The capital view of reputation recognizes a variety of financial activities related to reputation. Reputation can be invested in; strategic efforts can be made that can be shown to have a benefit through the added economic value provided by these efforts. A classic example of this is the *Exxon Valdez* oil-spill disaster. The giant oil tanker ran aground off the coast of Alaska in 1989. The oil company Exxon suffered more than just the estimated US$3 billion of financial losses from the catastrophe. It also lost its reputation, and this continues to impact the position of the company today, almost 20 years after the accident. The oil spill also tarnished the reputation of the entire oil industry, despite the fact that the *Exxon Valdez* ranked only 35th in the list of biggest oil spills.

For good companies, in other words, reputation is capital that should be invested in. Reputation should be managed and controlled, and this should be done actively. The loss of reputational capital can have serious economic effects. Therefore good companies should include reputational management in their business strategies and draw up a plan for minimizing any reputational risks.

Reputation as interpretation

Economics is by no means the only way to describe and define reputation. We argue that financial discourse is not enough when we want to describe the complex nature of the reputational relationships between a corporation and its stakeholders. The capital viewpoint fails to account for or capture the essentials of reputation-formation, i.e. how reputation is formed, and what the role of organizational communication is in that process.

Our main concern with the view of regarding reputation as solely capital is that it creates a false sense of control. An organization's reputation does not reside within the management of the organization, but among the organization's stakeholders. A second concern is that the capital viewpoint easily leads attention away from the fact that stakeholders want to see a company of good. The stakeholders perceive the organization as a character with more or less human characteristics. Good companies fight in the no-man's land between instrumental goodness and character goodness as they strive to succeed financially. As we pointed out in our introduction, a paradox lies at the heart of a good company's reputation: companies are expected to demonstrate both good character and the ability to operate psychopathically. Shareholders demand instrumental good, which is in turn created by good reputation based on intrinsic good, goodness in character. In this sense the instrumental good entails partially forgetting instrumental goodness or hiding its psychopathic pursuit.

To augment this limitation in the capital view, we propose that reputation should also be studied as interpretations among stakeholders: their stories, anecdotes, and other discursive elements regarding the organization. In addition, we argue that this interpretation is often related to storytelling of various kinds. The story aspect is key among all the discursive aspects of reputation, because reputational communication is not just sending and receiving messages but something that narratively builds up the corporate reputation. We will argue that reputation is not made by communication—the transmission of messages—but in communication, in processes of social construction.

The interpretive viewpoint of organizational reputation emphasizes that reputations are inherently subjective and socially constructed. Stakeholders give meaning to the organization through judging and sharing their emotions, worldviews, experiences, and stories. They constantly observe the environment and interpret their own needs and those of others, as well as make bridges across these with stories. They frame the organization in terms of the stories that reflect motives, wants, and abilities at play. With stories, they proactively seek to anticipate others' reactions in their own actions.

In the storytelling view of organizational reputation, we follow scholars who argue that reputation is not only an intangible asset and thus a cognitive formation, but also a narrative and communicative construct; that is, it consists of a "collection of stories told about an organization" (Smythe, Dorward, & Reback, 1992, p. 19).

The view which we promote recognizes the embeddedness of reputational discourse in various layers of culture (cf. Geertz, 1973). Cultural representations are constantly transforming to fit locally changing circumstances (Boje, 1991). Instead of involving a simple process of encoding and decoding information, representations of reputation involve complex, changing, socially constructed interpretation rules which are idiosyncratically enacted by individuals and groups (Weick, 1995), often guided by behavioral routines of various kinds (Vaara, 2002). The interpretation rules may be touched by universality, as these rules can sometimes be traced back to age-old myths and conceptions that cut across cultures, such as fairytales (Broms & Gahmberg, 1983). An organization's profound values and visions are kept alive in the collective memory and action of the joint community that is made up of its management, personnel, and external stakeholders (cf. Ravasi & van

Rekom, 2003), on the one hand, and the broader symbolic context of culture, symbols, and myths, on the other.

In this light, reputation consists of all the stories told about an organization, and it exists among people, in communities. Instead of reputation belonging to an organization itself, it is to a large extent controlled and distributed by the organization's stakeholders. Reputation lives inside our heads in a sense, but most profoundly it is constructed and re-enacted in speech. Reputational stories are produced and reproduced through talking and giving various kinds of presentations. At the heart of reputational stories is not money and its control but communication.

If reputation is stories, what are stories? In principle, defining stories is easy. A story is a verbal, written, or other kind of presentation that involves at least two people who interpret the past or past experiences. Stories can concern the past, the present, or the future. They have a beginning, a middle, and an end, and they present some kind of plot fixed in time on the basis of cause-and-effect relationships.

However, stories do not demand beginnings, middles, and ends. Each story is created in the interaction between storyteller and listener. Stories have many possible meanings, which allow participants the chance to create their own interpretations (Boje, 1991; Bruner, 1996; Gephart, 1991; Thachankary, 1992). Depending on context, different exclamations—even the smallest and most removed—can be interpreted as stories. For example, the words "May I have the salt?" spoken at the dinner table may mean the same as: "Mom has tried to feed us this tasteless food for years. She is a health tyrant. Enough is enough!" (example from Abbott, 2002).

Stories are not told for the heck of it within organizations either; instead, people can use them to create an explanation about themselves and their community. Stories form the development and significance of human organizations. Organizational stories are not uniform; they are formed in a struggle over meaning between groups of stories and interpretations. As Boje (1995) has noted, organizational life is more vague and chaotic than it is simple, systematic, and hierarchical.

Stories have power. It is claimed that the success of companies is not dependent only upon sales of products or services. Business thrives when stories, dreams, and emotions are sold. People make their decisions more on the basis of emotions than on common sense.

On the morning of March 30, 1999, trade was begun on the NASDAQ stock exchange in the US. Internet-based airline ticket seller Priceline.com went public. The listing price was US$16 per share, which immediately rose to US$85 when trade began. When the stock exchange closed the price was US$68 per share. The rise of the day was 425 percent. Priceline.com's market value was almost US$10 billion; more than United Airlines, Continental Airlines, and Northwest Airlines together.

The airlines like United Airlines or Northwest Airlines own their brands, airplanes, valuable air terminals, and other physical property. Priceline.com owned little software, a few computers and an unknown, untested brand. What about the business model of the company? Perhaps this was what was unique about the company.

Priceline.com began its operation on April 6, 1998. Until the end of that year, the company sold US$35 million worth of air tickets with costs of US$36.5 million. And this loss is calculated merely from business operations; the defeat figure does not include web systems' development costs, maintenance costs, or marketing costs. When including these expenses the company made a loss of US$54 million. In addition, in order to persuade the airlines to join to its system, the company gave them US$60 million in options. During its first financial year Priceline.com made a US$114 million loss. Against every dollar earned, the company lost.

A few weeks after going public, the value of the Priceline.com share was US$150. The net worth of the tiny dotcom company was more than the market value of the whole of US aviation. Two years later shares were sold at less than US$2 each; the value of the company was no more than two airplanes.

The Priceline.com case was "the greatest story ever sold," as the author John Cassidy put it. And as in every story, the Priceline.com tale carries a lesson. A good story and skillful storytelling are powerful business tools, and we can argue that in the modern business environment every firm should have a magnetic corporate story. However, the story, at some stage, should "meet the reality"—the story must keep the promises made and fulfill the expectations raised. Sooner or later publics should have good experiences alongside the positive image.

This view of the power of stories is nothing new. People have always told stories. Professor Walter R. Fisher discusses in his 1987 book *Human Communication as Narration* how stories are an integral part of human nature. Man is *Homo narrans*: teller, listener, and understander of stories. Without stories people would be nothing but information mills grinding up masses of data. The things that happen to people would be disconnected acts if they did not have some meaning. Stories create continuity and comprehension. Reality is built in stories.

The power of stories in the business world is likewise not an empty academic claim. The collective memories of companies are built in stories, and they are used to negotiate an understanding about the current state of companies and their visions for the future. Stories are also used to convey this reality to others. In other words, stories form an organization's identity and reputation. The basic essence of organizations is dependent on developing stories that are constructed and change their shape all the time. Stories also have a direct connection with organizational behavior. Different kinds of organizations can harness and utilize stories in different ways: for management purposes, for developing expertise and the organization itself, and in a variety of external communications. Sometimes corporate story-building is accidental, but highly effective:

> Before the war years, Finnish devoted fisherman Lauri Rapala had to fish in order to get food to his family. When fishing, he studied the fishes' ways of life. Because Rapala needed extra income, he had to get more catch. Because of this Lauri experimented with, carved, and ground different lure models which imitated a fish which had gone astray from its shoal, and swimming fish which had been wounded. Eventually, he found the model with which one was able to get more than 300 kilos' catch per day. The information about the wonder lure spread and Rapala started to make lures also for others. The stories about the lures of Rapala reached the US. A reporter from *Life* magazine came all the way to Finland to make a piece. The Rapala story was published in an extremely circulated number; in the same 1962 number the death of Marilyn Monroe was also told. After the story Rapala got about three million orders when the capacity of the production was about 50,000. The success story of Rapala, from Lauri's first lures to successful stock exchange company, started from this.
>
> (Reinikainen, 2002)

The daily reality of companies is a continuous struggle over which story is important and whose story dominates. There is no single truth about what a company is. Of course, this view of stories can be questioned, and "story generators" versus "real life" can be put in opposite corners of the ring to fight it out. This is not particularly useful, however, as stories are not the opposites of reality. A company's own stories and the stories told about the company must be based on actual operations: stories are not fictions or fairytales. For a corporate story to endure, it must be a realistic description of the organization. It must be credible, comprehensive, probable, and precisely told.

In the corporate world the smallest anecdotes can be blown up into big stories, just as big stories can be deflated into meaningless tales. Organizations become good or bad in stories—depending on the situation and the interpreter. The IT boom in the 1990s taught us that if corporate stories do not connect with reality at some stage, then the company in question does not have a future (Aula & Oksanen, 2000). For IT companies who did not have a history, stories that described what they would become in the future were vital. But for many companies, the future turned out to be just a pile of big talk with nothing to show for it. Stories became fairytales, and reality became myth.

The power of stories is based on our belief in their ability to convey effectively and in a memorable way views and information that are essential and hard to see. In the best case a well-told story can inspire perceptions and operational changes in people and organizations. In other words, stories convey information. However, stories are not simply a reproduction of events or transmission of information. Stories not only tell about reality, they also construct reality. John Durham Peters (2000) talks about communication as dissemination—the broadcasting of messages "into the air." In his model Peters states that essentials of communication are the free dissemination of the messages and the nature of the surrounding circumstances, where the messages are broadcast. Peters does not consider the communication as a sender-central operation in which the receiver is manipulated. Instead, more crucial to successful communication are the receiver's situation and background. The context of the receiver of the message, in other words their background and situation, are crucial.

As the discourse of reputation as capital rests on the idea that good deeds are like cash deposits in the bank, the discourse of reputation as interpretations rests on the idea of neighbors who gossip about an organization, whose operations they monitor tirelessly.

The perspective of reputational stories is extremely important, as stories are said to be not only the basis of human knowledge but of humanity itself. The narrative form in stories is considered one of the typical ways in which people make sense of reality. Alongside logical thought, the story form is another way of organizing experiences (Bruner, 1996). In fact, the narrative form may be the most essential property of humans, as knowing is based on listening to and creating narratives. Reality, for contemporary humans, is increasingly created narratively, and what we know about the world is a continuously developing story that changes its form over the course of time. From this perspective stories about companies are not just flowers and bees, sprites and gnomes. The concept of what a company is, where it is coming from, and where it is going to is constructed in a variety of diverse stories. Simply put, companies are created in stories, and they live and die according to how their stories are kept alive.

It is useful to discern between two kinds of reputational stories. On the one hand we can talk about corporate stories, which are the ways in which organizations say what they have to say in the form of stories. Corporate stories are based on products, people, the past, the future, heroes, and turning points, or any combination of these. What these stories have in common is their basic structure. They have a starting point or problem from which events proceed through various turns to a solution. A popular form of story is one in which a company founder or other key person is made a hero. Finnish communications professor Leif Åberg (2000, p. 122) talks about an organization's "framework story, the mother of all corporate stories," the story that links an organization's past to its future and positions the present. Framework stories tell about the future through visions, missions, and public goals. The present is positioned in the framework story by defining the company's identity: what the company is, what it does, and what it stands for. From history can be inferred organizational cultural factors, good heritage, and the value basis upon which the current way of operating is based.

Corporate stories, sagas, and great tales can be important symbols or, at the least, entertaining. Ultimately reputational stories are fragmented reports about companies that spread among people and that help people make sense of companies. This is the second sense of stories, the fragmented, often conflicting, everyday sensemaking we engage in (Weick, 1995). These stories are created in both large and small situations, from small and large fragments, in official and unofficial encounters, in official and unofficial communications. People do not encounter companies at face value, but instead through countless fragments of stories. Ultimately people, not organizations, build stories.

From the perspective of control, the remoteness of fragmented small stories is bad news. Reputational stories cannot be controlled or managed. Organizations can never be sure if the story world created by people about companies conforms to the story intended by the companies themselves. Good companies can use constructed corporate stories to try and influence their reputation, but ultimately reputation is formed in the heads of the audience. People interpret things in their own way and give them their own unique meanings. This means that on the individual level the reputation of each and every company is unique.

A good company's reputation is built from stories. A good company tells its story, which is reliable and true. A good company understands that stories both convey and create reality. A good company has a story, but it is aware of the mosaic-like story world of its audience. Its own story is so strong, however, that, even when the world of meanings among people disintegrates, it influences people's views of the company and creates an agreeable sense: a story that conceptualizes for the benefit of the company.

The interpretive view of reputation portrays an organization as a collection of people, a network, whose border with its environment is more or less wavering. Reputation is built in various public statements, but also above all in the interaction between ordinary customer service providers and customers, or between products and consumers. The organizational person brings to these encounters his entire value system; his world-view; his concept of self, of others, of his own organization and of that of others. In these encounters a person utilizes his identity.

The core: sufficiently uniform identity

> For sure if you can demonstrate that customer satisfaction is increasing, it gets people moving. Now that everyone knows that we are world champions, it is clear that we will ski fast on all trails. It motivates a lot.
>
> (Business area director of a major international corporation)

There is a well-known connection between organizational identity and external image, often used interchangeably with reputation (for example, Dutton & Dukerich, 1991; Gioia, Schultz, & Corley, 2000). Identity is the internal counterpart to external reputation or image. Revolutions in reputation cause changes to internal identity and so on.

Identity is central to the notion of a company of good, as it can be perceived as a "corporate moral philosophy" (Barney & Stewart, 2002). In terms of human beings, identity means a person's social self. We continuously seek limits for belonging to a variety of groups. An individual's identity is constructed in relation to various group social identities through membership (Wenger, 1998). Identities are continuously renegotiated. Even the individual's identity is not permanent but is instead in a state of continual change. Identity is a story that we use to make sense of the chaos of our lives (Weick, 1995).

When talking about the identities of companies and communities, attention is drawn to two main lines of thought. Firstly, identity is considered to be based on a common visual identity, and it can be communicated in some way outwards from the organization as a communicational project. In this case identity includes, for example, brands, logos, and slogans. Here we talk about a company's visual identity and its management. The concept of visual identity emphasizes a company's graphic image and the communication of that image. Indeed, graphic design provides the basis for corporate identity, and the heart of corporate identity is an organization's logo and other visual communications (Van Riel & Balmer, 1997). Visual identity is founded upon consistency and uniformity, which should extend to all internal and external communications. An organization's identity is thus the sum of all these visual messages, on the basis of which people recognize the organization (Bernstein, 1986). From this perspective (visual) identity is the companion of image. Identity is a kind of surface that should not be scratched. From the perspective of reputation the visual identity part can be recognized, but it is not at the core of this concept.

Secondly, the identity concept is considered to cover the views of an organization's members about what in the organization differentiates it from others and what is central and enduring (Albert & Whetten, 1985; Alvesson, 1990). In this case identity is an organization's essence, which is built on the current state of operations, on what the organization is felt to be, and on what and how it is considered to do things (Åberg, 2000). What is essential is how the members of an organization experience membership of the organizations, what kind of view they have about themselves as part of the organization. The feeling of a group effort is also important. The organization in general, but also its members individually, should have a feeling of a job to do, a kind of fate. The direction is forwards. In addition, a strong identity requires a feeling of permanence; identity creates a feeling of being rooted. Identity helps an organization maintain a feeling for its history, a connection with previous generations, which creates a feeling of continuity. We have a purpose.

An organization's identity is thus something that makes "us" precisely "us." It is something that "we" feel is our own and that differentiates "us" from others, "not one of us." Similarly, identity creates a feeling of continuity—the organization is the same organization as a year ago, even if a year ago not all the employees were the same. People change; identity continues. Illustrative examples are army units or student unions, whose members change all the time while adopting and repeating the same decades-old habits, stories, and attitudes. Identity is thus an organization's internal feature—it is like an organization's ego. In the same way reputation distinguishes a company from other similar companies and makes the organization unique and different.

Reputation and identity are thus in many ways sisters. An organization's identity can indeed be called "internal reputation," and reputation "external identity." When the idea of reputation being rooted in an organization's operations connects with the idea of the identity and reputation being related, we get to the core of reputation. An organization with a good reputation always has a strong identity. Many reputational advantages seem to be made concrete in a company's relations with the outside world. It could be, however, that the greatest advantage of good reputation is specifically its effect on the internal conditions of a company, the trust that is felt, the dedication, and the feeling of belonging together. Reputation affects a company's internal feelings about loyalty, unity, and morals (Aula & Heinonen, 2002). An organization's identity requires shared meanings, and these meanings are created in the internal structures of the organization. Identity is built in the interaction between the cultures and communications of organizations. As a result, the most important task of an organization is to continuously create itself and its identity.

Both an organization's identity and its reputation are based on two basic assumptions. Firstly, there must be a feeling of the importance and significance of existing within the organization. Secondly, there must be a small group of core values at the heart of identity to which people are genuinely attached. In a certain way the collective identity of an organization that generates reputation is something that people value more than the individual ego at any specific moment. If an organization wants its talented members to work and stay together, it has to have something that is considered more valuable than the self: a deep and shared understanding of the purpose of the organization's existence.

Organizational identity is often far from uniform, however. Organizations are not simple monoliths in which everyone thinks the same or even about the same things. Furthermore, organizations are not blank screens that reflect films that have been carefully produced for the pleasure or wonder of the audience. An organization's identity is diverse and constantly fluid (see e.g. Pratt & Foreman, 2000). And just as with strategies, also identity cannot be created for an organization from the top down; it is built upon an organization's local orientation. Identity comes from people, not organizational charts. What is reassuring, however, is that even with fragmented identities, organizations are fully operational. For the organization it is enough that its identity is sufficiently uniform (Aula & Heinonen, 2002), even if it can never be completely uniform.

The idea of sufficient uniformity, or rather the lack thereof, partly explains the controversy that repeatedly arises when discussing, for example, the interaction or lack of interaction between organizational subcultures (see, for example, Martin, 1992). A typical lack of interaction and direct collision can be seen in the apparent differences in the organizational cultures between the leaders and other members of an organization. The Central Chamber of Commerce of Finland published in January 2004 its third report on Finnish corporate culture. The report is harsh reading. A central deduction can be found behind its many individual conclusions: corporate leaders and employees live in two opposing organizational worlds. The views about the entity that is known as the company are like night and day. Such a major difference is naturally a problem, although not necessarily as big as one might imagine at first. The problem becomes more difficult if the goal is a single monolithic culture, or the exact same views about the same organization. If the goal is a sufficiently unified culture, and thus with cultural diversity, the problem no longer seems so catastrophic. "Like night and day" is not a good thing; the gray area is sufficient.

A good company's reputation is based on a good identity. Reputation follows from an organization's identity and is thus connected with each member of the organization. When a certain spirit, philosophy, and culture flourish within an organization, each member communicates this in all their interactions, both among themselves and with stakeholders. A good corporate identity is based on its members' shared beliefs about the organization's central and sustainable characteristics, which distinguish it from other organizations (Gray & Balmer, 1998). These characteristics include an organization's values, cultures, and general ways of relating to work and acting with stakeholders. These traits, and thus a good company's identity, are defined in an organization's practices—internally in the interaction between members of the organization, and externally in relations with other bodies. At the same time, where the organization is coming from, what it is now, and where will it go in the future are defined through a good company's identity. The building of identity is influenced on the one hand by the organization's understanding of itself and on the other hand by the organization's environment. External influences include, for example, social values, threats, and trends. The physical environment can also be seen as affecting identity. Especially in terms of an organization's reputation management, it is essential to be aware of identity and the mechanisms by which it is built.

An organization's storytelling networks are related to external reputation-building. For local organizations, the communicative capacities of stories engage in creating or destroying reputational capital that is linked to the experiences that stakeholders have of the organization. Stories and narratives are experiences diffused, or in the process of diffusing, among stakeholders, weaving webs of trust or distrust (Aula & Heinonen, 2002). Some scholars have actually argued that "reputational capital" has very much to do with trust and social capital (Carow, 1999; Petrick et al., 1999). Reputation management thus appears as trust and social capital creation at the top and lower levels of the organization.

Chapter 4

The arena model of organizational reputation

In chapter 3 we established a tension between two competing discourses over organizational reputation: the financial, value-driven capital discourse and the meaning-driven, interpretive discourse. However, we did not take an ultimate stand—which one is the "right way" to capture reputation and its formation processes? In other words, what do we think is the reputation of the good company? Is it money or stories? Our answer is that, in order to become good, a company has to pay attention to both aspects of reputation. We firmly believe that the tendency of mainstream reputation literature to collapse reputation to an economic view has led to an impoverished understanding of how reputations are built, improved, and destroyed. While we have been critical towards the dominant capital view, we readily acknowledge that a purely interpretive focus on reputation-as-stories, on the other hand, runs the risk of neglecting the fact that, first, reputations have real value to organizations, and, second, that reputation-building is often a competitive activity.

Our solution is to characterize reputation as a negotiation of meaning, taking place between an organization and a number of stakeholders. To give a satisfactory account of this we shall require two new concepts. The first of these is a market of meaning. The strategic management of reputation entails an understanding of an organization's environment and its internal situation. Strategic management tools are often founded on this synthesis of external demands and internal conditions—the most familiar of which is probably the SWOT analysis, in which internal strengths and weaknesses are connected with external opportunities and threats. However, traditional strategic management models have considered the environment that has strategic significance for an organization to be above all the market environment, the economic field of competition, whose phenomena are studied through microeconomic analyses.

Of course markets are important for reputation too, but the strategic management of reputation requires a parallel and quite different view of what constitutes an organization's environment. Accordingly, it should be seen above all as an environment of meaning (du Gay, 2000). Whereas the market environment of strategic management consists of such concepts as return on capital, transaction costs, value chains, resources, and market maturity, the environment of communicative meaning consists of the opinions, symbols, stories, myths, rumors, and other forms of communication that create and convey meaning about the organization.

The market environment has traditionally been described with the help of metaphors adopted from the natural sciences, most often biology. Accordingly, an organization is an organism that competes in markets over scarce resources as part of a certain population. The fast eat the slow, and only the strongest survive.

To depart from the biological metaphor in favor of a more communicative metaphor, we describe the environment in a market of meaning using the metaphor of arena, which is our second key concept. According to this view, organizations interact with their publics on different types of arenas, and these interactions create mental impressions that are important for each organization. To integrate the concepts of "negotiable reputation" and "reputation arenas" into our discussion we will use the help of communication and cultural studies (Hall, 1973; 1997; 1992) as well as semiotics (Greimas, 1987; 1991).

Arenas within markets of meaning

Organizational communication occurs everywhere: in exchange of texts, new and digital media, meetings, unofficial networks, the Internet, and so on. Ralf Stacey (1991) calls these places of organizational communication, the "arenas" of communication. Stacey uses the term "arena" within an organization's boundaries only by using it for internal meetings, hallway discussions, etc. Arenas can, however, be studied through the interrelationships between an organization and its publics. Thus arenas can be either inside or outside an organization. The media is an arena, as are interactions with stakeholders or between members of the organization. Arenas are places where the organization and its publics encounter each other and create representations and interpretations (Aula, 1999; 2000). In principle an arena can be formed wherever and whenever. Arenas can be regular and predetermined or irregular and spontaneous, official or unofficial in form, limited or open in terms of participation, and fluid and changeable or formal and consistent. All arenas are connected by the limited time affecting participants and the arena's communications. An arena is like a dish that has only certain possibilities to handle the things poured into it. New knowledge, interpretations, and thus also organizations themselves are created within arenas. Within the symbolic environment arenas are the birthplace of building reputation. The interactions between organizations and their publics that take place within arenas are at the heart of reputation (see

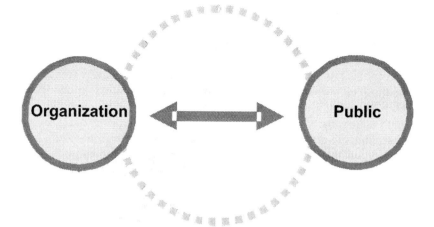

Figure 4.1 Reputation arena. Reputation is created when an organization and its public interact within the arena.

figure 4.1). For this reason it is appropriate to talk about an organization's reputation arenas.

An organization that is strategically building its reputation can be metaphorically envisioned to be involved in conversations in a large square where there are many others having conversations. An arena is like an old-fashioned market where local residents gather to take care of things and conversely, to share meanings. News reaches the market from inside and outside the kingdom, about faraway lands and about the neighbors' relationships. Amidst all the talking in the arena meanings are exchanged among conversationalists with influence both inside and outside the arena. At the right moment it can be easy to make one's voice heard above all the talking, but usually not. Statements that support or challenge an organization create stories that are transmitted among the public; these statements generally concern issues or themes that are interesting to stakeholders.

The communication of reputation is not only about sending and receiving messages in order to transfer information. The organization is interpreted through verbal, tonal, and visual perceptions and symbols in the arena. Representation of an organization is representation in the very first meaning of the word: bringing something into presence again. Representation can be understood as symbolism or illustration, i.e. when we present something as something (Lehtonen, 1996). For example, the thought of language as a representation emphasizes the fact that the symbols of language do not present their objects as such, but through the prefix "re-" the objects always become re-presented in language, as they are in fact being presented again or in another way. Each linguistic statement, such as organizational texts, refers symbolically to a whole set of meanings. Representation occurs not only on the level of single words but on the level of expressions as well.

Spoken language is raw material for making an interpretation. Language enables us to communicate with someone and about something. Thus it not only offers a means of communication but also the possibility to represent—e.g. give statements about an organization.

Language is often considered merely a medium, which people use for transferring various messages. Linguistic communication can, however, be successful only if the sender and the receiver already share knowledge on which to base their mutual understanding. It is interpersonal and intersubjective awareness. We give meaning to reality by language. Language divides the world into different realms, as well as forming and depicting it (Lehtonen, 1996). Communication thus always requires a certain mutuality among parties. Discourse means a special way of representing human reality and each discourse consists of characteristic presumptions. Different languages and the different discourses of the same language divide the world into meaningful parts in different ways. Discourses are thus culturally bound and change with time and place (Lehtonen, 1996).

We should broaden this notion of language in organizational reputation context. All reputational communication can be considered as the "reputational language" of an organization. An organization produces different forms of discourse about itself and its actions in respect of reputational dimensions.

Reputational communication is not a medium for sending a certain message to the public but an inseparable part of being an organization. Reputational communication originates from an organization's interaction with its members and publics and also with other organizations. Like language, reputational communication is also always a certain illustration of perceived reality and a production of reality. There is always the communicative aspect that has to do with meanings in all organizations' social activity. Meanings are thus not only time- and place-bound and time- and place-sensitive but also social. Subjects constantly modify the way they communicate according to how others have behaved ahead of them (Cappella, 1981). We are, at least to some extent, aware of what we are doing while communicating with others and this awareness can contribute to the size and direction of the next step in the system.

We make observations and get information by seeing, hearing, and reading. Then we shape and tone the information based on the credibility of the source, and color it with our own prejudices, experiences, attitudes, personal opinions, and/or convictions. Finally, we apply our "gut instinct" that we feel about something (Budd, 1994). Both direct and indirect encounters are, after all, about observing the target. Perception is not only a simple reflection of the target in the observer's mind. It is also based on interpretation and reasoning which are founded on the references at hand (Karvonen, 1999).

Arena is embedded in communication practice

On the reputational arena, an interpretation is formed of what the organization is about and this interpretation happens in communication. To increase the chances of building a public reputation as close as possible to its own identity, an organization needs to produce coded messages in the form of an expedient and functional discourse (i.e. it needs to encode the message in a favorable way). This set of encoded meanings is the one which affects, entertains, advises, or persuades and brings about cognitive, emotional, ideological, and functional consequences in the receiver (Hall, 1992).

An organization can, however, never completely control the meanings of its reputational communication. On the one hand, the messages that relate to a reputation can contain meanings that it has not purposefully included in them. On the other hand, the organizations that meet in the reputation arena always bring along their own cultures, worldviews, and experiences. The consequences are that an organization's messages can be interpreted completely differently from what was meant. According to the principles of reputation management, the organization ought to aim at presenting itself as accurately and favorably as possible. For example, as a reputation arena the media acts as an agent who creates a connection between the organization and its publics. However, it does not create the connection into a passive delivery channel but as an involved agent. The media interprets the information which comes from the organization, based on its own information structures and to meet its own ends. The media looks for further information, reformulates the issues, and selectively produces the texts which it offers to the public for interpretation (Karvonen, 1999).

An arena's communications are a diverse, dynamic series of overlapping interactions in which meanings are created, changed, and exchanged (Aula, 1999). The arena can be best understood through the communication practices, or language games, which constitute a "form of life" for the participants (Wittgenstein, 1951). This means that arenas are embedded in the practice of communication. They cannot be understood as instrumental communication media, nor as universal structures or boundaries for communication. The communication processes are determined by the premise of the parties that concerns communication, which is based on Goffman's (1983) idea of "interaction order." According to Kovačić's (1994) interpretation of Goffman's concept, social interaction is a mixture between customary verbal and nonverbal communication routines, which on one hand reproduces the cultural, financial, and political aspects of social order, and on the other produces new unexpected consequences and interpretations. Interaction is a micro-level world, where strategic, instrumental, and spontaneous as well as unconventional communicative actions occur. In addition, interaction is order without rules. Local contextually situated language games or communication practices are based on heterogeneous systems of rules. These rules produce separate, incommensurable, and/or loosely interrelated social realms as well as constant transfer of discourses—movement from one language game to another.

According to the so-called ritual view of human communication (Carey, 1985), the point of communication is not the transfer of information but the formation and preservation of a common, well-framed, and agreeable cultural entity. Communication is not directed towards the extension of messages in space but towards the maintenance of society in time, not the act of imparting information but the representation of shared beliefs. In the ritualistic view communication can be defined as a process, in which a common culture is created, re-formed, and regenerated. Communication portrays the core of culture and renews or represents it. Encoding and decoding messages is not possible until the sender and receiver share a common language and sufficiently coherent culture.

In the light of the ritualistic view of organizational communications, reputations can thus be seen as the production and renewal process of the conceptions and representations of an organization. If an organization is supported and highly appreciated by the public, its chances and operational conditions are good. However, should opposing ideas occur and begin to recur in stories, then an organization's chances deteriorate (Karvonen, 1999).

Reputation is negotiated in arenas

Reputation-building is not a process founded on consensus. It is a negotiation, which can at times be calm and subdued, although at other times, notably during corporate scandals, it is a struggle. How does this kind of interpretation or meaning-construction of the organization's reputation take place in the reputational arena? According to Hall (1980), the process of meaning-making can be analyzed with three so-called positions or codes.

Hall developed a theory of text which addressed "negotiated" or "oppositional" readings of the text by the audience. In particular he proposed a model of encoding–decoding of media discourses. In this the meaning of the text, which is located somewhere between its author and the reader, is framed (or encoded) by the author in a certain way, and the reader decodes the text's message slightly differently, according to his or her personal background and the various different social situations and frames of interpretation (McQuail, 1983).

In the context of reputational communication this means that publics do not simply receive a reputational message, accepting the meaning intended by the organization. Instead, they negotiate the meaning in the message; that is, they take in some of the meaning supposedly embedded in the message. However, they also infer some of their own meaning into it. Depending on various publics' cultural backgrounds, some people might accept most of the reputational message, while others reject it almost entirely, preferring an oppositional reading of the message.

Meanings are traditionally divided into denotation and connotation. The denotative interpretation of a sign is fixed by a certain code. The connotative aspect of a sign, in contrast, is more open and more prone to being actively changed. Every previously constructed symbol of this kind potentially can be converted into more than one connotative figure. Thus the situation-bound ideologies change and convert symbolization especially on a connotative level. Connotative codes cannot be equivalent with each other, however. Every culture is more or less a closed system, validating its own classifications of social, cultural, and political norms. These form the prevalent cultural order which, however, is not sound or indisputable. The different sectors of social life have been outlined as discursive areas, which have been arranged into hierarchically dominating or privileged meanings.

In a communicative situation, the receiver often interprets the meaning differently from the sender's intention. In other words, the receiver does not act upon a valid or preferred code. In reputation management, the most preferred communication is completely transparent. In order to solve misunderstandings on the connotative level we must—through code—refer to the orders of social life, financial and political power, and ideology.

In sum, the notions of Hall's theoretical ideas contribute to our reputational arena model as they capture the characteristic of reputational communication as a process where meanings are contested and negotiated in interpretation. An organization is able to offer reputational messages to the arena using a certain code or position, but the meaning of the messages is always negotiated. The public may share the organization's reputational code and broadly accept "the preferred reading." However, the public may also resist and modify the reputational code in a way which reflects its own position, experiences, and interests. Negotiation over organizational reputation is often a process of contestation, full of conflicts. According to Hall, the majority of so-called "misunderstandings" are due to conflicts and mismatch between hegemony-dominating decodings and negotiated group-specific encodings.

Negotiating between "seeming" and "being"

Relying solely on Hall's theory of negotiation would lead us to an incomplete view of the arena. Hall's theory is based on a demarcation between "text" on the one hand and "interpretation of a text" on the other. The interpretive viewpoint, on which our arena model is based, does not make this demarcation, however. It would be misleading to regard the organization, or some other party, as the "producer" of a text, and others as "interpreters." There are many authors of the "reputation text," and the process of interpretation is the process of text-authoring itself. Hall's views are very illustrative in the view they have allowed us of negotiating meanings, but the limits of their applicability in the present context must be kept in mind.

Therefore, in order to understand the processes of reputation-formation as a collective process of text-production, i.e. "what happens in the arena," we need to elaborate our arena model further. As stated, an organization cannot fully control the meanings associated with it, and it is only one player among the producers of meanings attributed to its reputation. The perceptions are not the property of the publics either. We argued that meanings associated with the organization, and thus interpretations of the reputation, are created between organization and public.

To comprehend the differences between an organization's own notions about itself ("what we are"), the way the organization perceives how others see it ("how they see 'what we are'"), and how the public perceives the organization ("what it is"), we should differentiate between "being"—factual reality—and "seeming"—expressions about reality (Greimas & Courtés, 1982). As there are multiple authors of reputation, neither the organization nor its audience members have an "ontological monopoly" over "being" in a realist ontological sense. The tension between "being" and "seeming" captures our relations with others on the arena, however. We believe we have better access to our own being than others. It is easy to believe that all of us feel we have privileged access to what we are, while others are much more in control over what we seem to be.

Tension between "seeming" in opposition to "being" is present in Greimas and Courtés's (cf. Courtés, 1991) so-called semiotic or "veridictory" square, which is a device which helps us to both understand conceptually and describe the basic situation of reputational encounter between the organization and its public (Hébert, 2006). The veridictory square

> may be described in simple terms as the opposition being/seeming projected onto the semiotic square. It allows us to examine the dynamics of true/false evaluations in a semiotic act, particularly

a text. The main factors it takes into account are (1) the evaluating subject, (2) the object being evaluated, (3) the specific characteristic evaluated in the object, (4) the veridictory categories: true (being + seeming), false (not-being + not-seeming), illusory (not-being + seeming) and secret (being + not-seeming), (5) the time of the evaluation and (6) transformations or changes in one or more of these factors. For example, when a cabaret Elvis goes into to his dressing room after the show and then comes out, he goes from seeming + not-being Elvis (illusion) to not-seeming + not-being Elvis (falsehood).

(Hébert, 2006, para. 1)

Finnish communication researcher Erkki Karvonen (1999) has adapted the veridictory square to create a grammar for the social negotiation of meaning, suitable to our current reputation arena model. With the square we are able to capture the "fundamental syntax" (Gahmberg, 1986, p. 62) of an arena's meaning-constructing processes. For our purposes, we can describe the four possible situations as in table 4.1.

From the point of view of reputation, the positions True (1) ("being + seeming") and False (3) ("not-being + not-seeming") are more or less trouble-free. In the first case (True), for example, an organization makes a promise to its public and also keeps it in the eyes of its audience. The reputation-related act ("being") is considered to be true ("seeming"). From the standpoint of reputation management, the organization should do its best to safeguard an action first, and then communicate it. For example, as reported in wikipedia.com (read June 13, 2007), the cosmetic manufacturer Body Shop offered, from the beginning (first store opened 1976):

homemade skin care and moisturizing lotions advertised to be made with natural ingredients. Product names, descriptions, and promotional material were very similar to the original US namesake. Thus, products featured exotic ingredients such as jojoba oil and rhassoul mud from local herbalists and had simple, descriptive names such

Table 4.1 Being vs. seeming—the arena's meaning-construction positions.

		Position 1 TRUE		
	BEING		SEEMING	
Position 4 SECRET				Position 2 ILLUSION
	NOT-SEEMING		NOT-BEING	
		FALSE Position 3		

as tea tree oil Facial Wash and Mango Dry Mist. In contrast to high street retailers, the packaging included details about ingredients and their properties. Customers could return to the store to refill product containers for a 15 percent discount.

To understand the relation between positions Illusion (2) and False (3), let us consider the story of "Bonk Business," the imaginary corporation made up by Finnish artist Alvar Gullichsen:

> Bonk Business Inc. is a multiglobal industrial conglomerate employing 13,000 in 52 countries. BBI is the world leader in pioneering Third Millennium technologies such as fully Defunctioned Machinery, Cosmic Therapy, Repacking, ADS (Advanced Disinformation Systems) and LBH (Localised Black Holes). The Bonk story is closely interwoven with the history of Uusikaupunki [a small town in Finland]. The company was founded here more than a century ago, and the Bonk Vertical Reality assembly plant still provides local employment.
>
> In his founding speech of 1893, Pär Bonk declared "I shall make machines that make Man happy." But the roots of the company are even older. The Bonks were a simple fishing family from the island of Helgoland, not far from Uusikaupunki. They made several discoveries, based on the anchovy, which were to change the region completely. Firstly they re-invented Garum, an ancient Roman fishy relish based on the Baltic anchovy. Garum is still made and exported worldwide today. A by-product of this process was Anchovy oil, an extremely viscous lubricant ideal for the harsh Northern climate, which greased the wheels of nascent Nordic industries. Overfishing led to the extinction of the Baltic anchovy, but imported Giant Peruvian anchovies were bred in heated rock pools revealing the existence of the Anchovy Effect—a marine dynamo. So began the rapid growth of an industrial empire that has brought forth a cornucopia of inventions.
>
> (Quoted from: www.bonkcentre.fi, read June 31, 2007)

Whether the audience buys into the Bonk story determines whether the relation between seeming and being is Illusion (2) or False (3). If they interpret Bonk as real, the illusion is maintained, if they become suspicious and find that it is an illusion, the dynamic is changed and Bonk becomes a false image.

Is the second position, Illusion ("not-being + seeming"), about lying or deceitfulness? In one sense, yes, Bonk is claiming to be something it is not. However, in the case of many other organizations, corporate communications are constantly built upon stories about a future which has not yet come to be. This was the case at the time of the last IT boom. During the time of the IT boom, everybody knew that they were betting on promises not yet realized. It was a time when an illusion of a future that never came to be was maintained. After the fact, it is easy for us to judge the players as fools who believed in a lie, yet few had the nerve to question the *Zeitgeist* back then.

> At that time, even taxi drivers gave investment advice about quick wins . . . Soon, all this will be forgotten and investors will be carrying truckloads of money to hot firms again.
>
> (Founder of a "hot" IT startup that went bankrupt)

In the strictest sense, a statement is only a lie when the person making the statement does not believe what he or she is stating. In this sense, a false prediction is not a lie unless the one stating the prediction does not believe in it. When illusions are blown from (2) to (3), it is easy to frame this as the uncovering of a lie. This uncovering causes disappointment among the public, which often causes problems with reputation.

Building an illusion is always a reputation risk. For instance, an organization uses marketing tools to communicate only the good qualities of the organization and tries to hide the possible problems. The public understands organizational selling purposes and, instead of "buying the message," turns to more objective or contradictory information sources. In addition, the media plays this role often. It takes the position of the critical public and teases the truth out from various sources. This position can be used to explain criticism of image-building or "spin doctoring". The organization is made to look good.

> Boo.com was a United Kingdom Internet company founded by Ernst Malmsten, Kajsa Leander, and Patrik Hedelin that famously went bust following the dot-com boom of the late 1990s. Boo.com's intention was to sell branded fashion wear over the Internet; however, after spending vast sums of its venture capital, it eventually had to liquidate and was placed into receivership on May 18, 2000. The boo.com website was widely criticized as poorly designed for its target audience, going against many usability conventions. The site relied heavily on JavaScript and Flash technology to generate pseudo-3D views of wares as well as Miss Boo, a sales-assistant-style avatar. The first publicly released version of the site was fairly hefty—the home page alone was several hundred kilobytes which meant that the vast majority of users had to wait minutes for the site to load (as broadband technologies were still not widely available at this time). The designers had forgotten that getting people to use the website and purchase items outweighed the "sexiness" of the design. The

warning on their front page—"this site is designed for 56K modems and above"—apparently did not appease their would-be customers.

The complicated design required the site to be displayed in a fixed size window, which limited the space available to display product information to the customer. Navigation techniques changed as the customer moved around the site, which appealed to those who were visiting to see the website but frustrated those who simply wanted to buy clothes. As a result, although the boo.com brand received a lot of press coverage, potential customers were quickly turned off when they visited.

(Quoted from www.wikipedia.com, read June 15, 2007)

In the fourth position there is a secret ("being + not-seeming") at play. In other words, the organization is something but this something is not outwardly manifested in any manner. This follows common sense, in that people tend to hide negative matters about themselves—crime or divergence, for example. The secrets of organizations are, of course, titbits to the critical media and gutter press. However, in many conditions, "the hiding of one's goodness" is a workable reputation strategy: modesty makes one beautiful. Furthermore, many organizations choose to keep their nature in the dark for a variety of reasons. Secret services, security police forces, and secret societies are of course obvious examples of companies that have elected to remain in the dark. However, there are less self-evident and more mundane examples.

Is it a good idea to keep your company's true nature a secret? Is it necessary to communicate actively regarding one's reputation? Would it be better to say nothing? When German discount supermarket chain Lidl entered the Finnish market in 2002 the move created a lot of interest. Some Finns reacted to this mysterious foreign firm with feelings of true fear. Lidl's official policy was to communicate nothing about itself. The company's reputation strategy thus relied on silence, in which a dialogue between the public and the company's reputation was not even attempted. The company's Finnish managing director explained this policy in part by stating that "a company with a light organization does not have time to spend time with the media when there is lots of work to do" (*Kauppalehti Presso*, June 11, 2005). In June 2005 Lidl's Finnish managing director finally appeared before the public in the business publication *Kauppalehti Presso*. The director nevertheless refused to have his picture taken, explaining that "I don't want these issues to be associated with me personally. Lidl in Finland does not want to publicize any single person from among our 1,600 employees." The company can thus be seen to be seeking anonymity.

The managing director admitted the problems created by choosing this strategy of silence. The interview continues: "The mysterious nature of the retail chain has fed rumors and fuelled controversy. There has been talk of harsh pricing and personnel policies that discourage innovativeness and threaten safety."

The managing director has taken all the punches that have been thrown at him without saying a word, just as the company's information officer has done. The words have hurt, however: "At times it has felt pretty lousy," he admits.

The claims have seemed unjust, as Lidl feels that this feedback reflects ungratefulness. The company says it has created at least 1,600 jobs, a remarkable number, in Finland within a very short time. It is one of Finland's biggest foreign investors (*Kauppalehti Presso*, June 11, 2005). Lidl's choice is characterized by the fact that it has left managing relations out of its reputation strategy completely. It would be interesting to know why the company consciously wants to hide its face. Is there any advantage to being mysterious? On the surface it would seem that this kind of reputation strategy only leads to problems—and to the managing director feeling lousy.

If an organization's goodness is not communicated outwards, or is not shown anywhere, the public cannot get a good impression about the company, and thus act accordingly.

Integrating and contradicting in the negotiation of reputation

On one hand, reputational negotiation in the arena takes place between "seeming" and "being." As shown in our discussion of Hall's theory, negotiation takes place between different parties; that is, the organization and a specific audience, a sender and a receiver (Karvonen, 1999). We argue that two elementary communicatory acts can be identified in this negotiation: "integrative" and "contradictory."

Communication can be argued to carry out a dual function (Aula, 1996; 1999; 2000). The central purpose of communication is to keep the organization up to date, to enact and re-enact beliefs, and to make sense of complex, unordered meaning-structures (e.g. Weick, 1995). Nevertheless, communication can also break the existing meaning-making structures and create intentional disintegration, which can foster emergent properties. Therefore communication includes both integrating and dissipative elements, with which one can create or reduce the diversity of the existing meaning-structures, and, consequently, increase the chance of the emergence of new meanings in the unfolding interaction (Aula, 1996; 1999).

The notion of the dual function of communication is founded on the idea of dissipative systems (Jantsch, 1980; Prigogine, 1976), as well as the dissipative structure model of organizational transformation (Leifer, 1989), according to which change emerges when internal or external conditions of the system are unstable enough to throw the system off balance. In transformation, the existing form and structure of the system break and seek new forms and constructions. Despite the seemingly chaotic condition, the system retains its internal capacity to be restructured and this restructuring will take place after change periods when it is faced with far-from-equilibrium conditions (Leifer, 1989).

According to the dissipative structure model, the growing structural instabilities of the system caused by the turbulence of the environment, by loss of control, or by the lack of resources creates a critical state or condition that can be characterized as the breaking of the symmetry or the bifurcation point of the system. Prigogine and Stengers (1984) argue that the bifurcation point gives the system an opportunity to adapt itself to the new demands of the environment. The conditions of the bifurcation point provide the opportunity for the creation of the new dynamic order, which makes dealing with the growing uncertainty potentially successful. The behavior of the organization is directed by the human operation, which makes it possible to rise to the challenge caused by bifurcation instabilities (Leifer, 1989). From our point of view, this "human operation" is synonymous with "human communication," which in turn is the essence of leadership (Aula & Siira, 2007).

The core idea of the dual function of an organization's communications is that communication is characterized by two simultaneous counter-forces (Aula, 1996; 1999). On the one hand, communication integrates the organization's forms and structures by reducing contingencies and thus increasing the organization's ability to manage complexity (table 4.2). On the other hand, communications destroy existing forms and structures, breaking old and creating new ones. Thus communication's dissipative quality increases contingencies and decreases the organization's abilities to control complexity.

If an organization's goal is, for example, shared understanding (e.g. "balance in meaning-structure"), effective integrated communications are a tool that the organization can use to handle outside pressure for transformation. Following the idea of organization as meaning-structures this could be achieved, for example, by aiming at literal, intentional, controlled, and monophonic communication. Dissipative communications work the other way, deliberately increasing organizational disorder by breaking down the existing meaning-structures. The way to do this is to diffuse rich, metaphoric, impulsive, and polyphonic communication content. This can work favorably for an organization, but also harmfully, leading the organization down the wrong path of development at the bifurcation point. However, controlled disorder can sometimes be the objective. Order in itself is not necessarily advantageous for organizations, or disorder disadvantageous. Thus, according to dual function, communications can be used to control an organization's structuring,

Table 4.2 The dual function and its qualitative properties (Aula, 1999).

Integrative communication	*Dissipative communication*
Literal	Metaphoric
Reactive	Proactive
Intentional	Spontaneous
Controlled	Impulsive
Monophonic	Polyphonic
Monologic	Dialogic

as well as its diversity, and we argue that human communication plays a vital role in both determining and maintaining the complexity of the organization (Aula, 1996; 1999).

Dissipative communication is effective when the organization is in crisis and problem-solving needs innovation and creativity. Integrative communication is productive when the crisis is over and the organization needs control and planning. Dissipative communication is indirect and dialogical and it allows communicative partners to present alternative views and interpretations. It permits new intellectual structures to emerge. Dissipative communication tends to show, rather than tell, how things are (Aula, 1999).

Integrative communication presents the content directly, logically, and efficiently and it creates feelings of continuity and consciousness of control. Integrative communication is a monologic process, in which a sender communicates to a receiver, instead of involving true interactive participation. Integrative communication is systematic and structurally conservative. It is more telling than showing. Dissipative communication is suitable for unique tasks which presuppose imagination and integrative communication when tasks are continuous and routine (Aula, 1999).

The dual function of communications can be easily applied to our inspection of the dynamics of the formation of meanings in the reputation arena. For the sake of simplicity, we can discern two types of statements in the reputational arena: unifying and contradictory. Unifying statements aim to make opinions conform and to provide a comprehensible interpretation of how the organization is perceived in the arena. The public statement "Nokia becomes the world's leading mobile phone company" is an example of a unifying statement—and a rather strong one at that. Contradictory statements, on the other hand, shatter uniform interpretations, present challenging new perspectives and create uncertainty. "Nokia's social responsibility activities in China do not stand up to scrutiny" could represent the kind of public statement that challenges the official corporate view. Both unifying and contradictory statements can be made by an organization that is managing its reputation, as well as by other actors in the arena—the organization's publics.

We can demonstrate this further by comprehending media as a communication arena and media texts as forms of unifying and contradictory communication. Gentzkow and Shapiro (2006, p. 281) use the following example when describing media bias and its effects on reputation:

> On December 2, 2003, American troops fought a battle in the Iraqi city of Samarra. Fox News began its story on the event with the following paragraph: "In one of the deadliest reported fire fights in Iraq since the fall of Saddam Hussein's regime, US forces killed at least 54 Iraqis and captured eight others while fending off simultaneous convoy ambushes Sunday in the northern city of Samarra" (Fox News 2003). The *New York Times* article on the same event began: "American commanders vowed Monday that the killing of as many as 54 insurgents in this central Iraqi town would serve as a lesson to those fighting the United States, but Iraqis disputed the death toll and said anger against America would only rise" (*New York Times* 2003). And the English-language website of the satellite network Al Jazeera began: "The US military has vowed to continue aggressive tactics after saying it killed 54 Iraqis following an ambush, but commanders admitted they had no proof to back up their claims. The only corpses at Samarra's hospital were those of civilians, including two elderly Iranian visitors and a child" (Al Jazeera.net 2003).

As Gentzkow and Shapiro point out, even thought the news stories were based on the same actual event, each conveys "a radically different impression of what actually happened" (2006, p. 281). In the same way an organization is under scrutiny in relation to "reality" or "what the organization actually is."

A good company's activities involve active participation in these arenas and even making passionate statements of its own. An organization that maintains a good reputation strives to unify scattered views according to the interpretation of a good company. A company suffering from a reputation crisis aims to challenge the public verdicts creating the bad reputation and to contradict the unanimity in order to start over. New knowledge, interpretations, and thus also organizations themselves are created within arenas. Within the symbolic environment arenas are the birthplace of reputation-building. The interactions between organizations and their publics that take place within arenas are at the heart of reputation.

Summary: three implications of the arena model of reputation

Our purpose in building the arena model has been to reconcile the interpretive and economic viewpoints of reputation. However, the arena model involves a number of reorientations in the conceptions of organizational reputation.

1 An organization is not a matter, "a thing," or a commodity in the traditional meanings of the words

An organization is an artifact produced by human cognition (Taylor, 1993). Even though an organization is represented through various physical manifestations (buildings, logos, brands, trademarks), in practice all that is known about an organization is necessarily based on symbolic expressions and thus secondary information. From this point of view, reputation is a process of social construction. People categorize their experiences of an organization and by doing so create their own "subjective reality" concerning this organization (Gilmore & Pine, 1999). Instead of being affected by some external "objective reality," various publics interpret experiences to form for themselves subjective realities about the identity, image, and reputation of the company. From this point of view, reputation takes the form of continual production and reproduction of representations by various stakeholders concerning the actions and impressions (Aula, 2000; Aula & Rapo, 2001) of the organization in specific operational contexts (Goffman, 1974).

2 Organizational reputation is, by definition, intangible

> [Reputations] are not a tangible commodity like a physical product, but are subjective. A sense, a feeling, the signals you send are critical whether it's a story, an action, a report, an event or a meeting—all are pieces of the persona puzzle, the sum of which, at some point, will evolve into a reputation, one way or another.
>
> (Budd, 1994, p. 12)

Rather than being directly observable by the natural experiments of a researcher, an organization's reputation is always mediated. Reputation is always the public's interpretation of an organization's ability to meet with its challenges and conditions.

According to Perelman (1971), rotations of the elements of an argument to fit the requirements of a certain viewpoint can radically transform a reputation for persuasive effect. Because one framing of the organization's existence and actions will focus the persuasive power of the organization's reputation differently from other framings, the management of framing can be considered an organizational tool to both understand and socially rotate messages in particular cultural contexts. There is wide evidence that (external) organizational image and (internal) organizational identity are reciprocally interlinked—image is best built on core identity and image reflects back on identity (Dutton & Dukerich, 1991; Dutton, Dukerich, & Harquail, 1994; Gioia, Schultz, & Corley, 2000; Gioia & Thomas, 1996).

3 We comprehend and define reputation as the production, reproduction, and renewal process of the representations of an organization

Reputation is constructed within the encounters between the organization and its publics. Everyone having to do with an organization creates his or her own perception of it through subjective interpretations and thus never has absolutely the same idea of it as someone else. Thus to manage the organization's reputation is to politically and symbolically conquer a leadership position for how reality is produced and reproduced, defined and redefined (Aula, 2000; Aula & Mantere, 2005; Aula & Rapo, 2001).

The Swedish researcher Johan Fornäs argues (1995) that we are humans by virtue of being able to understand and interpret what we perceive, i.e. through producing symbols for things. Through symbols we can think of what cannot be grasped and are thus able to ponder our history, plan our future, observe others, and make speculations about the unknown. Together we form these kinds of models, build the world and establish our place in it. Fornäs describes appropriately the foundational importance of meanings to our lives, which was already well understood before humans were able to write. From the beginning of humanity, people left marks for other people in order to communicate something. For example, a branch that was stuck into the ground was supposed to tell the direction the person going ahead had chosen. Or the stones piled up on a grave were to symbolize that this was hallowed ground.

The manifold rivalry in the world of meanings is not merely restricted to the interpretation of the actual signs per se. People also give meaning to their world through judging and sharing their emotions, worldviews, and experiences through storytelling. People constantly observe the environment and make assumptions about it. They interpret their own and others' needs, motives, wants, and abilities as well as anticipate others' reactions in their own actions.

The production, presentation, and understanding of meanings belong to the most repetitive of human actions. We judge reality, social situations, and ourselves, and thus produce concepts for ourselves and for others of what this world is about and of our role in it. Meanings,

values, and theories become established in institutions, social relationships, belief systems, habits, and customs, and the ways the material
world and its objects are utilized. All of these together form cultures,
whose meaning-landscapes help their members to give sense to the world
(Lehtonen, 1996).

Throughout the next chapter, we will discuss the implications of the
arena model for strategic reputation management. The dynamic view of
reputations offered by the arena model helps us focus on the activities
involved in building organizational reputations, and the management
implications of these activities.

Chapter 5

Reputational arenas within markets of meaning

We have discussed the arena model of reputation as a synthesis of the interpretive and capital views of reputation. Next, we will explore what kinds of reputation arenas can be envisioned. Our model is based on a simple division between two kinds of communication, as discussed in association with the double function of communication, and between two parties: the organization and an audience.

Different reputational arenas are formed, based on the kind of communications practiced by the organization on the one hand, and the communication practiced by its public on the other. Both the organization and its publics can use either unifying or contradictory communications, and can strengthen or contest the company's existing reputation.

To illustrate reputation-strategizing in various symbol environments, we differentiate between four specific arenas which represent the arenas the organization may find itself in (table 5.1). The model is based on two elementary acts in a communication system—integrating current meaning or dissipating it (Aula, 1999)—and two sets of actors—the organization and its public(s). In terms of reputation, integration builds on existing reputation while dissipation seeks to disrupt its foundations. In terms of the arenas, each actor may focus on either reputation strategy.

In the previous chapter we drew from Hall's theory of communication to illustrate reputation-building as a process of negotiation, and in particular, drew out the conflict element in this negotiation. In similar terms but from a public-relations angle, the relationship between an

Table 5.1 Reputation arenas for reputation-strategizing.

A public \ An organization	seeks to integrate reputation	seeks to dissipate reputation
seeks to integrate reputation	Arena 1: Peace	Arena 3: Attack
seeks to dissipate reputation	Arena 2: Defense	Arena 4: Riot

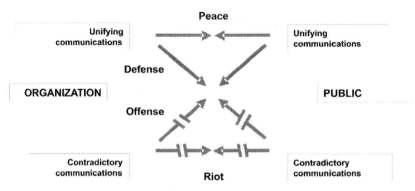

Figure 5.1 The reputational conflicts between an organization and its public.

organization and its publics can be described by James E. Grunig's (1992) notion of two-way symmetrical communication, where communication is used to negotiate with publics, resolve conflicts, and promote mutual understanding and respect.

Four arenas

Through a somewhat ironic lens, by applying the military-historic roots of strategic management, we can think of an arena as a battlefield of meanings in which an ongoing skirmish is being fought over the organization's reputation. And as with all battles, the battle for reputation goes through different phases. This reputational conflict can be dominated by peace, by defensive battles within the arena, by offensive attacks, or by riot (figure 5.1). As we have seen, a company's reputation is the relationship between the company and its stakeholders.

Arena I Peace on earth and goodwill among publics

A company and its publics live in a peaceful relationship when both the organization and its publics share the same meanings that are applied to the organization—in other words, when they are relatively of one mind about the issues affecting the organization, when they talk the same talk, just like Donald Duck's nephews Huey, Dewey, and Louie. In terms of Greimas's semiotic square, the peace arena can be coded as a situation where the reputational messages of an organization ("being") are accepted as genuine and true by its audience ("seeming"). The story told by the organization itself conforms with that told by its publics without creating any major contradictions. These stories change over time, but there is no quarrel about their meanings; instead, all statements create a uniformly positive image of the organization (figure 5.2).

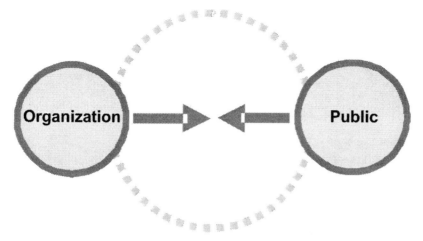

Figure 5.2 Peace in the reputational arena.

For example, most Finns cannot, will not, or do not want to dispute Nokia Corporation's reputation as the nation's savior during and after a wide economic depression in the 1990s. Similarly, who can look at the panda symbol adopted by the World Wildlife Fund when the organization was founded in 1961 and at the same time question the reputation of the WWF as an agent of good and a voice of conscience?

Many organizations would like to be in the peace arena. The views of the organization and its publics are sufficiently unified about what kind of citizen the organization is, where it is coming from, and where it is going. Communication between the various parties is straightforward and mutual. There is no direct contradiction between the organization and its publics; the relationship is in harmony.

Arena 2 The defensive battle

Every so often the peace is broken, however. In today's arenas someone is always opposing something that others prefer to defend (figure 5.3). Using the semiotic square, we can frame this situation in terms of the organization facing the danger of landing in a position where its reputation is regarded as false, "seeming" and "being" landing in conflict with each other.

It can be argued that a state of peace is frequently desirable, yet rarely 100 percent possible. There is always a war, or the threat of war, somewhere. For one reason or another, the harmony between interpretations and meanings is shattered, and the parties gear up for war to either defend or attack reputation. The organization or some part of its public is dissatisfied with the reigning perception of the organization. One of

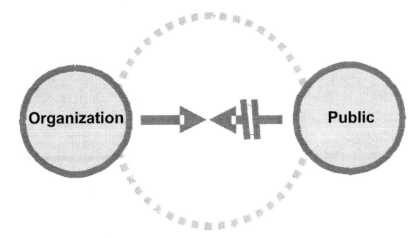

Figure 5.3 A company is forced into a defensive battle in the reputational arena.

the parties begins to smash the structures of meaning that currently rule the arena. The story loses its plot, and competing voices begin to demand recognition and application of their own interpretation. Some of the public are confused, while the most active choose their troops. In the battle over reputation the interaction between organizations is uncertain and disordered. Both established formal and non-established informal channels of communication are used. There are lots of contradictions and uncertainties in the relationship. Communications are both unified and contradictory, and communicative contents create paradoxes. A peaceful relationship becomes a reputation battle. And as in all battles, the opposing sides can either withdraw to defensive positions or charge forward to attack with their communicative sabers in hand.

The arena becomes a defensive battleground for an organization's reputation when parts of the public challenge the organization's reputation while the organization itself strives to hold on to its previous, unified, and favorable perception.

Tire manufacturer Bridgestone/Firestone Inc. was faced with a major product recall after discovering the treads on several of its models were separating from the tires. The case involved more than 14.4 million Firestone tires, most of which had been installed on sport utility vehicles (SUVs). Ford's SUV Explorer models constituted a major portion of the recall. Future investigations linked the faulty tires to 1,400 complaints, 88 deaths and more than 250 injuries. Both companies were forced to take action.

The problems started in 1997, when several accidents were reported in Saudi Arabia and Venezuela that involved Ford Explorers and Firestone tires. The companies knew about the product problems but decided not to announce them publicly. This was the same "strategy of silence" that Firestone had chosen in 1978, when the company recalled a vast number of tires without specifying the exact reasons.

The companies did not react until a TV station reported a number of similar accidents in the US. The first response was to accuse the station of spreading false information about the accidents and products. But again this strategy did not pay off. The scandal was very pricey for both corporations. Bridgestone's stock value crashed from US$100 in 1999 to US$40 in 2000. For Ford, the tire exchange expenses were estimated at US$500 million. After a long and fruitful business relationship, the companies blamed and turned against each other. For example, Bridgestone/Firestone's CEO Masatoshi Ono argued that the victims died because Ford's SUVs swerved off the road, and not because of the problems with the tires made by his company. In proportion, Ford's CEO Jacques Nasser shifted the blame onto Firestone, because it had not told about the tire problems earlier. According to Nasser, Ford had to tease out the information from the tire manufacturer. In May 2001 Bridgestone/Firestone announced that it would end its relationship with Ford.

From a communication standpoint, the Ford/Firestone case is considered to be a good example of badly managed crisis communication. For example, Ford trickled information under pressure from the media; it started with a partial instead of a full recall of the flawed product. The companies suspended important information and pointed fingers, and instead of putting the customer's safety and security first they made litigation strategy more important. Their strategy clearly turned heavily against the companies. From the reputation point of view, Firestone had the worst reputation in 2000, and Ford, after being the sixth-most-admired company in 1999, dropped down to third in the list of disreputable companies. In 2002 both companies were still holding their positions at the bottom of the reputation listings.

During the defensive battle the public (or, for example, competitors) try to bring forth new and contradictory meanings for the previously unified image of the organization. For many companies, being forced into this kind of defensive position can mean a reputational crisis. In the minds of its publics, the organization's operations have diverged from the course of good practice. Many aspects of the organization that were once considered good now look bad. The reason may lie within the company itself: perhaps its operations really have changed and good standards have been sacrificed. The reason may also be wholly independent of the organization: perhaps the values of its publics, and thus the demands placed on the company, have changed, and the company's operations have not kept up with the changes.

Arena 3 The offensive

The war over meanings is not always just a defensive battle. Organizations can also go on the offensive within the reputational arena. An organization attacks inside the arena whenever it tries to smash unified meaning of its reputation among publics (figure 4.5). In other words, it wants to change its reputation in a situation in which the "old reputation" is no longer accurate but is still firmly embedded in the minds of its publics. In terms of the semiotic square, the organization is either (1) seeking to challenge fixed views of "being" and "seeming" being in contradiction, that is, a fixed reputation according to which the organization represents a false image; or (2) seeking to upset a coherent reputation (true) that the organization wants to escape from.

An offensive battle is called for especially when a reputational crisis has created a unified yet unfavorable perception of the organization. However, it does not have to involve a reputational crisis as such, as many organizations simply want to get rid of entrenched reputations. For example, hamburger giant McDonald's stirs up strong emotions. Over the years its expansion to every corner of the globe has aroused heated debates over the rights of workers, US cultural imperialism, and the impact fast food has on health. For example, the documentary film *Super Size Me*, directed by Morgan Spurlock, received a lot of attention when it was released in 2004. In the film, the director eats nothing but McDonald's products for one month, resulting in the collapse of his health. The perceived threat when international corporations expand is that these companies, which are often owned by faceless investment funds, will neglect the well-being of local communities in the name of maximizing their financial advantage. McDonald's marketing is strongly focused on families with children through the character of the Ronald McDonald clown. In our least charitable moments it is possible to think that this global megacompany is set on destroying the health of our children.

McDonald Corporation-related The Ronald McDonald House Charities (RMHC) is a prime example of a company's concerted attack on all or part of its reputation. According to the charity's website (http://www. rmhc.org), they do good "by creating, finding, and supporting programs that directly improve the health and well-being of children." Although McDonalds do not own the charity (the charity programs are owned and operated by local RMHC chapters), the corporation

> provides RMHC with free use of its facilities, equipment, materials, and limited services. The free goods and services provided by McDonald's Corporation partially defray certain costs that the Charity would otherwise incur to conduct special fundraising events as well as for program services, fundraising, and management and general expenses.

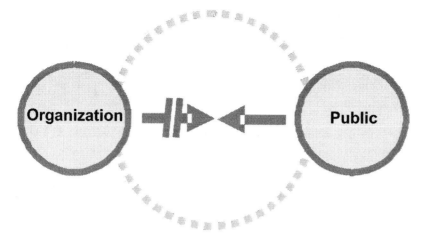

Figure 5.4 Companies can also go on the offensive.

RMHC's children's homes no doubt offer support for seriously ill children and their families, but they also represent a strategic reputational tool. It is no coincidence that the target of the company's philanthropy consists of the families of seriously ill children. The company, whose marketing is directed at children and families and whose products have questionable health effects, solves the problem by establishing children's homes to serve seriously ill children and their families. The Finnish Ronald McDonald House website (www.rml.fi, read May 6, 2007) describes the purpose of these children's homes as follows: "The main idea of the Ronald McDonald House is to allow you and your family to live in a home-like environment in the villa district of Meilahti while undergoing treatment at the HYKS (Helsinki University Central Hospital HUCH) Children's Hospital." This global mega-corporation, which for many represents the faceless power of capitalism and creates fears that it will harm the local community, establishes a charity foundation because "it was a principle of founder Ray Kroc that a portion of the company's earnings are returned to the community" (www.rml.fi/toiminta/tavoite_ja_taustat.html, read May 6, 2005).·

The reputational arena can thus be at peace when the company and its publics see and experience the company in sufficiently the same way. In other words, the organization is unanimously considered to be a suitably good company. As we have seen, however, there can be strong fighting within an arena over what a company's reputation is or is not. In this kind of reputational battle a company becomes either good or bad. In addition to peace and two kinds of fighting, there is one further kind of reputational arena: there can be rioting.

Arena 4 The riot

Rioting occurs in the reputational arena when neither the public nor the organization tries to unify their perceptions of the organization, or when both strive to shatter the existing perception at the same time (figure 5.5). In these circumstances the image of the company has splintered on both sides. It is interesting to consider whether this kind of riot reflects the failure of an organization's reputation strategy. In other words, has the organization failed in its attempt to unify perceptions, and are its communications hopelessly confused? In some cases an organization is unable to communicate logically through official channels, while in other cases an organization's official message is essentially different from its operations close to stakeholders, for example in terms of customer service.

The story of the New York Port Authority published by Jane Dutton and Janet Dukerich in 1991 is familiar to many organizational researchers. Port Authority workers viewed their organization as a good citizen and a pillar of the local community whose task was to keep the port clean and safe. This was also the organization's official message to its public. However, the heavy-handed treatment of homeless people by Port Authority guards created the exact opposite image among its public. When the Port Authority realized that its external reputation and internal identity were in stark contrast to each other, it began taking active measures to help the homeless get back on their feet. In this way the Port Authority began repairing its reputation by doing what it said.

The Port Authority case is a prime example of the riot arena, in which an organization builds its reputation contradictorily by saying one thing and doing another. However, organizations may also want their operations to be considered unpredictable so that its reputation has to be reinterpreted all the time, like a work of art.

The relationship described by this kind of riot is typical of new companies. One of the basic theses of reputation is that it takes a long time to build. Indeed, it can be questioned whether new companies can have a stable and prepared reputation, or does reputation always emerge out of a riot? IT growth companies at the end of the 1990s employed precisely this tactic, at least in part. For example, the mission statement of much-hyped SMS mobile-phone game producer Riot Entertainment Ltd (Riot-E) was "We don't make games. We create riots."

The story of "Riot-E"

I got an education worth 21 million in this business.

(A founder, Riot-E)

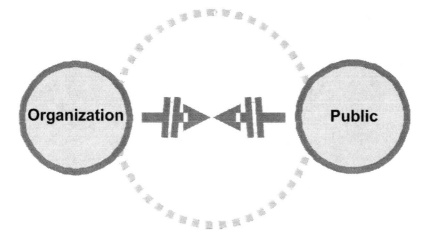

Figure 5.5 A riot breaks out in the reputational arena when neither the public nor the organizations try to unify their perceptions of the organization.

Riot-E was founded at the beginning of 2000, when the IT-market, "the new economy," was at its peak. The first wave of Internet business was over, but markets went into overdrive. Riot-E founders started writing a business plan. Right after founding, they found themselves at negotiation tables with major investors and business angels. Getting the money was enormously easy.

Now Riot-E had the money, but basically nothing else. Riot-E had to find an office, furnish it, and have somebody to work there, sell, and market. And they had to do this very fast. Investors did not want to wait. Riot-E had to build the whole company from scratch for a market that did not exist. There was no such market as "mobile entertainment." The challenge was to find good people. At that time, it was very difficult to find skillful personnel. Riot-E recruited students, friends, and relatives to do tasks nobody had done before. Two weeks after the founding, the staff numbered over 40. Spirits were high and employees were empowered to build roles for themselves. Riot-E was able to pay competitive salaries.

Riot-E skyrocketed. During the first six months everything went up. By the summer of 2000, Riot-E had offered work to over 60 people. Company spirits were positive and extremely enthusiastic and self-confidence was high. At the same time, rapid growth incurred management problems. The wrong people were hired, and the right people were placed in the wrong positions. But organizational difficulties were not seen as crucial. People outside the firm kept on saying how good they were, and that mobile entertainment, and thus Riot-E, would be the next big thing. Nobody bothered to ponder the consequences of the burst Internet bubble. On the contrary, the mobile world was seen to be the savior of the new economy. Markets, media, and research firms confirmed the picture; mobile markets continued to grow at a fast rate. The mobile business could not burst, for the simple reason that it was not a bubble, it was the real thing. Skeptics were silenced. Riot-E represented the "elite of the new economy," as one business daily wrote. The company CEO announced that the company would go public.

After six months, Riot-E received millions in venture capitalists' impatient money. The second round of investment took place between June and September 2000. Riot-E did very well. The process was said to be the most successful in Finland's financial history. It was an easy round, even though there was not much to sell. The business plan was basically the same as in the first round. The second round started Riot-E's second growth boom. The number of personnel exceeded 100, and the company went international. Riot-E established offices in London, Berlin, Paris, Rome, Singapore, and Los Angeles. Also, the firm obtained major international deals with big players from, for example, Hollywood. The parties arranged at Riot-E's impressive Helsinki headquarters achieved an almost legendary reputation.

In the summer of 2001 things started to change. Rumors started to circulate. The first people were laid off. The expenditure structure was untenable; the tide of success was about to turn. Soon it was realized that the capital markets were not the same. Riot-E understood that in order to succeed with the third investment round, the firm must be put in order and more people would have to go.

It was a time of cuts and spiritual stagnation; the managers somehow lost their touch. The problems inside the firm were swept under the rug. Qualms about the company's future had an immense effect. People started to feel burned out. Bad news was everywhere, markets were going down, and there were no alternative openings in the industry. Some of the founders left or were forced to leave the company and founded new startups. This affected company morale. At the same time, Riot-E were about to run out of money.

But Riot-E was willing to fight. Their last few months were like a survival game. The spirit was, "if we go down, we go down with style." They searched aggressively for new investors. However, the firm divided into cliques. While the powerful company spirit of the early days returned for a little while, on the other hand some regarded the struggle as very frustrating, unfair, and poorly managed. But even the good spirit of one group did not help. Business operations came to an end in the spring of 2002, after two and a half years, two rounds of financing and more than €22 million.

Two years later, the people involved in Riot-E produced an award-winning documentary about the company's journey titled *Riot On!*

(2004), with the tagline "sex, lies and mobile games." Even after the film the late company was still in the riot reputation arena. The document, and thus the existence of the company, were questioned. On March 3, 2005 a troubled public started discussion in popular website www. suomi24.fi. Lauri H. (a pseudonym) wrote:

> How long we have to wait until the hoax of the Riot-E movie is exposed in public? The Finns have been hustled over a year now, even though it is widely known that all of this is framed, and that commercial registers prove that there has never been such company in Finland which the "documentary" is supposed to be about.

Eight reputation strategies

When the relationship between a company and its publics is being formed, the kinds of communications practiced by the different parties are important. As was shown earlier, depending on the type of communicational meaning (contradictory or unifying) an organization and its publics struggle in all kinds of ways to define the nature of the company. These battles are fought in different reputational arenas.

Just as different types of business environment require different types of business strategy, different reputational arenas require different reputation strategies. In offensive situations the megaphones and big guns are brought out, whereas when there is peace agreements are signed and coffees are sipped. Defensive battles require shielding and the ability to negotiate, while offensive attacks require sharp words and more unconditional rhetoric to achieve success.

Choosing the right reputation strategy therefore depends partly on what kind of arena an organization is in and partly on the type of relationship between the company and its public. A company's public relationships can be described as either institutional or personal. An institutional relationship is coherent, transparent, and explicit. The purpose of communication is to distribute, often to a considerably broad audience, a message that is available to all and presented in the same way to all. Institutional relationships utilize commonly agreed communication channels that are known to all members of the organization, and the organization uses these channels to direct its operations. In an institutional relationship communication adheres for the most part to official communications processes, according to which communication channels, for example, are in principle accessible to members of the public. The official communications of an institutional relationship are often based on established, unilateral, "from-one-to-many" communication channels: the press, radio, television, Internet, publications, and press conferences. There are many examples. Basically all forms of communication typically labeled "official" can be classified as institutional. For example, Nokia Corporation's website communicates the importance of corporate culture and reputation-building:

> Shaping corporate culture, minimizing risk, enhancing efficiency, and building reputation are all aspects of CR which give it a significant position when setting agendas to increase our business value. We have long understood that this added value is the result of taking responsible corporate actions. Our goal is to establish proactive, integrated programs within our core business which always keep sustainability in mind.
>
> (www.nokia.com/A4254194, read May 15, 2007)

In a personal relationship communication is typically less formal, interactive, and with desirable parts of the public. In a personal relationship prewritten and openly available information content holds less value. Often the goal is mainly to construct a unified view of an organization in dialogue with members of its public. A personal relationship is not a synonym for covering up or withholding information, but rather another form of dialogue that is suitable in certain situations.

It should be noted that in neither relationship is communication between the company and its public fixed on any specific channel. The official communications of an institutional relationship can be seen as seeking a unified message, a factual form of expression, and an appropriate appearance. An institutional relationship's communications are dominated by official message-carriers—spokespeople. Often it is the CEO or managing director who provides the official explanation of how things are. Communications are often connected with careful planning, the goal being that the exact same information is simultaneously available to everyone. An institutional relationship can also be seen as seeking to control meanings. These organizations have strict guidelines for managing relations. Often no one is allowed to say anything without official permission. A joke in one multinational IT corporation runs: when a friend asks you how you are doing, the model response would be "please contact [company name withheld] corporate communications." In this way, the official nature of institutional communications is determined by the sender, the organization as official communicator whose operations and methods are regulated by the organization's power and decision-making hierarchy.

The division between institutional and personal relationships is essential in reputation strategies. On the one side, reputation is built in newspapers, on television, and through high-volume statements with unified messages. On the other side, reputation is built through unofficial interactions among parties that may know each other, be partially familiar

Table 5.2 A company's public relations and reputation strategies.

		Company's public relations		
		Institutional	Personal	Reputation management objective
Type of arena	Peace	Strategy 1: the senator	Strategy 2: the old-boy network	Sustaining status quo
	Defense	Strategy 3: the defense counsel	Strategy 4: the negotiator	Maintaining story coherence
	Offense	Strategy 5: the champion	Strategy 6: the stirrer	Disrupting story coherence to renew reputation
	Riot	Strategy 7: the chameleon	Strategy 8: the turncoat	Destroying story coherence in order to tease out the element of surprise and creative chaos, and to communicate implicit messages to: • tease out the element of surprise and create chaos • communicate implicit messages

with each other, or be complete strangers. A company can orient itself according to the four aforementioned reputation arenas emphasizing either institutional or personal relationships. Eight alternative reputation strategies are thus formed (table 5.2).

The peace, defense, attack, and riot arenas can thus be approached from the perspective of either an institutional or personal relationship. In order to maintain peace, defense, attack, or riot, one can broadcast the news to everyone or fly below the radar. Emphasizing different relationships creates different operating processes for each arena.

Peace

Strategy 1 The senator

The institutional emphasis during times of peace can be referred to as the senator strategy. The organization acts like a statesman, spreading his message openly and deliberately through official channels. An excellent example of the senator strategy is the Finnish Red Cross. Founded in 1877 to take care of wounded soldiers, the Finnish Red Cross has achieved the position of arguably the nation's most recognized organization representing asocial conscience whose public legal position is defined by law. In other words, its reputation is without refutation. The

President of Finland awards the organization's medals of honor and can act as its patron. The Word War II hero, wartime Commander-in-Chief Marshall Mannerheim, was for a long time chairman of the Finnish Red Cross. The organization has incomparable institutional communication channels at its disposal. Its campaigns reach a large body of the public at one go, supported by the state media and a large army of volunteers. It can even utilize the noncommercial national public-service broadcasting company (YLE) to market its operations, unlike most other organizations. The Finnish Red Cross has also recognized the importance of managing its environment of meanings. It formulated its first brand strategy in 2003:

> The communications environment has undergone rapid change. The amount of communications has grown exponentially, the pace has picked up, and the competition for attention and people's time has intensified. The impact of images and stories has increased. It has become more common to broadcast news about negative events and to monitor these systematically. In order to effectively meet these new challenges and to stand out from other actors in the humanitarian sector, the Finnish Red Cross should: utilize the mechanisms of the image society to make communications more discernible and to increase the storytelling factor—also through visual communications.
>
> (Aula & Mantere, 2005)

Strategy 2 The old-boy network

When there is peace in the arena, the seeds of an organization's reputation can also be sown behind the scenes. Here the organization's representatives rely on personal relations and build reputation through their networks. We can refer to this strategy as the old-boy network. Things are agreed among familiar faces in the proper way. These activities are flexible but not transparent. Furthermore, the loss of key persons can easily cast the organization adrift. An example of this could be a small consultancy firm that relies on its good reputation in certain customer segments and protects this reputation precisely through personal contacts. Many service businesses are dependent on an old-boy network. The most important thing is to be known and to become known. Deals are often made among familiar people, and the key success factor is having a direct influence on key stakeholders.

Larger and institutional companies also rely on the strategy of the old-boy network. Take pharmaceuticals companies, for example. Especially before legislation in Finland became too restrictive, pharmaceuticals companies and doctors enjoyed a rather symbiotic relationship. Although new laws have made it harder for pharmaceuticals consultants to entertain doctors at lavish banquets, pharmaceuticals companies still play an important role in training doctors. Within specific medical segments the relationship between a specialized pharmaceuticals consultant and their client can become quite personal over time, as the total number of clients is limited. Doctors who prescribe medications are important gatekeepers for pharmaceuticals companies, as their decisions have a direct impact on major purchases. Therefore it is crucial for pharmaceuticals companies to create a personal relationship with each individual doctor. In the following example, a Pfizer pharmaceutical sales representative describes his typical day:

> My workday begins between seven and eight in the morning. The highlight of the day is meeting clients, in which we listen, discuss, and try to assist the client in the best possible way. Interactive social skills are very important. I like to think that the representative's job is also to brighten up the client's day: a bit of humor and a light lunch are always appropriate.
>
> (www.pfizer.fi, read June 15, 2005)

Defense

Strategy 3 The defense counsel

In the defensive battle arena the defense counsel relies on official channels in order to maintain institutional relationships and to consolidate reputation against possible attacks. The defense counsel makes official public statements to try to correct misunderstandings and present information that is favorable to the client. Typically the defense counsel will claim to be acting in the right. The reason for misconceptions lies elsewhere: in general misunderstandings or mistakes made by the media.

A fairly recent example of a successful defense-counsel strategy is provided by the Finnish family-owned meat-processing company Oy Snellman Ab. At the end of 2004 the company was faced with the public fear of mad cow disease (bovine spongiform encephalopathy or BSE). Health inspectors in the service of the Finnish Food Safety Authority made a series of mistakes when taking samples to test for the disease in the company's facilities. The inspectors sought to cover up their mistakes by replacing the damaged or unsuitable samples with practice specimens (Finnish news broadcast, December 1, 2004). Naturally, health concerns can be fatal for food industry companies.

Snellman was in what seemed like a truly unfair situation. There was grave danger that the customers would project the faults of health inspectors who were supposed to be supervising Snellman onto the company itself. In many cases the association of BSE withSnellman would motivate the customer to steer clear of Snellman's product, just to be on the safe side. In Snellman's case its potential customer segment included the entire Finnish population, so its defense strategy had to be open and unified. It was crucial to demonstrate that Snellman was not party to the misconduct, as those who made the mistakes were in the employ of another organization, and Snellman was not aware of their activities. On December 1, 2004, immediately after the news was broadcast, Snellman held a press conference that included a health inspector from the Finnish Food Safety Authority. The press release of December 1, 2004 stated the following:

> Food safety in meat processing plants is monitored by health inspectors under the Finnish Food Safety Authority. Oy Snellman Ab is not able to influence the activities of these health inspectors. Oy Snellman Ab does not have the right or the possibility to influence official working methods and practices. . . . The impression given that Oy Snellman Ab has fired the health inspector who blew the whistle is incorrect, as the person in question was not an employee of Snellman but of the Food Safety Authority. Only the Food Safety Authority can comment about the termination of this person's employment.

In addition, it was pointed out that **"All Snellman products are completely safe and tested according to the guidelines of the Food Safety Authority"** (in bold in the original source, www.snellman.fi, read May 25, 2005). In Snellman's case it was essential to present clearly the facts demonstrating that the company itself had made no mistake. The bolded section demonstrates the key point of showing how the news in no way suggested that Snellman's products were harmful to health. The presence at the press conference of a state official responsible for the misconduct was also essential. In its press release the following day (December 2, 2004), Snellman stated the following:

> The health inspectors who inspect the meat before it enters production are under the supervision of the Finnish Food Safety Authority, which in turn operates under the Ministry of Agriculture and Forestry. The health inspectors are public servants and operate independently of Oy Snellman Ab. The company does not have the possibility or authority to influence the activities of these health inspectors. They operate independently. Suspicions of misconduct by these health inspectors have cast a shadow over our products. Snellman products are completely safe. The company tests its raw ingredients and products regularly to ensure the highest quality.
>
> (www.snellman.fi, read May 25, 2005)

Later it was reported that Snellman was considering suing the health inspectors for damages. The course of events illustrates again how dependent companies are on their reputation. Indeed, reputation can be immeasurably valuable, as the Finnish agricultural-sector publication *Farmi-Uutiset* reported on December 17, 2004:

> Snellman will most likely seek damages from the two health inspectors who switched BSE samples while inspecting Snellman's facilities. According to the company, it is still impossible to estimate the extent of the damage or to determine precisely if the company's brand has been impaired.

In this example it was clearly a case of someone else's mistake, so it was crucial for the company to avoid misconceptions regarding its own role. In reputation crisis situations it is quite common to rely on this kind of defense strategy: "we haven't done anything wrong." A less common defense strategy is to openly admit one's own mistake. The fear of being stoned to death may easily prevent such a confession. The same strategy can be found in a much larger context. In 1982 Johnson & Johnson experienced a major crisis. Altogether seven people in the United States died after taking Extra Strength Tylenol headache medicine which had been laced with cyanide. The Tylenol case stands as a prime example of how a company has to operate when a crisis happens. Johnson & Johnson without delay expressed commitment to and concern for customers and pulled capsules from the market. The company was not afraid to lose sales in the short term in order to protect public safety.

Tylenol is nominated one of the classics of good crisis management and communication. Tylenol controlled almost 40 percent of its market, but immediately after the cyanide poisonings its market share was reduced to 7 percent (Mitchell, 1989). After losing a huge amount of money and a market-leader position, Tylenol came back comparatively rapidly, and came to be a market leader again within months. Honesty and commitment elevated customer trust and reputation damage was minimal. However, as in Snellman's case, the cause of the crisis lay outside the company.

One of the most important modern arenas is undoubtedly the "blogosphere," which refers to the collective nature of the Internet's blogs as a social network or community. From the reputation point of view, the blogosphere is very hard to handle, but still requires special attention. One blog posting can make all the difference. A disappointed customer posted a criticism on his blog of the traditional, well-reputed Finnish restaurant Lehtovaara in August 2004. He posted his critiques after writing a letter to the restaurant and waiting six months for a reply:

Don't you just get mad after bad service at restaurants? I don't mind if the service is bad at a lunch cafeteria. But in a gourmet restaurant one part of the high price of eating is service. Avoid the Lehtovaara restaurant in Helsinki. I had my worst restaurant experience at Lehtovaara and decided to write to management. After 6 months they haven't responded to my letter. Although it has had a good reputation, lately I have heard of many disappointed customers. Let's see if they react after reading some reviews on the Internet. Please share your experiences.

(http://hietanen.typepad.com/, read May 28, 2007)

The restaurant answered with a letter from lawyers demanding financial compensation for the damages at the rate of €5,000 per month of online accessible criticism. They justified the demand by appealing to both tangible and intangible losses:

It has come to the knowledge of the management of the Ravintola Lehtovaara of a letter of slandering [sic] in nature has been posted on the net by you in which you have in a [sic] improper manner and continuously maintained a writing, which gives a substandard picture of the restaurant's kitchen and service, lessens and jeopardizes the business of the restaurant and labels the professional skills and abilities of the chef and main chef (the current chef has nothing to do with your restaurant visit). The same applies to defamation of the management of the restaurant and the head waiter and the head waiter's professional qualifications.

(http://hietanen.typepad.com/copyfraud/files/
lehtovaaraEng.pdf, read May 28, 2007)

The blogger, who is a lawyer and a long-time member of the Finnish online civil rights organization Electronic Frontier Finland (EFFI), posted the claim to his blog immediately. This started vivid blogging around the blogosphere, and the link to the blog was at the time of writing still (May 28, 2007) the second hit in Google.com after the restaurant's official presentation.

Even though "case Lehtovaara" is not strictly comparable to the global, more dramatic corporate cases, it is a good example of the magnitude and sensitivity of the new settings of reputation arenas. Clearly the restaurant wanted to defend its reputational assets, but without proper understanding of the nature of communication and its context, the defense went totally wrong. It is a clear case of how not to manage your reputation in the age of the Internet, and an example how even a small firm can find itself in the middle of reputational battle. It demonstrates yet again that reputation is not something a company can control in a strict sense. To attempt this in this day and age just communicates to the stakeholders that the company disregards their views and concerns. Lehtovaara sought to control its reputation among its external constituents. Another example of trying to control a company's reputation among its stakeholders, in this instance its employees, can be found in the human resources practices of Finland's largest and most well-beloved amusement park, Linnanmäki, which could be labeled "Helsinki's Disneyland." In contrast to Disneyland, however, Linnanmäki is not owned by a multinational corporation but by a non-profit organization, the Children's Day Foundation (Lastenpäivän säätiö), the mission of which is to collect funds for child welfare work (http://www.linnanmaki.fi/en/linnanmaki/amusement_park/foundation, read June 27, 2007).

As the Finnish winter prevents Linnanmäki from operating outside the summer season, it relies to a significant degree on seasonal staff, many of whom are young students working to pay their tuition fees during the summer break. In April 2007 Linnanmäki managed to arouse media attention when the employment contract the employees sign got out in public. The contract involves a section where the employee promises not to say a bad word about the park during or outside working hours. The executive director of the foundation commented about the fuss in *Helsingin Sanomat* newspaper (April 25, 2007) when asked what kind of bad talk had been around about the foundation: "Nothing bad has ever come out, but we want to keep it that way."

While an amusement park run by a philanthropic foundation is right to value its reputation, again we see how an attempt to control one's reputation, to control meanings among a company's stakeholders, conveys a rather distorted message: we don't trust you, you are a liability, if you misbehave, we will sue. The contractual controlling of organizational reputation, even among employees, seems a rather risky business.

Strategy 4 The negotiator

In defending reputation the aim of the negotiator is to counter conflicting messages from organizational audiences among key stakeholders. The negotiator persuades key stakeholder representatives in their own fields, and tailors messages to each context. The activity is based on careful identification of select key players and the forceful channeling of activity in their direction. In situations where organizational audiences are not essentially sympathetic but demand continuous persuading not to diverge from the shared story, the negotiator strives to maintain the unity of the reputational story. The negotiator's role is made easier if the key stakeholders who create reputation form a limited group that can be identified easily. Negotiators' tactics have connections to lobbying. However, it is important to make a clear distinction from what is usually meant by lobbying.

The negotiator strategy may be founded on corporations' "off-the-record" communications conventions and stakeholder relations. For example, confidential meetings with journalists, unofficial gatherings with analysts or potential investors, and discussions with activist groups are forms of negotiator strategy in practice. Negotiator strategy often utilizes personal communication networks, where direct and indirect contacts help the negotiator in achieving desired goals. However, it is more difficult to find well-known, current cases of reputational negotiation as a strategy as it is embedded in personal, informal practices of managers.

Negotiator practices do not have to be based solely on off-the-record communications. The key is to maintain personal communications, designed to address different stakeholders. One such example of negotiator strategy in defending corporate reputation can be found in the story of how Jeffrey Immelt succeeded Jack Welch as CEO of General Electric (GE). Welch's choice was something of a surprise to many, as another GE top management team member, Robert Nardelli, had already gained the nickname "Little Jack,"[1] as many considered him to be Welch's natural successor. In his article in the *Wall Street Journal*,[2] Alan Murray praises Welch's foresight, because while Nardelli was known for his ability as an operating manager, Immelt turned out to be able to defend GE's reputation in the immediate aftermath of the Enron scandal (Immelt's choice was made public on September 7, shortly before the Enron scandal was fully realized). Murray writes:

> Subsequent events have confirmed the wisdom of Mr. [Jack Welch]'s choice. . . . Mr. Immelt has played the CEO's political role with great skill. He has tied his own pay closely to performance. He has eschewed the kind of employment contract that is now rewarding Mr. Nardelli. He has reached out to a wide range of constituent groups. And he has adopted a number of popular initiatives, such as his "eco-imagination" program which, among other things, includes an effort to reduce GE's emissions of greenhouse gases.

The reputational crisis GE faced involved the very nature of corporate America and CEOs. He managed to defend both his own and his company's reputation through a personal addressing of the concerns of different stakeholder groups. Another CEO praised in the same respect in Murray's article is Procter & Gamble's CEO A. G. Lafley, who according to Murray:

> instead of catering just to shareholders . . . makes a broad appeal to "stakeholders"—a group that, by his definition, includes shareholders, employees, customers, consumers, and the communities in which all these people live. When I asked him last year whether that makes

his job sound like that of a global politician, he responded: "Like it or not, we are in a global political world. I've concluded I'm in it anyway, and I might as well deal with it anyway."

In his new office as the CEO of Home Depot, Nardelli did not do as well in this respect, according to Murray:

> What Mr. Nardelli missed, however, is that in the post-Enron world, CEOs have been forced to respond to a widening array of shareholder advocates, hedge funds, private-equity deal makers, legislators, regulators, attorneys general, nongovernmental organizations, and countless others who want a say in how public companies manage their affairs. Today's CEO, in effect, has to play the role of a politician, answering to varied constituents. And it's in that role that Mr. Nardelli failed most spectacularly . . . Mr. Nardelli's failure to do so reflects, at least in part, his inability to adapt to a new era of greater scrutiny. "I used to play football," he said when asked about the challenges of being a public company CEO today. "In football, you always know the score. Now, it's like we are ice-skating, and you've got a bunch of judges on the sideline shouting out the scores."

Offense

Strategy 5 The champion

The strategy of the champion is useful when an organization wants to challenge a reputational story that has become fixed in the minds of the public and is unfavorable to the organization. The champion plays with an open hand, talks in a loud voice, and uses public channels to make his challenge. An example of this is provided by the world's largest banana producer, Chiquita, which has worked for years to change its reputation. The goal has been to get away from its old reputation of exploiting third-world farmers. On the verge of bankruptcy a few years ago, the company has spent US$20 million over the past decade to improve its social responsibility. After years of hard work the company was finally granted international SA8000 certification for its banana plantations in Costa Rica and Panama. This certification requires adhering to basic international work guidelines. Chiquita's Environmental Director George Jaksch has stated that

> good reputation for us is both risk management and a prerequisite for success. Our shareholders and investors are also aware of this. European retail trade companies are much more enlightened than

their US counterparts when it comes to social responsibility. Certification is not a legal requirement for our plantations, but it is noted
positively.

(business daily *Kauppalehti*, October 22, 2004)

In the first quarter of 2005 the company posted its strongest result for
over a decade.

An entrenched reputation that a company tries to get rid of does not
always have to be negative. A former state agency that is deeply rooted
and respected may change its activities and image and consciously convey
a youthful and dynamic image that contradicts its former reputation in
order to enter new markets. A prime example of this would be Finland
Post Corporation (nowadays Itella Corporation). The organization has
probably never suffered a single direct reputational crisis in its entire
history. Finland Post has been fortunate to operate in a relatively appre-
ciative business segment. So long as it has taken care of its basic tasks its
customers, who are many, have generally been kept satisfied—after all,
it is always a pleasant experience to receive a personal letter through the
mail. Most Finns still associate Finland Post with jovial postmen who
always have something nice to bring us in their yellow vans. We can quite
safely assume, then, that Finland Post has no need to attack its reputation
due to any perceived negativity. However, Finland Post is not what it used
to be. The company's new mission statement is to provide "solutions for
reaching people." Accordingly, "Finland Post is the leading provider of
delivery and logistics services in Finland and selected markets in north-
ern Europe. The Group is seeking growth, particularly in information
logistics, comprehensive logistics solutions and international business."
According to its vision it "seeks to be the best industry player, in terms of
expertise, innovativeness, and customer satisfaction" (www.posti.fi, read
May 6, 2005). The jovial postman has given way to a solutions consultant, and fun letters and packages have become value-adding delivery and
logistics services.

Strategy 6 The stirrer

Offensive attacks are not always open. You can also attack behind the
lines, instigate new reputation discourses which disrupt the coherence
of reputation narratives. Just as with pioneers in wars, the stirrer picks
out important targets from the public. He then tries to sow non-uniform
views of the organization's story to help destroy the company's harmful
or entrenched reputation before a new reputation can be built. This influence is asserted "off the record." An appropriate tip to a journalist about
things getting out of shape or a couple of contradictory messages to different parties can help provoke a debate and change perceptions.

A new company, building its reputation, can often take an offensive strategy. Igglo (www.igglo.com) is a Finnish real-estate broker startup. The firm was founded early in 2006, and it is currently operating in Finland and Norway. Igglo relies strongly on the Web. It offers a Web housing-location service with photographs and data of buildings plotted on a map, where customers can bid for sites that are *not* for sale. By using the Internet as a tool they promise to halve real-estate commissions. This novel business concept gives customers the possibility to express their interest towards a site, and house-owners a way to monitor how the price of their property develops.[3]

Igglo's reputation-building communications resemble the stirrer strategy. When they launched their operations, they "forgot" a printed Power-Point presentation about "Igglo's top secret business concept" on the men's room toilet seat in the Hilton Hotel, Helsinki, while attending a real-estate broker's annual convention. The word about the "new revolutionary concept" spread out rapidly among the brokers, and the startup gained vast media coverage. Igglo got its voice heard, and its toilet-based instigation started a vivid public debate about, for example, the industry's invoicing practices and the quality of the services of established broker companies. Igglo has understood the utilization of varying reputation strategies. The firm's reputation-building strategy also includes champion elements. It has spent a lot on provocative TV and print advertisement campaigns.

Riot

Strategy 7 The chameleon

In a riot a company can choose between the reputation strategies of the chameleon or the turncoat. The chameleon changes form and booms messages about the organization's reputation in a loud voice that challenges current interpretations of its reputation. Just when the public had gotten used to thinking about a company in one way and begun constructing a credible story about it, the company sends out a contradictory message. The chameleon's strategy is typically part of a company's advertising methods, particularly in strong image advertising. Surprising the public captures attention. Advertising in which the connection between the advertisement itself and the product being advertised is at least ostensibly remote provides plenty of opportunities for the audience to create a product image. Indeed, advertisers often use the element of surprise to their advantage. "Far-fetched" ads can be seen on TV all the time. A low-calorie soft drink is advertised using a car driven by a monkey, mobile-phone subscriptions under the slogan "life is," and Italian clothing with images of AIDS-infected mothers.

The chameleon's reputation strategy is more than just surprise product advertising, however. A monkey driving a car is a surprising twist to the ad, but this image is unlikely to change our perception of the soft drinks manufacturer. In our minds the soft drinks company simply has funny advertising. Chameleons are companies that strive to prevent the formation of a clear core reputation by changing the public's perception of themselves.

Chameleon companies are not that common. Reputational chameleons show up most often in the fields of fashion, culture, and the arts. Chameleons object to a strict definition of their reputation. For example, many pop bands want to avoid being categorized to prevent their fans from knowing exactly what to expect from their next release. Established rock bands that rest heavily on their core reputation, such as AC/DC or the Rolling Stones, who have made dozens of albums that sound the same, are often criticized for their inability to "reinvent" themselves. They surprise no one, and listening to their records can be regarded a pastime for toothless old people trying to relive their youth. The same duty to transform can be found in the fashion industry: fashion changes all the time, and the most successful designers are those who can "ride the wave" of fashion yet whose next creations can never be predicted.

Even major corporations are capable of shedding their skins. Apple is a prime example. When Microsoft Windows began dominating graphic user interfaces, few consumers could predict that Apple would come to dominate the field of digital music distribution by creating the iPod. It became a hit product that everyone wanted. The computer company had become a key distributor and equipment manufacturer for music and moving images. A comparable Finnish example would, of course, be Nokia, the "rubber boot" company that transformed itself into the world's leading mobile-phone company.

Such changes, of course, are not particularly uncommon. It can be debated, however, whether such business transformations are a question of reorienting reputations due to new business strategies or actual chameleon strategies in which a company opposes the definition of its reputation in the same way that a rock group or fashion designer objects to their work being predicted and categorized. We are prepared to claim that a company is a chameleon if its public expects the unexpected from it. It is not sufficient to surprise the public; instead, the chameleon's public has to expect to be surprised, to view the company in a completely different way tomorrow than it does today.

There are few real chameleons among well-known companies. In fact, marketing and reputation management literature emphasizes the importance of a strong core reputation, the kind that chameleons do not even attempt to construct. Chameleons are often companies that are just starting up operations and that like to tease the public by acting unpredictably. An example of this kind of company is the controversial Finnish advertising agency Bob Helsinki, which was founded in 2002. In autumn 2004 Finns were moved by news of the impending termination of the baboons at Helsinki Zoo. Finland's leading daily *Helsingin Sanomat* reported on October 9, 2004 that the renovation of the zoo's monkey house would leave the baboons homeless, as a result of which they would have to be put down. Bob Helsinki employed a journalist with a PhD in political science for a period of one month to develop a plan for saving the baboons. Bob Helsinki used this trick to gain a tremendous amount of publicity that would have cost the company a lot more than one month's salary if purchased through advertising.

Bob Helsinki's next coup was to recruit a grandmother in spring 2005. The public was astonished to hear that the advertising agency had placed ads to recruit an old woman to sit in a rocking chair, tell stories, brew coffee, and prepare homemade food. In *Bisnes.fi* magazine (March–April edition, 2005), the company itself explained the reasoning behind this as follows:

> What does an ad agency whose workers have an average age of 29 need from a grandmother? "Grandma instills spiritual balance in our team. Grandma is living proof that hard work can be combined with soft values. Right now slowness is a virtue, as in the slow food trend," Parkkinen [the CEO of Bob Helsinki] begins. "Slow food is offered once a week when Grandma gets to cook in the kitchen. Today Grandma is whipping up a ground beef macaroni casserole." In addition to cooking and sitting in her rocking chair, Grandma provides a shoulder for Bob Helsinki workers to lean on when they are having a bad day. Grandma can take only so much of this, however. "We were looking for a grandmother who was also strict, the kind who would wash our mouths with soap if we used bad language," explains the company's graphic artist, who was on the selection committee.

It is hard to imagine that Grandma has anything to do with the "core business" of Bob Helsinki. Indeed, we could be led to believe that the company was playing with the opposite stereotype of that expected of a young advertising agency. In this sense the chameleon's surprising message did not really come "out of the blue," but instead as a counterpoint to the public's expectations. In the same way the baboons of Helsinki Zoo probably also played a more concrete role in terms of associations. Bob Helsinki promotes itself as a soft player in the ruthless world of advertising. The baboons that won over the public were a perfect symbol for distinguishing the advertising agency from the superficial masses.

In addition to advertising, another conscious effort to defy expectations and communicate through contradiction is provided by the small

Finnish clothing and design company IVANAhelsinki. It manifests itself in the form of story which is an open fiction. IVANAhelsinki is a boutique label that promotes the idea of localism and uses it as a selling point. Their website (www.ivanahelsinki.com) opens with a text of "Ivana Helsinki: Homemade in Finland," and a pop-up narrative of the company's origins:

> In 1938 manufacturer Ivan J. Paolovski arrived by train in Helsinki from Vyborg, which was under Russian occupation at the time. He founded the Globe's most northern match factory into the dark uninhabited wildwood of Eastern Helsinki. Ivan's ideology of ascetic, genuine everyday life gained many supporters in the form of motivated factory workers. And every other Saturday they went camping. In his match factory the light of life was growing and the factory grew into an entire sector of town; Eastern Helsinki was born. Today IVANAhelsinki is one of the biggest match factories in the world. By the way, IVANAhelsinki also manufactures clothes.

The firm has been open about the story being a fabrication. There has never been a match factory.

> It's a great story, though, and doesn't it create a more romantic image than the thought of sweated labour churning out cheap copies of Marc Jacobs's latest three-month must-have? Perhaps this is the point. IVANAhelsinki's 'history' exists to define the brand as a design-oriented lifestyle, rather than disposable fashion. The IVANAhelsinki factory is located in Lahti, Finland, and uses highly-skilled seamstresses, who enjoy healthy working conditions, maternity leave, and pension benefits. Many IVANAhelsinki items are hand-finished—even the prints for the brightly-patterned knee socks are individually designed in-house,

comments *Contemporary Magazine*[4] in its feature on the company.

In addition to its ethical values of regard for the good life for its workers and customers, the IVANAhelsinki story is essentially about the aesthetic values represented by the designer. It represents *fennofolk*, a tradition in design which is based on the reassessment and re-legitimation of the Russian influence on Finnish design, which has traditionally been oriented towards Scandinavian minimalism rather than the luscious folklore from the east. The "arrival" of the illusory founder is a metaphorical representation of the "return" of the eastern influence to Finnish design (www.fashionfinland.com, read June 18, 2007).

Both the IVANAhelsinki and the Bob Helsinki cases are instances where a fictional or absurd story, while deceiving audiences on the surface level, communicates the core values of the company: in Bob's case it is innovation and surprise, in IVANAhelsinki's case it is *fennofolk* aesthetics and a human way of life.

Strategy 8 The turncoat

Although the chameleon's message changes its form from one moment to the next without forming a coherent and continuous story, each message at any given moment is clear and comes from one mouth. The turncoat in turn offers messages that can be interpreted in many ways or are even contradictory, messages that accept no single interpretation at the moment that they are conveyed. In other words, chameleons change their form and surprise the public by appearing different from before, whereas the turncoat makes it hard to determine what color the company is at any one time.

One way of implementing a turncoat strategy is to say one thing and to do another, to communicate the rhetoric of goodness while doing bad. At their worst, those carrying out turncoat strategies are real PR "spin doctors." Behind their mystical messages lies a clear and cynical motive. Building reputation is based on the idea that things have to look good regardless of whether they actually are good. It would be easy to think that turncoats are simply reputation strategy amateurs who have not yet realized that words should be applied to deeds and not the other way round. This kind of assumption should not be made too soon, however.

Can you think of any company that claims the products it is promoting are dangerous? A company that would seem to be a good citizen by openly admitting that it spends large amounts of money advertising products that are damaging to your health? That claims it is trying to make legislators limit the availability of its products? A company that supports projects that help people stop using its products? Such a company is Altria Group, the parent company of Philip Morris International, Philip Morris USA, and Philip Morris Capital Corporation, one of the world's largest tobacco companies.

Altria is very aware of the importance of reputation. The website of Philip Morris International, which runs its tobacco business outside of the US, features a number of headers warning of the dangers of cigarette-smoking to one's health. For example, the company claims it wants to prevent young people from smoking:

> We don't want children to smoke. We understand that you might be skeptical. After all, we're one of the world's largest tobacco companies—why would we want to stop anyone from smoking? Our answer is simple: youth smoking prevention makes sound commercial sense. It's what our employees, our shareholders, regulators,

adult smokers and society as a whole expect from us. You don't run a successful business by flouting society's expectations. So yes, youth smoking prevention is in our business interests. But it goes well beyond that. We also believe that stopping children from smoking is the right thing to do. In fact, because of the serious health effects of our products, we believe we must stop children from smoking.

(www.philipmorrisinternational.com, read May 23, 2005)

This text is fascinating. The company claims it believes that it is sensible to prevent children from smoking, because this promotes a good reputation, which is good for business, and above all because it is the right thing to do. Is it then less bad to market cigarettes to adults? The Philip Morris International website continues: "If you don't want young people to smoke why don't you simply stop marketing your products altogether? We believe that we should be able to communicate with adult smokers" (www.philipmorrisinternational.com, read May 23, 2005). No explanation is actually given. The company repeats that people who want to look after their health should avoid smoking or give up the habit. Why, then, does it want to "communicate" the positive aspects of its products if it thinks that no one interested in their own health should use them? Is this ethical?

Is the belief that "it is good for business and above all the right thing to do" logical? Philip Morris International is a tobacco company. If developing its reputation is good for business, it will sell more cigarettes. According to its own words it does not want to sell more cigarettes to children and young people. Is it then right that it sells more of its products to adults? The messages would be at least somewhat logical if the company wanted to save children from the dangers of its products and turned to its adult customers to help do so.

The company's website's FAQ column nevertheless contains the following message for smokers:

What are you doing to make cigarettes safer? There's no such thing as a "safe cigarette." If you're a smoker and you're concerned about the health effects of smoking, you should quit. That said, we're devoting a lot of resources to the research and development of what health officials call "potential reduced exposure products"—that is, cigarettes that might reduce smokers' exposure to toxic smoke constituents and so reduce some of the health effects of smoking. For more about this topic, please see the Reduced Risk Products page.

(www.philipmorrisinternational.com, read May 23, 2005)

The company's message is that of the oracle: if you are interested in your health, don't use our products. It would seem, then, that Philip Morris believes that only consumers committing slow suicide should be its customers. The idea is absurd. Of course, not everyone is interested in their health, or they prioritize other things. Nevertheless, it would seem clear that few consumers would consciously want to shorten their lives.

Philip Morris International is an extreme example of reputation management carried out according to the turncoat strategy. Accordingly, an image of the company's reputation is created without in fact forming any image at all. The company advertises its products as a lifestyle while at the same time affirming that they will destroy the user's health. It does not even try to propose the possibility of "moderate use," as alcohol companies might do. Neither does it try to present tobacco as an intermediary product for building a bridge to a better future, as oil company Shell does, for example. Shell tries to create a positive story about the future by pointing to the energy needs of the third world. In the name of social justice it is necessary to meet all energy demands by utilizing the methods that are available today, including the burning of fossil fuels. Ultimately this is just an intermediary phase, Shell tells us, as the company is investing heavily in research into renewable energy sources.

The right strategy at the right time

We have presented eight reputation strategies that companies use when creating an image of themselves as good companies. We have not yet described how to choose between these strategies. We also have not touched upon the situation in which the public is passive or divided into factions. A radical renovation of a reputation can lead to an offensive or riot arena. Why do companies try to destroy their existing reputations? Furthermore, what factors influence the official or unofficial emphasis in communications?

When to attack, when to riot?

Do companies change their reputations only when the reputation is spoilt? The descriptions of the offensive and riot arenas can give the impression that a good offense is the best defense in situations where an organization's reputation has been tarnished. It is true that the offensive strategy becomes relevant in a situation where a negative reputation has become rooted in the big story told by the public. The traditional strategy for cleaning a dirty reputation is to identify the core of the tarnished reputation story and to create a new contradictory image in its place. If an image of the organization as a greedy money-grabber that does not give a damn about its stakeholders has become fixed in the minds of the public, the organization's message is to focus on painting the opposite picture of itself as a doer of good. If an organization is thought to be polluting the environment, its strategies of sustainable development should be emphasized—just as Shell is always going on about its research work into renewable energy sources. If an organization is seen as threatening health and the local community, build a Ronald McDonald House. The idea is to emphasize good deeds that are insufficiently known about among the public and to soften or explain any possible misdeeds. Going on the offensive does not always entail a tarnished reputation, however. Sometimes a company just wants to renew itself, to create a new skin, as we demonstrated using the example of Finland Post.

The word "riot" has a negative connotation. A riot is something bad, damaging, unpleasant, unwanted, or harmful. But can the word "riot" have a positive connotation seen from the perspective of reputation? Is it possible to consciously start a riot? Can an organization on purpose smash its reputation? A conscious riot suggests the idea that the object of the reputation wants to be interpreted in many ways, almost like a prophetic statement that is continuously reinterpreted. Riots can indeed sow the seed of a good reputation. For example, a new-growth company in undeveloped markets can consciously create an image of itself as mysterious, interesting, and attractive by promoting confusion. Something is told about the new company, but a lot is consciously left untold or contradictory things are also told. Since the new company has no history, the symbolic world affecting it is not yet built and is therefore from this perspective transformable.

A conscious riot for established organizations is also not as far-fetched as might at first appear. Consciously keeping a reputation fluid can be an advantage when adjusting to a particularly stormy environment. Reputation in this regard can be seen as strategic capital. Competence capital, another form of strategic capital, may require confusion in order to help the organization adjust to unexpected or rapid changes in the environment. It can be advantageous, therefore, for an organization not to define its areas of expertise too precisely, as sudden changes in the competitive environment can shipwreck a crew that is overly specialized. Nevertheless it can be claimed that some kind of core competence should be safeguarded and that uncertainty should be limited to concrete applications of this expertise (Hamel & Prahalad, 1994).

In the same way it can be considered that a company's task is somehow to unify, reinforce, and protect its core reputation, but around this the company consciously creates waves of multiple interpretations. It is not good to be known for just one thing, although a strong brand is useful—for example, one of the key lessons of marketing is that one strong brand is better than a dozen weak ones. Reputation should form an umbrella under which unexpected visitors can fit when needed, and where no places are reserved in advance.

In addition to an analogous connection between reputation and core competence there is a practical connection. Good reputation is always based on good operations, and focusing on core competence means building a kind of core reputation. In other words, an organization has the best possibilities to carry out good operations in areas that it commands well, in its core areas of expertise. Sowing the seeds of core competence can thus be seen, with certain stipulations, as sowing also the seeds of reputation.

When institutional communication, and when personal?

Strategies based on personal relations are extremely appropriate in situations in which the public is so small that it really is within reach of dialogue. Reputation becomes a negotiation that relies on building a unified meaning. Small organizations that do not even want a public reputation but whose success is dependent on a few key clients often undertake reputation-negotiations through their social networks. A perfect example of this is small consultancies whose best gambling chip is their reputation as good companies among select potential clients.

Big companies also build reputation in personal and unofficial ways among core publics. Lobbying political decision-makers is an essential example of this. However, big companies nearly always have to have in addition an official institutional reputation strategy for the general public, a big strategy that interacts with its unofficial personal strategy.

Personal strategies are ideal in situations where an organization is strongly interconnected with social institutions. Organizations like the Red Cross that rely on public goodwill and trust have to make sure that they are not caught negotiating behind the scenes about things that have not been discussed with their main stakeholders. In the same way, companies that are subject to strong public regulation, for example producers of hazardous biomaterials or food industry companies, also rely on public confidence that is fostered through unified, open, and official communications among the general public.

State administrative organizations represent the highest degree of institutionalism and must demonstrate total transparency in their decision-making and communications. The foreign ministry or president's chancellery cannot afford to rely on unofficial communications for public issues. Instead, they are expected to communicate their message to all citizens in the same way.

Strategies change: "Who dares trust the Finns anymore?"[5]

The choice of reputation strategies is not final. Strategies change, just like arenas. No battle or peace is eternal. There is a road to peace for even the deepest reputation crisis. An example of this is the doping scandal

Table 5.3 Timeline: From one lost case, to two doping cases (adapted from
Helsingin Sanomat international edition, February 26, 2001).

February 2, 2001	The Finnish cross-country ski team returns from a World Cup event in Estonia. A Finnish Ski Association physician's bag goes missing. The bag contains Haes-steril plasma volume expander and a good deal of other medications, some of them banned for use in sports.
February 15	The Lahti World Championships get under way. Finnish skier Jari Isometsä is called for a doping test after his fourth place in the men's 15 kilometer race.
February 17	Isometsä admits having used Hemohes, another plasma expander that reduces an athlete's hemoglobin levels. He loses his silver medal in the pursuit event held on Saturday and will face a two-year ban.
February 20	The lost FSA bag is delivered to a Helsinki police station from the gas station where it was found.
February 21	The head coach of the Finnish men's skiing team, Kari-Pekka Kyrö, goes to collect the case and signs for it. It was not handed over to one of the FSA's two physicians, as the bag was the property of the FSA. The same morning, Kyrö is absent from the press conference for the men's relay team. According to another member of the coaching squad, Kyrö was "taking a breather" after the whirlwind of the past few days in the wake of the Isometsä incident.
February 24	The physicians announce their resignation from their positions with the Finnish ski team.
February 25	A second Finnish athlete tests positive at the games. It is a male skier. The FSA refuse to divulge the name until the B-sample has been analyzed. Head Coach Kari-Pekka Kyrö assumes full responsibility for what has happened.
February 26	The Finnish skier is confirmed as a member of the victorious men's 4 x 10 kilometer relay team. The skier, Janne Immonen, will face the same ban as Isometsä, and presumably the relay team will be stripped of its gold medal.

connected with the Finnish Ski Association after the 2001 Nordic World
Ski Championships in Lahti, Finland.

The scandal arose during the world championships when six skiers
were caught using illegal substances. The scandal blew up in the public
arena as more and more layers were revealed, like peeling an onion (table
5.3). On Sunday top Finnish cross-country skier Jari Isometsä is caught,
but he assures the public that he alone is responsible for his actions and
that no one else is connected. On Monday a mysterious medical bag is

dropped off at the lost-and-found office. Inside, six drip-feed bags and other key doping supplies are found. On Thursday another Finnish cross-country skier, Janne Immonen, fails his blood test, as a result of which the entire Finnish cross-country skiing team is subjected to a surprise doping test. The following Wednesday other team members are caught, among them legendary skiers Mika Myllylä and Harri Kirvesniemi, as well as top female skier Virpi Kuitunen. The skiers themselves, their head coach, and team physicians take it in turns to deny everything, refusing to discuss the matter or confess. The scandal is a tremendous shock to the Finnish nation, which arguably loses its trust in Finnish cross-country skiing altogether. Matti Häyry, then professor of philosophy at the University of Kuopio, says on the radio that challenging the honor of cross-country skiing is equally serious to the prestige of Finland as challenging the miracle of the Winter War. The scandal's financial consequences for the FSA were dramatic, the government took back a significant proportion of its support, and practically all the corporate sponsors pulled out of their cooperative agreements.

The following year, 2002, the Finnish Ski Association adopted a new set of values: "fair play, openness, co-operation, expertise and Finnishness" (www.hiihtoliitto.fi, read June 18, 2007).

The next head coach of the Finnish cross-country skiing team, Reijo Jylhä, was given the task, following the Lahti doping scandal, of rebuilding the sport's reputation both within the organization and in its public relations. The role of reputation manager is not often one of a ski coach's main activities. "I really have not had time to do all the work that is traditionally expected of a head coach, but these are exceptional times," he later explained.

Reijo Jylhä wrote the essay "The importance of reputation management in my own leadership role" as part of his eMBA course in Oulu that was taught by present co-author Saku Mantere. We will use the essay, where Jylhä relied on the arena model taught on the course, as a source in analyzing the Ski Association's reputation strategy. All statements reprinted here are with the permission of Reijo Jylhä.

The Ski Association's progress from one arena to the next towards a state of peace is an exceptionally interesting example of how reputation can be reconstructed following a seemingly crushing reputation crisis. Following the scandal the Association's first choice of strategies was that of the defense counsel. Instead of attacking in order to change its reputation, the organization tried to hold on to its reputation:

> Initially we were in the defensive arena in which we tried to maintain our previous reputation. After 2001 we succeeded somewhat in these efforts. Externally the organization explained that the scandal was created by a few individuals and that there was no similar problem

in the activities of the organization itself. Together with the Finnish Olympic Committee and the Finnish Anti-doping Agency we drew up a list of regulations and public statements according to which we pledged not to use intravenous methods or oxygen doping. The reactions to this were quite surprising: in addition to committing ourselves to anti-doping activities, we also agreed not to use permitted recovery methods that were generally used by other teams. We were considered stupid for handing the competition such an advantage.

The defensive arena ultimately failed when top female skier Kaisa Varis tested positive for doping in spring 2003. The organization succumbed to a state of rioting, as the public assumed that it had been carrying out the turncoat strategy—saying one thing but doing the other:

> Following the new doping scandal connected with Kaisa Varis in spring 2003 it was clear that our previous strategy could no longer be used, and our credibility among sponsors and other partners in particular was in the red. We had to build up everything again from scratch. For a time we found ourselves in the riot arena in which no logical impressions were created.

The example of the Finnish Ski Association demonstrates how an organization that enjoys major institutional trust and whose reputation is important for the nation cannot and does not want to play with the idea of having its reputation interpreted in multiple ways in the riot arena. The organization's response was to attack, to begin systematically building a new reputation, and to challenge the public to accept its new reputational story. It worked to "create an entirely new image of cross-country skiing." In other words, it shifted the emphasis of its reputation strategy from competitive skiing to skiing as a collective recreation. It adopted a new vision: "Success, recreation and fun for everyone!" The main tool of this reputation strategy was to train a sports journalist and actor, Risto Kaskilahti, to ski as part of the Elixir program on national television. "Risto will save Finland's skiing reputation," the show advertised on its website:

> One of the main goals of the Kaskilahti project was to destroy the perceptions of our reputation. For a moment we shared the offensive arena with our public. We used the TV show to destroy the perceptions of our recent reputation. As of spring 2005 we have succeeded in this project so well that in this particular area we have almost returned to the peace arena. Both the organization and the environment are maintaining our new reputation and its related image.
> (www.elixir.fi/liikuntatarina/risto_maajoukkueeseen,
> read June 14, 2005)

Shifting the focus of the reputation strategy also created peaceful conditions for the competition: "Competitive skiing has enjoyed peace during this chain of events, and credibility is gradually being restored with the success of our athletes. Our PR campaign culminated in Risto Kaskilahti participating in the Finnish Championships in the 50-kilometer cross-country skiing event."

The Finnish Ski Association's reputation strategy is an example of successful reputation management, a successful recovery after a major failure. It teaches us that reputation arenas change just like reputation strategies (figure 5.6). It also demonstrates how an institutionally strong organization emphasizes institutional communications, conveying the same message to all members of the general public. The "Kaskilahti Project" utilized television, a strong institutional tool that provides the general public with a unified message.

Most interesting about the Finnish Ski Association case is the reminder that the offensive strategy is based on building a new reputation when the old one is no longer useful. The organization recognized that cross-country skiing was not like ski jumping, which is viewed but not practiced by most members of the public. Cross-country skiing to Finns is not only a focus of collective interest but also a collective experience. After a long period of rebuilding reputation, peace was finally restored and new credibility created for Finland's skiing elite.

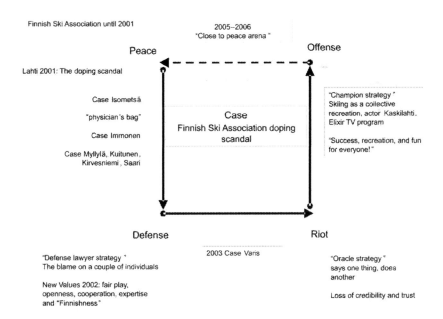

Figure 5.6 Reputation dynamics. The case of the Finnish Ski Association

The puzzle of disassembled publics

Thus far we have only looked at situations in which the public either builds a unified story together with the organization or then objects to doing so. For simplicity's sake we did not add a further dimension to our strategic model in which the public is passive or in which there are many publics. For strategically managing good reputation this possibility must also be considered.

Even a small but active section of the public can destroy the reputation of a large organization. A familiar example of this is Shell, whose reputation was put to the test in the mid-1990s due to the activities of a single organization: Greenpeace. In 1995 Shell planned to dispose of one of its North Sea oil rigs, the Brent Spar, by sinking it into the sea. In the same year the execution of Ken Saro-Wiwa, a Nigerian environmental activist who had criticized Shell's drilling operations, received a lot of international attention. The environmental organization Greenpeace was an active participant in both controversies.

It is reasonable to claim that Shell lost its reputation in the mid-1990s. In the reputation arena an active party, Greenpeace, arose from among the public and crushed in two blows the relatively positive perceptions of the company held by other parts of the public. At least for a moment Shell came to represent the model of corrupt big business in the eyes of many citizens, a company that purchased weapons for a totalitarian leader, on the one hand, and tried to sink its own oil rig, on the other. In Finland this reputation lives on among many music fans through the words of the hit song "Ken Saro-Wiwa on kuollut" ("Ken Saro-Wiwa is dead") by the popular Finnish band Ultra Bra.

Following these scandals Shell has gradually built a new reputation. The new story features an interesting turn towards the future. From one year to the next Shell has assured us that it is a pioneer in the development of renewable forms of energy. On its website it describes its strategy of sustainable development in the following words:

> By far our biggest contribution to sustainable development will come from delivering the energy needed for development without pollution levels that damage health or threaten vital natural systems. With energy demand set to double or even triple by 2050, mainly because of exploding demand in the developing world, this is a daunting challenge. It means continuing to provide oil and natural gas; helping provide access to modern energy for the two billion people who currently live without it; and offering more customers cleaner products, such as low-sulphur petrol and diesel, and hydrogen for new fuel cell vehicles. It also means helping the world gradually shift to a low-carbon energy system by providing more natural gas, and

lowering the costs of alternatives like wind, solar power, and fuels from plants.

(www.shell.com, read May 25, 2005)

Shell's sustainable development strategy creates an image of a transition stage in which social justice entails a lesser evil in the use of fossil fuels that the third world would get to use as part of its development. This transition stage would be followed by a "low-carbon energy system" relying on the use of renewable and other low-emission forms of energy. In this sense, Shell, while openly admitting to be a party to the green-house effect, creates a narrative much more optimistic than the one offered by Philip Morris, discussed earlier.

Shell replaced its tarnished reputation with a new image by turning the volume up to 11, through repeated and unified ad campaigns and press releases. Shell is a good example of how, in a networked society, even a small but active section of the public such as Greenpeace has the possibility to attack an enormous corporation. Rebuilding the reputation of this colossus required a lot of work over a long period of time.

"Issues management," associated with Professor James Grunig of the University of Maryland (for example Grunig & Repper, 1992), offers a conceptual methodology for making sense of disjointed and latent audiences. The theory provides answers about strategies that companies use to deal with reputation arenas that have passive or heterogenic publics. Grunig & Repper (1992, pp. 146–147) argued that organizations "use the process of issues management to anticipate issues and resolve conflict before the public makes it an issue." In other words, companies concoct plots for their story that can be revealed to meet anticipated challenges from the public. The story is adapted to meet the challenge before a controversy has time to arise.

Issues management and anticipation have a lot to do with communication and the formation of meanings. As a result they can be applied in part to our inspection of the environment of meanings surrounding companies. In other words, issues management is a tool for reputation researchers to use to understand not just reputation management but also reputation strategies. The ability to analyze reputation arenas enables strategic reputation management.

Grunig has studied the creation of activated publics in an organization's environment and their activities with the help of various concepts of the public. According to Grunig, publics consist of people who recognize an issue related to a certain organization, and if they find this issue to be a problem they are ready to organize themselves to do something about it. According to Grunig (Grunig & Hunt, 1984; Grunig & Repper, 1992),

- apathetic publics do not pay attention to themes related to an organization. An apathetic public does not see any problems in an organization's issues;
- latent publics are aware of an issue but do not see it as a problem. A latent public is aware of an issue that could cause a conflict but still does not think of it as a real problem;
- aware publics are activated by one or more small issues or problems that do not interest the general public as such;
- active publics are activated by one or more issues or problems that affect in some way the entire general public and are widely publicized, for example in the media.

An organization's situation could be one in which an issue related to the organization has become so significant that an active public is created. Greenpeace's activities against Shell are an example of this. The active public has decided to do something to solve the problem (Åberg, 1997). In terms of reputation management this public can be seen as a problem group for the organization, as it tries to organize in order to solve the problem, and the information it produces often has an agenda and is almost always strongly emotional.

In terms of an organization's reputation, the most common situation is one in which there is no direct conflict between an organization and its environment, although as Professor Leif Åberg (1997, p. 135) points out, "no matter how legitimately things are done, some groups (in the organization's environment) are nevertheless activated."

Network strategies

Thus far we have focused on the problem of a single organization, managing its reputation among an audience or a set of audiences. A recent trend in strategic management (see chapter 6) emphasizes the role of networks in strategic management, and strategy as the collective endeavor of a number of companies.

Organizations operate within networks formed by customers, partners, subcontractors, legislators, and other stakeholders. Networks have intruded into companies' sales, logistics, social influence, and acquisition of information. They have become part of companies' production processes due to more complex subcontractor and partner relationships. An organization's reputation does not matter in the customer interface alone. In fact, reputation is a resource in all phases of traditional production processes: in sourcing materials, in production, in distribution, and in sales.

It would be convenient to think of organizations as black boxes that process defined inputs and spit out the desired end products. Unfortunately, in many cases time has passed this classic metaphor by. The products of most organizations are produced within various networks. The production process itself is thus often permeated by networks.

Organizations have always been a part of different kinds of networks. They have always had partners, competitors, customers, and legislators as their stakeholders. The management of stakeholder relations was a core management process in Venetian merchant houses in the 1600s just as much as in our networked companies today. It is typical of our network society that these networks are growing bigger and more complex.

An organization that is known as a good partner has an advantage in negotiating partnerships in all stages of the production process. For example, a company that is recognized as good among its subcontractors has a strong position when demand for subcontractor services is greater than supply, as a result of which subcontractors can choose whom they serve. It is even more obvious that a subcontractor possessing a good reputation is going to get orders.

When a multiple number of other operators participate in a company's production process, in its core operations, the organization's boundaries become blurry, and the company becomes a network in itself. Take the famous example of Nike (www.nikebiz.com, read April 6, 2005), for example. The footwear manufacturer does not make footwear, it only designs and sells them. As a result, our traditional view of organizations as black boxes that transform inputs into end products becomes more complex. Where does the interface of Nike's core process begin, where is the border of the black box? Nike's products are manufactured in over 900 factories around the world. The number of production personnel is around 660,000. Nike designs and markets the products, while production takes place primarily in third-world countries. In this sense Nike is a perfect example of a network company. Nike also strives clearly to communicate that it is a good company. The website Nikebiz.com lists the company's ethically sustainable operating principles. Special attention is paid to opposing child labor and to promoting general criteria of honest work. The impression is formed that being a good company for Nike means especially managing its network. The Nike code of conduct (www.nikebiz.com, read April 6, 2005) emphasizes that the company only cooperates with manufacturers that are prepared to act in compliance with Nike's principles. "Our goal is to do business with contract factories that consistently demonstrate compliance with standards we set and that operate in an ethical and lawful manner" ("Workers and Factories," www.nikebiz.com, read April 6, 2005).

Nike's ethical principles, which emphasize the control and obedience of the network, are without doubt a reaction to the damage done to the company's reputation regarding charges of low wages and child labor. A famous example of the criticism against Nike is Michael Moore's documentary *The Big One* (1997), which provoked wide debate about Nike's labor policies.

Exchanging reputation-capital

As networks permeate throughout organizations, networks also concern their reputation capital. We have acknowledged that while reputation cannot be fully collapsed into an economic view, it does have an economic component. This component of reputation is an asset, which is close to what some sociologists use to denote "firm status" in a market, for example "the perceived quality of [a] producer's products in relation to the perceived quality of that producer's competitor's products" (Podolny, 1993, p. 830).

Rindova, Petkova, and Kotha (2007) found that new firms build reputation, by, for example, obtaining endorsements from high-status or prominent third parties. This approach opens the door for a wider line of inquiry: what kinds of exchanges are made by using reputation capital? We argue that one key property of reputation has not been properly addressed by literature: when viewed as a form of capital, reputation may be exchanged in networks between different parties. In this sense, reputation can be exchanged, sold, bought, bartered, stolen, and borrowed between organizations.

Even if literature on reputation management has not given much attention to them, reputational exchanges are nothing new in a more general discourse. Consider a politician retiring and "willing" her votes to a junior candidate. This can be regarded as a move where person X transfers to person Y some reputation capital.

Burt (2005) has shown that reputation is a mechanism which creates trust within closed networks, as the fear of loss of reputation reduces misbehavior. From such a standpoint, reputation is a property of individuals within networks. It is a form of capital, the safeguarding of which motivates the members of a closed network to behave themselves. However, individuals—be they people, groups, or organizations—also use their reputation as a commodity in social exchanges. The objective may be to transfer reputation into some other good, to collaborate with others to transfer other goods into reputation capital, or to create more reputation through reputational collaboration.

Within a circle of reputation

When the reputation of your worst rival is smeared, do you benefit from it as customers flock to your doorstep, or can this actually harm you as the loss of a reputation of one of the key players damages the reputation

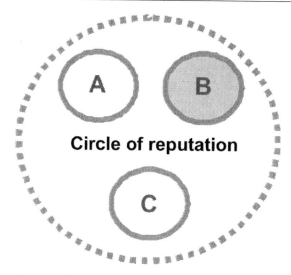

Figure 5.7 Sharing reputational capital within a "circle of reputation."

of the whole population of firms? For instance, if you are in the tourist business in a specific area, will you benefit from the reputational misfortunes of a competitor, or will the misfortune of this competitor deter tourists from visiting your whole area? Conversely, if a rival does exemplary work in serving his or her customers, will this not affect the reputation of the whole area in a positive manner? The post-Enron downturn in opinion regarding big business is another key example. While Enron's competitors have no doubt benefited from the plight of their rival, they too have had to face the collective loss of reputation of big corporations among various stakeholder groups.

The above speculation is to demonstrate that stakeholder attributions may not be directed at a specific company, but at a specific group of companies: the firms operating as parts of a specific value chain, in a specific geographic area, or even in a specific business. Reputation capital may reside within what we call "a circle of reputation" (figure 5.7).

In the case of reputation-sharing (figure 5.7), companies A, B, and C share collective reputation and thus form a circle of reputation. When one intra-circle organization flourishes in its reputations, the other members enjoy some of the positive limelight. Conversely, when the reputation of one of the organizations is smeared, the others also suffer a reputation loss.

Reputation-sharing could be defined as a partnership between companies inside the circle. It is reasonable to argue that every business partnership is always a companionship of reputation as well, and forming a partnership should always take reputational aspects into account.

We will next outline four types of reputational exchanges, which

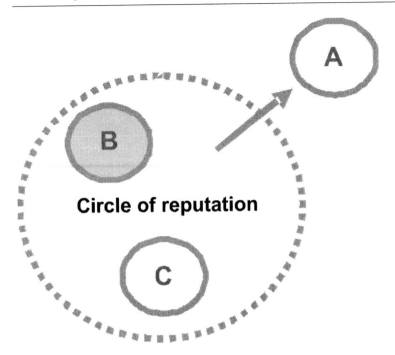

Figure 5.8 Borrowing reputation.

address different dynamics to and from the reputational circle: borrowing, allying, outsourcing, and stealing.

Borrowing reputation

A company borrows reputation when members of a specific circle of reputation allow it to employ some of their existing reputation. A startup firm is often in need of a reputation, for instance. A firm that has not had the opportunity of building a network of stakeholders or aroused the interest of the media is often in desperate need of reputation, in the sense of both visibility and credibility.

In the case of reputation-borrowing (figure 5.8), companies B and C share a reputation and they are willing to lend it to company A, which is not inside the circle, but still can benefit from the goodness of reputation—for a price. This is the case in the Microsoft certifications system, where Microsoft has generated a multilevel system to establish a network of qualified IT companies. In addition to ensuring a good-quality network, Microsoft markets the system in relation to reputational benefits to the potential certificate candidates. According to the Microsoft website:

Microsoft Certified Professionals (MCPs) stand apart from other IT personnel. They've demonstrated undeniable expertise with Microsoft products and platforms to colleagues, employers, and—most importantly—to themselves . . . Microsoft Certified Professionals are cut from a different cloth than their IT counterparts. They not only thrive on the continuing challenges of the IT field, but they also have taken it upon themselves to develop and hone their skills—to stay a step ahead. The practical expertise that is gained through the certification process provides individuals with the kind of know-how that gets recognized—on the job, among peers, and by future employers.
(http://www.microsoft.com/learning/mcp/default.mspx, read May 2007)

By giving certificates the company lends its reputation as well.

Reputation-borrowing can be viewed from company A's perspective also. In the case of Microsoft Certified Professionals the reputational benefits are comprehensible: it is reasonable to assume that it is easier to build reputation as a skillful IT-supplier as a "certified partner" of Microsoft than as an independent IT-worker.

As reputation-building is often slow, startup firms often seek to acquire it from external sources. A typical example is to rely on the reputation of a respected financier. Indeed, many financiers specializing in startups have included this aspect in their services. They may even open doors by letting the startup share parts of their personal networks. Many startups also recruit well-known, senior professionals into their boards of directors. Mobile operator Blyk (http://about.blyk.com/) is a startup, the first pan-European ad-funded mobile network. It plans to offer customers free mobile phone calls and SMS messages in return for receiving advertising on their mobile handsets. Blyk is run by Pekka Ala-Pietilä, former president of Nokia Corporation and Nokia Mobile Phones, and Marko Ahtisaari, the son of the former president of Finland, acts as a director of brand and design. By making the presence of these prominent people as visible as possible in their communications, Blyk is clearly trying to make good use of the reputation history of these famous key figures.

Building reputational alliances

Companies A, B, and C form an alliance (figure 5.9) in order to achieve good reputation, as they step into the same circle of reputation. Reputation alliance is a specific form of reputation-sharing between companies, as this involves a voluntary linking of reputation, enabled by the coherence or at least complementarity of goals. Reputational alliances are, like many strategic alliances, conducted in many different contexts: starting a new line of business together, consolidating different aspects of each

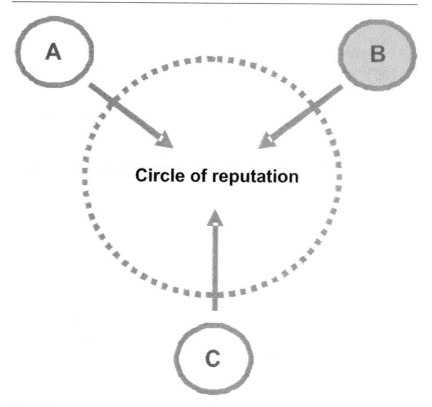

Figure 5.9 Reputational alliance.

other's reputation, sharing legitimacy in different environments, and so on.

When the United Nations Children's Fund (UNICEF) engages in reputational alliances with business firms such as furniture retail group IKEA, it takes a reputation risk. It needs to trust that the activities of its partners stand the light of day.

Reputation exchanges involve risk, as the example of IKEA demonstrates. The reputation risk connected with child labor applies to subcontractors, as a result of which it is in the parent company's interests to control its subcontractors in order to protect its reputation. IKEA has had to face reputation risks, as it employs a lot of contract factories. IKEA has published its ethical codes for subcontractor activities entitled *The IKEA Way on Purchasing Home Furnishing Products*, which includes a chapter entitled "The IKEA Way of Preventing Child Labour" (www.ikea-group.ikea.com, read June 20, 2005). IKEA's rhetoric is friendlier in tone that Nike's, yet it is still firm. In its general ethical guidelines it states the following:

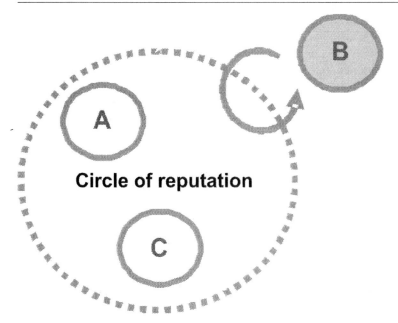

Figure 5.10 Outsourcing reputation.

> The IKEA Group believes in long-term relationships with suppliers who share our commitment to promote good practices, and who want to grow and develop with IKEA. We expect them to respect fundamental human rights, and to treat their workforces fairly and with respect.
>
> (www.ikea-group.ikea.com/corporate/responsible/conduct.html,
> read June 19, 2005)

IKEA has apparently succeeded rather well in fighting child labor, as UNICEF considers the company to be a successful example in its guide on preventing child labor (www.unicef.org.uk/publications/clrg/, read June 20, 2005). It would be hard for a company to receive better institutional support than this. Sporting goods manufacturer Reebok and clothing manufacturers Levi Strauss and Pentland Group are mentioned in the same context.

Outsourcing reputation

From IKEA's standpoint, the reputational alliance it has formed with UNICEF may also be considered as a form of "reputation-outsourcing" (figure 5.10). It consolidates a position where it is more difficult to confront it again with child labor charges—at least without solid proof.

While it is not building its core reputation as a friend to children, and while most of its operations are not directed at this end, it secures one corner of its reputation through this operation. It outsources a part of its reputation risk to UNICEF, and UNICEF accepts this risk itself.

Reputational outsourcing is in a sense a response to what is regarded as Milton Friedman's "competence argument" regarding corporate social responsibility. According to Friedman (1970), as companies are not experts in the "ethics business," they should stick to the business they know and let the other stakeholders use a part of the accumulated wealth to do the ethics part. In reputational outsourcing, the company accepts that it is not the ethical expert but wants to enlist the services of an expert to manage the matter for the company. In return, the company is willing to pay good money and even allow access to its vulnerable core processes.

While UNICEF engages in reputational outsourcing only as a "minor venture on the side," there are organizations specializing in reputational outsourcing of specific kinds. One well-known example is Fairtrade Labelling Organizations International. It is "an association of 20 Labelling Initiatives that promote and market the Fairtrade Certification Mark in their countries" (http://www.fairtrade.net/, read June 14, 2007). The organization is divided into two branches: a nonprofit "development branch" and a company-form "implementation branch." The first branch, FLO International e.V., is an association of experts which develops and reviews standards and assists producers. The second branch is a limited company that specializes in the inspection and certification of producers and trade.

The certification process for a producer operating in the third world, as well as for an importer in the developed world, involves the implementation of a set of standards maintained by the Fairtrade organization, as well as fees paid to the certification branch. The standards involve issues such as work conditions, pricing, and various contractual problems like favoring long-term contracts, etc. (cf. www.flo-cert.net).

While there is no reason to doubt that Fairtrade is driven by an ethical mission, the certification process can also be viewed as a reputational outsourcing service. The key is that Fairtrade accepts a reputation risk in return for compliance with its standards as well as a set of monetary fees. They too regard the producers and traders as "customers" and make assurances that they are continuously improving their "services."

The "carbon offsetting" fares, offered for instance by many airline companies, are a further example of reputational outsourcing. Airline passengers are reminded by their airline providers that, by traveling by air, they are taxing the environment. A solution is offered by adding a voluntary extra fare, calculated on the basis of the length of the journey and number of passengers. The notion of "offsetting" the environmental damage caused by the airplane is based on the activities of the offsetting organization, which conducts or funds a variety of projects that plant new forests, implement sustainable energy sources, and so on.

One of many such acts of outsourcing reputation is the partnership between British Airways and Climate Care, an offsetting company. Climate Care is a financier, which provides funding to a number of projects aimed at reducing CO_2 emissions or their effects. British Airways reminds the customer on its website (www.britishairways.com, read June 25, 2007):

What impact does your flight have on climate change?

Every flight you take has an impact on climate change that arises from the carbon dioxide (CO_2) from burning kerosene and other effects in the upper atmosphere. British Airways supports a long-term approach to tackling this impact which you can read below.

You can take responsibility for the impact of your flight

British Airways has joined forces with an organization called Climate Care to enable you to offset the CO_2 emissions created during your flight.

You can click on the calculator button to calculate your share of the emissions created during your journey and the cost of neutralizing the impact of those emissions. If you decide to pay this cost, the money raised will be used by Climate Care to fund sustainable energy projects around the world on your behalf.

Climate Care (http://www.climatecare.org/ read June 25, 2007), on the other hand, allures its potential business partners by offering them, among other things, "a cost-effective—or cost-free—way to engage consumers in products or services." The company assures that it is "committed to leading best practice in our approach to offsetting emissions. Our Environmental Steering Committee has played a key role in guiding our work." The Environmental Steering Committee, which is brought up as a source of legitimacy, consists of representatives of a number of legitimate environmental organizations, such as WWF, Forum for the Future, and the British foreign secretary.

In a sense, the mechanisms of the offsetting business are not unlike the sale of indulgences in the Catholic Church—the environmentally aware airline traveler is able to pay up to repair his or her guilty conscience. It remains to be seen whether the mechanism actually produces tangible results—for now the evidence is mixed. The offsetting companies have an impressive range of projects. Many critical voices have been raised, however. The *Financial Times*, for instance, (April 25, 2007, www.ft.com, read on June 25, 2007), laments "the industry being caught in carbon smokescreen" in an article reporting an investigation which found:

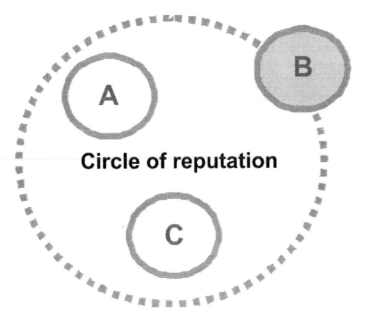

Figure 5.11 Reputation-stealing.

- widespread instances of people and organizations buying worthless credits that do not yield any reductions in carbon emissions;
- industrial companies profiting from doing very little—or from gaining carbon credits on the basis of efficiency gains from which they have already benefited substantially;
- brokers providing services of questionable or no value;
- a shortage of verification, making it difficult for buyers to assess the true value of carbon credits; and
- companies and individuals being charged over the odds for the private purchase of European Union carbon permits that have plummeted in value because they do not result in emissions cuts.

Stealing reputation

Reputation-stealing is what happens when an organization is able to make use of another organization's reputation without its consent or even against its will (figure 5.11). Reputation-stealing may sound like a hypothetical exercise, yet real-life examples do exist. Rows within family businesses are one example. A relatively recent example can be found in our native Finland.

Paulig[6] (www.paulig.fi) is likely to be the premier coffee company in Finland. It also produces a range of seasonings and ethnic food. Paulig is a family business with a history that traces back to 1876. It has been a conservative family business both in its external communication—advertising and corporate communications—and in its corporate culture. It has, for instance, built an advertising campaign which emphasizes the virtues of craftsmanship among handicraft professionals of different varieties (who take breaks to drink coffee which has also been produced with care), which it has maintained for decades.

In 1986 Robert Paulig, a board member and cousin of the then-CEO, wanted to list the company on the stock exchange. This breach of family values led to Robert Paulig's dismissal from the firm. He even had to sell his stock. Consequently, in 1987 he started his own firm, Robert's Coffee, focusing on special coffees and a modern chain of coffee shops. The company has become the biggest coffee shop chain in the Nordic countries.

Almost 20 years later, Paulig responded. They sued Robert Paulig for the use of the name "Robert Paulig" on the coffee packages. According to the Paulig lawyers, Robert's Coffee had exploited Paulig's good and established reputation. Their lawyer argued that their customer services has been receiving questions and complaints about Robert's Coffee products and that "market polls have clearly shown that customers confuse the two brands" (Finnish economics weekly *Talouselämä*, October 10, 2006).

Robert Paulig's lawyer's response was plain: a man has to be able to use his own name. "'Paulig' is what I say when I answer the phone," notes Robert Paulig in an ironic vein in the *Talouselämä* article. The courts found in favor of Robert Paulig on October 6, 2006.

Summary: towards the management of a company of good

The question of whether reputation can be managed at all is often raised. What exactly is done when reputation management is exercised? It is an interesting question. After all, according to its definition "reputation" is something that is ultimately or to a significant degree in the minds of its stakeholders as an image, piece of information, experience, or similar, depending on perspective. Therefore, in order to be effective, reputation management requires the use of a "surgeon's scalpel" instead of a saber. It is true, of course, that reputation cannot be directly and absolutely managed, if by management we mean control. Reputation cannot be controlled like a piece of machinery or equipment. If we want to be precise, no communicational activities or activities with a communicational aspect can be controlled. All forms of communicational activity, whether they involve advertising, public relations, stakeholder relations, or communications, hold within them an element of uncontrollability.

A message never gets across the exact same way that its sender intends. For example, it is impossible for a company to control stories that are formed by the public. This idea can be further clarified by thinking of the opposite: if one of us knew how to control people's minds, he could play us like puppets on a string. However, just like images, reputations can be influenced. Therefore reputation management is also possible, albeit indirectly.

Part III

Managing the company of good

At the end of Part II, we proposed the arena model of reputation to reconcile the tension between economic and interpretive conceptions of reputation. The arena model is dynamic, as it accounts for activities where organizational reputation is negotiated in markets of meaning, in different reputational arenas where stakeholders interact. In this part we focus on what organizations do as parts of these negotiation processes; that is, how they seek to manage their reputations. As we have argued on many occasions, reputation management is not a discrete function of organizing, and as such attributable to a single function such as corporate communications or PR. Instead, organizations build their reputations in a variety of activities across functions.

The previous part of the book was focused on building an account of reputation as an extra-organizational phenomenon. We have built a model of strategic reputation management based on the notion that reputation is constructed by multiple stakeholders in communication arenas. These arenas can be conceptualized from the standpoint of strategic management as "marketplaces of meaning," where reputations are negotiated in cooperation or contestation among organizations and their audiences.

In Part III we will concentrate on what characterizes the company of good itself: what it is, how it is managed and led. Our focus, while not purely intra-organizational, is now on organizational reputation-building activities. While we hope to have convinced the reader that reputations do not reside within actors but between them, it goes without saying that companies strive for good reputations within their activities.

We build our case on three kinds of activity. We argue that the basis of a good company is good deeds. This has some radical consequences for how we conceive the activities belonging to reputation management. Corporate reputation cannot be collapsed to corporate communications but is based on the organization's core activities: the products it creates and services it provides. We explore this challenge by founding reputation management in strategic management.

In addition to the founding dimension, however, reputation always

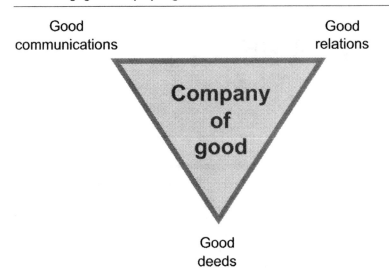

Good
communications

Good
relations

Good
deeds

Figure III.1 The reputation of a good company requires good deeds, good communications, and excellent public relations.

has a communicative side. According to its definition, reputation is established within the general public. Reputation represents the stories that
are told about a company. In this way, the activities of a good company
do not yet automatically guarantee a good reputation. These activities must always be communicated to the right people at the right time.
Companies have to master good communications. As we have shown in
Part II, when a company and its audiences communicate, an interactive
relation is established. This is where good relations play a key role in
terms of a good reputation and a good company.

We have based this book around these three dimensions of good management, the "triangle of good" (figure III.1). We begin by accounting good deeds of companies through a strategic management lens. This
creates a venue for us to revisit the contradiction between instrumental and
intrinsic good, presented in the first chapter, and revisited in Part II, where
it was manifested in the capital and interpretative views on reputation.
Since we are interested in reputation strategies, we pay special attention to
how concepts of strategies that emphasize traditional material value can
be assessed in order to create unified goals for the activities of a company's
employees. In the sixth chapter we focus on the role of corporate communications in reputation management. We conclude Part III of the book by
looking at relations between organizations and other companies and their
broader audiences. It appears that reputation, while extra-organizational,
can be transferred and bartered from company to company.

Chapter 6

Doing good deeds

Rindova et al. (forthcoming, p. 2) present two key dimensions to an organization's reputation: "(1) the extent to which stakeholders perceive an organization as being able to produce quality goods; and (2) the extent to which the organization is prominent in the minds of stakeholders." The first dimension illustrates that the challenge of managing reputation is founded on its core operations—in a sense, the deeds it commits.

A good company's reputation is a valuable resource. Like any other resource, reputation can be wasted or increased. Managing good reputation is simple in a way: in principle it is sufficient that an organization does its work well in the eyes of its stakeholders. A good bricklayer is recognized on the basis of the work he has performed as a good bricklayer, and in a society of stories rumors of work performed well are increasingly picked up by the ears of potential customers. If an organization is known for its good products, quality customer service, and reliable deliveries, its reputation thrives among customers. In other words, one of the key prerequisites for good reputation is that work is performed well within an organization. In the best case each member of the organization is a plank of the organization's reputation. This is made possible in part when an organization is managed well on the whole.

Managing reputation therefore does not involve tricks or gimmicks that can be separated from other effective management practices. If a product is lousy, a media campaign can create short-term profits, but long-term success will be compromised. Good deeds and good management are thus necessary, yet still not sufficient for guaranteeing good reputation. Good deeds must also be demonstrated to others. In this sense reputation management is communications, communicative actions.

Reputation should therefore to a large extent be the focus of management's attention. Although reputation is built on the basis of good basic operations, it is still in management's interest to support a positive image. If all the basics are in shape, there is no point in being bashful. Good deeds should be communicated.

Reputation management is particularly crucial in crisis situations. In a reputation crisis an organization becomes the focus of public attention due to the revelation of misconduct or a catastrophe. One of the key wisdoms of crisis management is that it is not worth covering anything up. Our own conscience tells us that the rhetoric of reputation without an honest mind and goodwill will lead to a communicational contradiction if the PR department says one thing while management and operative personnel do something else.

Reputation can be saved even after a major crisis or failure so long as honest and thorough communications spare a company from uncomfortable revelations. Cover-ups can blow up even the smallest mistake, making a mountain out of a molehill. If the public loses its trust in a company, its reputation is more seriously threatened than after admitting its errors.

Finnish design house Marimekko Corporation describes itself as "a leading Finnish textile and clothing design company that was established in 1951. The company designs, manufactures, and markets high-quality clothing, interior decoration textiles, bags, and other accessories under the Marimekko brand, both in Finland and abroad" (www.marimekko.fi/eng). The company is considered to be one of the country's most important exporters and an ambassador of Finnish clothing design. Its CEO Kirsti Paakkanen is among the most recognized business leaders of the country and the company has always been of high repute. The corporate story has been very well taken care of, and it is full of dramatic but positive turns and heroic management details. Marimekko is a classic example of a company that is founded upon its reputation. The leading Finnish business magazine *Talouselämä* stated in February 2005 that Marimekko is a company "whose publicity value is greater than its size." Marimekko's turnover increased by around 15 to 30 percent between 2001 and 2004.

In 2001 Marimekko decided to make a strategic turn, and go into the fur business. When Marimekko acquired the fur company Grünstein on August 20, 2000, it seemed like a natural strategic move to the board members of Marimekko. In its stock exchange release, the company explained its purchase:

> According to Marimekko President Kirsti Paakkanen, Grünstein is well suited to the image of the Marimekko brand. Grünstein's products represent a high level of design and quality . . . The increased product selection, volumes, and new sales channels create synergies that will improve both companies' profitability and business opportunities internationally.
>
> (Stock exchange release, August 24, 2000, www.marimekko.fi, read June 6, 2005)

Apparently, the company really did not anticipate the controversy and the "Bloody Marimekko" (*Marimekko—verimekko* in Finnish) campaign carried out by anti-fur protestors. One particular controversial reputation story was created when internationally acclaimed Finnish film director Aki Kaurismäki refused to accept an honorary doctorate from the University of Art and Design Helsinki, because Kirsti Paakkanen was to receive her own doctorate at the same event. According to Finnish business magazine *Talouselämä* (February 16, 2005) "Grünstein Product was an image thorn in Marimekko's side for over four years. The media produced a constant stream of images of animal activists carrying 'Bloody Marimekko' banners. Paakkanen also reported disturbances against herself personally."

Finally, on December 17, 2004, four years later, Marimekko sold its shareholding in Grünstein, recording a loss of €1.3 million. In a stock exchange release dated December 17, 2004, the explanation for dumping Grünstein was rather laconic: "Marimekko acquired Grünstein in August 2000. The company's business operations have not met the targets set by Marimekko. Prior to the final decision, Marimekko negotiated with several potential buyers for the sale of Grünstein for a couple of years" (Marimekko, 2000).

Paakkanen admitted herself later that the acquisition of Grünstein was a mistake, and that she was relieved when the company was sold. "This is a really big relief for me. I regard the purchase of Grünstein as my only big mistake." She said that the merger of Marimekko and Grünstein turned out to be all but the great alliance that had been envisioned. Gradually, the fur business turned into a burden that tarnished Marimekko's good image. The profits did not meet the targets, either. In addition to the adverse animal-rights publicity gained by the acquisition, Marimekko discovered that Grünstein was not opening up new markets for it after all. "The results were a zero. I have to admit, however, that eventually we did not invest in the company, either. I just hope that it will be more successful in new hands," said Paakkanen in a *Helsingin Sanomat* newspaper interview (June 13, 2007).

Marimekko's strategic move into the fur business turned out to be a severe reputational crisis, but demonstrates quite well how a reputation crisis can be successfully handled. Having admitted its error openly through the words of Paakkanen and taken corrective measures, Marimekko has probably been able to continue to coexist in peace with anti-fur activists.

The most essential pillar of a good company is good deeds. Founding an organization's reputation on something else is to accept a reputation risk. What is hidden behind these good deeds? Are companies good simply because of their own virtuous character, or do they have ulterior motives? What, then, is goodness? How are companies viewed if they are thought of as good? Can good deeds be managed "strategically," or is "strategicness" itself an impediment to good deeds?

Instrumental goodness or intrinsic goodness?

> I have divided the problems in this field into three categories, and when they appear, everything goes to hell. There is hatred, greed, and stupidity. Stupid people just react, they don't think what they're doing—they can be easily led by others. Angry people want to dominate and control—they are twisted. And greedy people don't want anything else but "me, myself and I"—they don't understand that "no man is an island."
>
> (Founder/manager, multimedia company)

There are several different kinds of goodness.[1] We focus here what we consider the two most essential types for our study: instrumental goodness and intrinsic goodness, or natural virtuousness. The virtues of a good golf club as a tool are different from the virtues of a good Samaritan. A golf club's virtues have to do with how it performs, whereas a good Samaritan's virtue suggests goodness by having a character of a specific kind. A golf club is a good instrument that allows the user to win a game, while a good Samaritan is a person who is respected by his or her community, perceived as leading a good life.

In business ethics the concept of a good company refers clearly to the second type of goodness: to virtuousness and a good nature. According to classical Greek ethics, *aretē* goodness refers to virtuousness that describes a good person. Accordingly, Greek philosophers described four key elements of this kind of goodness: wisdom, modesty, courage, and justness (Sedley, 1998). In classical Greek ethics goodness was often connected with living a good life in harmony with one's self and one's environment.

When companies are considered good, they are often thought of as people whose natural characteristics are considered worthy of respect. The ideas of social responsibility, business ethics, and responsible operations are all connected with this perspective: a company is like a person whose life history can be ethically assessed by us in order for us to see if this is worthy of our moral appreciation. Buying into the good life, the first component of the market value of goodness as described in the beginning of this section, emphasizes the meaning of goodness according to the classical Greek concept—as an estimation of a company's goodness. Consumers want to buy things from companies that reinforce their own values and lifestyles.

Although business ethics emphasize a good nature, the world in which companies operate transforms companies in the opposite direction, that of instrumental goodness. This can be seen particularly clearly in strategic management, undeniably the most popular management ideology of our time.

The company as a good citizen

In some circles, reputation is considered a parallel concept for responsible business operations. In this sense good reputation is based on an organization's ethically sustainable operations that are seen and heard. Idealistically, the reputation of responsibility is based on the idea of a company's good conscience, an unselfish way of behaving, altruism according to which a company makes decisions for the good of itself, the environment, and society, even by sacrificing a degree of financial success. In this way organizations, even hard-core businesses, become good neighbors who look after others and who care. Companies are no longer institutions but citizens. In fact they are even more: good corporate citizens.

The concept of corporate citizenship is widely used when talking about responsible business operations. According to the original idea, corporate citizenship is comparable to the citizenship of individuals. Companies are subject to the same rights and obligations that apply to individual citizens as members of communities and/or society. However, the idea of corporate citizenship alone does not make an organization good. Individual members of society (people) continuously act contrary to good principles. They steal, fight, kill, lie, pollute, hurt, rob, and rape, yet they are all citizens. In the same way companies can be "citizens" but still act immorally.

Corporate citizenship does not mean that citizenship itself produces socially acceptable and desirable operations. Paying attention to stakeholders does not automatically guarantee good stakeholder relations or doing good deeds for stakeholders. Acquiring knowledge about corporate citizenship and the values, wants, likings, and desires of citizens and reacting to this knowledge does not ensure good "citizenly operations," good reputation (Zadek, Hojensgard, & Raynard, 2001). Instead, the idea of being a good company is made concrete through good corporate citizenship. Corporate citizenship can be considered the symbol of reputation management. A good corporate citizen maintains good practices and has ethically sustainable operations. It is particularly important that a good corporate citizen maintains good relations with all its stakeholders and is in continual dialogue with these. For example, a company establishing long-term stakeholder relations would do well to adopt the role of bearing responsibility within society, which is a part of good citizenship (Karvonen, 2000).

The idea of companies as citizens is connected with the discussion about corporate social responsibility. Reputation and responsible business operations are also closely entwined when talking about corporate social responsibility. Corporate social responsibility is based on the idea that in business operations things other than the psychopathic pursuit of one's own advantage are important. Companies have to operate in an ethically sustainable way and take care not only of nature but also of their employees, community, and broader social issues (Aula & Heinonen, 2002). According to the reigning view, socially responsible operations are guided by financial, environmental, and social dimensions according to a so-called triple bottom-line view.

We seem to be living in a situation in which companies all over the world are emphasizing the ethical and responsible sides of their business operations. There are many motives for doing so. The most visible of these are public pressure and active audiences, economic and cultural globalization, ethical investors and investment funds, knowledgeable and demanding employees, consumer activism, and various state and suprastate regulations. The case is clear in terms of reputation: responsibility lies at the core of good reputation, and responsible operations reduce a company's reputational risk. There is broad consensus regarding this. Companies cannot be irresponsibly good.

Social responsibility has nevertheless developed into a transformable mantra whose continuous repetition has clouded the importance of responsibility. Responsibility is often harnessed to the pursuit of selfish goals. The principle of virtuosity, according to which the advantage of another (for example, employees) may in certain situations be placed above that of oneself (or the owner), seldom receives support when discussing an organization's decision-making. Altruism cannot compete with egoism; selfishness and a company's own advantage have become a precondition for responsibility in modern business life.

Which is prioritized, which follows which: financial success before responsible business operations, or responsibility before success? According to Nokia's former CEO (present chairman of Shell and of Nokia's Board of Directors) Jorma Ollila, "responsible business operations make sense for Nokia. They help us create a sustainable lifecycle for our products, sustainable employment relationships and a good corporate reputation—and that way we can pursue sustainable financial growth" (www.nokia.fi, read October 23, 2003). The Confederation of Finnish Industry and Employers (TT) has published a report entitled *Corporate Social Responsibility: What Is It?*, which paints a more cynical picture of the basis of social responsibility. TT states that "the ability to perform well financially also provides the foundation for other factors of social responsibility." The financial factor of social responsibility refers primarily to "responding to the profit expectations of owners."

Taken to its extreme, this view, according to which financial performance is a prerequisite for socially responsible operations, leads to some radical conclusions. If TT's report is interpreted sympathetically, it can be inferred that a company incapable of operating profitably simply cannot operate at all—neither responsibly nor irresponsibly. This is a rather trivial assumption, however. Radically interpreted, the principle of "financial performance first" liberates a company from all responsibility on the grounds of economics. Social responsibility can be neglected if it cannot be afforded. Exempting reasons could include the current market situation or uncertainty regarding the future. Furthermore, the profit expectations of owners may be so extreme that the pursuit of financial responsibility leaves no room for other forms of responsibility. Responsibility escapes, or it is easy to escape from.

Against this background the whole notion of a triple bottom line is in danger of trivialization. All responsibility is subordinate to economic "responsibility," which in its most extreme form can be simplified as responsibility for meeting the profit expectations of owners. Virtue becomes a luxury that can be afforded only when the financial situation is healthy. The same kind of argument applied to society would be that poor people can kill, lie, and steal if things are going badly enough for them. Despite all the business ethics gloss, much of today's rhetoric about general responsibility is in danger of remaining a veneer, subordinate to Milton Friedman's (1970) maxim of corporate ethics. According to Friedman, companies have only one social responsibility and obligation: to maximize profits for owners.

Responsibility in operations does have implications for business performance. Countless examples around the world in recent years—from Enron to Boeing, Worldcom to Martha Stewart—have demonstrated that irresponsibility does not pay. Managers are faced with the complex task of navigating between maxims urging responsibility and maxims urging profit-maximization. The most important profit-driven management discipline of our time is called "strategic management."

Strategy-as-*Zeitgeist*: instrumental value

> We use tactics to take care of everyday things—tactics are used to win battles, whereas strategies are used to win wars.
>
> (Member of the management group of a Finnish insurance company)

Among management discourses, strategic management is a success story without compare. In a way it has become an ideology, a set of values and a worldview that has become so self-evident that its existence is hardly noted these days—"we have to have a strategy!" (cf. Knights & Morgan, 1991; Mantere & Vaara, forthcoming; Shrivastava, 1986). When an organization or nation creates a strategy, they are tempted to conform to the basic principle of strategic management, according to which success in competitive markets is the most important (if not the only) valuable goal of management.

In *The Concept of Corporate Strategy*, one of the early classics in the canon of strategic management, Kenneth Andrews, who is considered to be the inventor of SWOT-analysis, writes (Andrews, 1971, p. 238): "Corporate purposes are by definition a projection in part of the leader's own personal goals and a reflection of his character . . . a corporation is essentially the lengthened shadow of a man."

Like other ideologies, strategic management generalizes certain interests to apply to everyone. Strategic management is organically related to managerialism, an ideology according to which an organization's interest is the same as the interest of management, which serves the financial interest of shareholders (Hardy & Clegg, 1996). According to managerialists the decisions of management are essential, and challenging them is the same as challenging the interest of the organization. The voice of managerialists can be heard particularly loudly in situations concerning major layoffs that are designed not to save an organization but simply to increase productivity or streamline operations, for example. When appealing to an organization's strategy it is no longer necessary to explain tough decisions in terms of saving the company, only in terms of improving the viability of the organizational tool.

When confectionery company Leaf announced in May 2005 that it was closing its otherwise profitable factory in the Finnish city of Turku, the reason given was not to save the parent company. Jaap van den Bent, president of operations at Leaf International, explained the closure to Finnish business daily *Taloussanomat* (May 25, 2005) in terms of "a low utilization ratio, old machinery, logistically inefficient production buildings and expensive wage costs, even compared with other Western European markets." When Perlos, a stock exchange company and a manufacturer of components for mobile phones and the pharmaceuticals industry, announced in spring 2005 that it was closing its production unit in the Finnish town of Ylöjärvi, the reason given by Managing Director Isto Hantila was "excessive production capacity" (*Taloussanomat*, April 28, 2005).

Strategy is the lingua franca of today's management.[2] It is also a secret science whose initiation rites are revealed by consultants and MBA courses. When learning "strategy talk" students become familiar with such magic words as "transaction costs," "return on assets," "core competencies," and "value chain integration." Demonstrating a command of these concepts elicits satisfied murmurs among upper management, and the initiated student is accepted into the inner circle. In some cases, of course, students are set tasks to prove their decisiveness and resourcefulness—they may be sent abroad to manage a local factory or made to carry out stringent rationalizations at home.

New managing directors are expected to bring with them a strategy that will determine the fate of their organizations. Lasse Kurkilahti, a leading Finnish executive who is known for his rapid actions at the head of major corporations, emphasizes in Kemira's stakeholder magazine (January 2004) that "a Finnish company that strives to be the world's best has to have a sharp strategy" and that his most important task as Kemira's new managing director is to "assess and possibly hone current strategies."

Strategy as a worldview

What is strategy? Well, managers in particular are expected to adapt themselves into a rapidly changing environment.

(Head of department of a Finnish government ministry)

Strategy describes the world as a battleground or playing field. Strategically managing a company contains within it the most important choices, based on which an organization can succeed amidst competition, in other words win the game or destroy the enemy. The history of strategy goes back thousands of years to military literature. The Greek word *strategos* refers to a general or his professional competence.

There is an important connection between strategy and the network society—in fact, they can be regarded as competing characterizations of the same society, and harmonizing the two can create problems. The strategic nature of society is based on the fact that, even though interdependence has become increasingly apparent due to networking, the fierceness of competition is the other reality of life. Even if within networks a good reputation is a market advantage and a company that is considered good sells more to the general public, the strategic spirit of the times is to keep life a game in which the lives of other players usually do not hold much significance. Strategy's goal is to win the game in which others are just playing pieces.

These days companies are not the only ones who demand a strategy. Public organizations and even entire nations emphasize the importance of strategies—strategy has become a question of fate. Even Michael Porter, perhaps the biggest name in strategy literature, was inspired to write a book on national competitive strategies (Porter, 1990). Nokia's former CEO Jorma Ollila emphasized the importance of strategy for small nations in the face of globalization: "If there is no strategy, decisions will be made not on the national level but elsewhere" (www.finpro.fi, read November 10, 2004). Strategy's siren song makes it clear: those who do not make strategies will wither away.

All the talk about strategy in connection with managing organizations arose after World War II, when the global markets opened up and competition intensified in a way that it had never done before. American corporate leaders, consultants, and economists invented a new lexicon—mainly for the needs of American M-form corporations—to try to describe and control the problems and challenges created by the new competitive situation. Economic historian Alfred Chandler is considered to be the father of organizational strategy, having studied the development of American M-form corporations. Chandler's most famous theses include "structure follows strategy," in other words strategic goals determine what kind of organizational instrument is built, what line of business the organization operates in, and so on. Chandler proposed the idea that a changing competitive environment makes companies form strategies, plans, and policies for the future, which organizations use to succeed within their respective environments (Chandler, 1962). Organizations could no longer be seen as machines that managers tune like engineers. Instead of machine-like efficiency, the competitive advantage became anticipating the changing demands of the environment and adapting to them. Management that was based precisely on making decisions connected with adaptation to the environment began to be referred to as strategic management.

> You can't go around making strategies by deciding that we're going to make a strategy that forty people believe in. That just turns out to be so much nonsense that it's not worth even starting. That kind of situation doesn't even exist. Not everyone has to believe in it. It's enough that I believe in it and a couple of other key people buy into it. And then if you succeed well, everyone starts believing in it.
>
> (Development manager of a major corporation)

In the social debate, referring to strategy means hardening values. Managers are more credible decision-makers than politicians, and market discipline dominates in politics too (Kantola, 2002). When public organizations or nations form strategies, they are in essence reviving the lessons of business management developed in the US in the 1960s, according to which the pursuit of profit is the main goal of management. Oakes, Townley, and Cooper (1998) present an illustrative example in their case study of a Canadian museum. A strategic planning process was introduced according to the "modern way of managing." Unfortunately, when the managers began focusing on financial capital, they forgot that the organization was supposed to be the caretaker of cultural capital. When everyone discovered that they had to have a strategy, the original purpose of the organization was forgotten—to take care of culture by studying, maintaining, and presenting history.

Corporate strategies and society have a two-way relationship. When talking about society's influence on a company's strategy, we usually talk about social responsibility. It can be seen that social institutions have the chance to partially lead a company by the hand in its strategic choices.

Socially responsible operations are a part of reputation management as it builds public opinion and views about the organization.

The other side of the coin is that companies strive to promote their strategic advantages by influencing society. This is what is meant by a company's political strategies. The basic idea behind political strategies is that companies must be able to compete not only in business markets but also in political markets. Political decision-makers make decisions that affect corporate competitiveness all the time. As a result, companies must protect their interests also within the political arena.

Corporate political activity literature studies how companies protect their interests in political markets (cf. Getz, 1997). While lobbying and campaign funding are already quite traditional phenomena, connecting strategies with political activities at its worst can mean dirtying society, turning social life into a game or a great military campaign as political decision-making begins to serve the interests of corporations.

The success of strategic management reflects the worldview of market-oriented Western industrial nations that became the dominant worldview after World War II. The world is a tough place in which money determines the most important choices. This helps explain the success of a symbol like strategy within the management debate. During the last half-century management trends have come and gone, but strategy has remained and succeeded in renewing itself.

Strategic reputation management of the good company

> It is a piece of shit we got from management.
> (Finnish telecom mechanic when asked to define "strategy")

Strategy and the network society are not very good partners, even if they are two of the most important phenomena describing our times. We showed earlier that in a network society goodness has a market value in terms of both customers and potential partners. A perception of being good is a strategic resource.

On the other hand, it is hardly a good idea to show an openly strategic face if you want to be labeled as good by customers and other stakeholders. Few customers want to buy a psychopath's products. A company with a good reputation "values its customers and employees" and cares for the environment and the future of our children. These values also instruct industry how to demonstrate its own socially responsible operations. According to a booklet published by the Confederation of Finnish Industries[3] a few years ago, "the good or bad management of social responsibility has a rapid effect on corporate image. For this reason social responsibility means managing both the company and its risks . . .

Some companies even utilize social responsibility to improve the image of themselves and their companies." The booklet highlights the importance of integrity ("presented information has to be relevant, accurate, and understandable") and respect ("good practices and cooperation within corporate networks"), as well as communication ("open dialogue and co-operation with stakeholders") and excellence ("some companies aim to turn social responsibility into a competitive advantage"). And above all, social responsibility "is part of a company's strategy and daily operations." An ironic parenthesis to this is based on the fact that Enron's values were respect, integrity, communications, and excellence (cited in Cruver, 2002).

Therefore those making reputation strategies have to reassure the surrounding society that it is forsaking the mercilessness suggested by strategy and transforming it into a genuine desire to increase the well-being of all through honest entrepreneurship. The challenge of a good company's strategy is to discard the tradition of violence and cold analysis, at least in part, and to see strategy instead as the sensible activity of a good-hearted person, "with a healthy mind and a big heart."

In other words, a good company's strategy has to maintain a distance from the militaristic and instrumental roots of strategic management. This entails looking more closely at these encrusted concepts of strategy.

When talking about reputation, interest is often focused specifically on the external stakeholders of organizations. In terms of reputation, however, an organization's most important stakeholder is its own personnel. An organization is its own most important public in two ways. Firstly, an organization's employees want to create a good life for themselves through their careers, to be in harmony with the core values represented by the organization. For example, a pacifist could find it hard to work for a company that produces weapons, especially if he or she does not believe that the weapons are being manufactured purely for defensive purposes.

Secondly, a company's good and bad deeds are made by its personnel. Particularly in service industries, a company's reputation is built through encounters with its employees. To manage a company as a good company, the central challenge is to create and implement a good strategy. This kind of strategic management of goodness cannot rely simply on classic lessons of strategy, as they are built purely on the basis of instrumental goodness.

Strategic organization: a tool or a community?

Our views of an organization are directly affected by what we think about the organization's management. Few things influence management as much as our understanding about what we are managing.

The root of the word "organization" is the Latin *organum*, which refers to a tool. This is in fact what is often meant by organization—a tool that is used to achieve goals that are perceived as being useful. For example, an NGO organizes and distributes roles among activists in order to promote its issues more effectively. "Organization" is used to mean structuring, as in structuring roles, resources, and technology into the most effective form. An organization can thus be seen as a tool with which a certain interest group achieves its desired result. Business economics considers the most important interest group to be shareholders, whose pursuit of gain is supported by the organization. For a manager too, the organization that works beneath him is a tool for achieving the goals that have been approved by the shareholders.

Views about what an organization is change over time. In the early 1900s a manager who was inspired by the then-dominant ideas of scientific management was essentially an engineer who tuned his organizational machine to run more efficiently. In the second half of the century the strategic manager became a player who actively studied the competition situation and contemplated various strategic moves. The fact that this leadership style that emphasized the competitive environment began to rely on the lessons of war reflects a worldview whose values are success, growth, conquering, winning, and analytical sharpness—*cogito ergo sum* ("I think, therefore I am"). This worldview also suggests primitiveness; the struggle often requires sacrifices, including laying people off.

Rational and humanist management discourses

> Strategic decisions are concerned with the long-term health of the company. Tactical decisions deal more with the day-to-day activities necessary for efficient and smooth operations. But decisions, either tactical or strategic, usually require implementation by allocation or reallocation of resources—funds, equipment, or personnel.
>
> (Chandler, 1962, p. 11)

A rational and analytical manager lies at the heart of both the organizational machine and the strategic organization. Strategic work, the most important work that has to be done within an organization, means analyzing the environment, sensing development trends, and applying the organization's competencies to threats and possibilities. Strategic work is often conceived as analytical thought work, the concerted decision-making of an alpha-male general (Mantere & Vaara, forthcoming). The importance of strategic work also means an implicit demotion of the importance of so-called "operative" work. It can be considered that strategy has inherited its ideal of rationality from old-fashioned and somewhat out-of-style scientific business management, or "Taylorism."

> It is not the cash that fuels the journey to the future, but the emotional and intellectual energy of every employee.
>
> (Hamel & Prahalad, 1994, p. 127)

An organization is a tool, but it is still a work community. Most people do not want to see themselves simply as tools, but rather as thinking, feeling, and intrinsically valuable beings. People today live their entire lives in different types of organizations, from the cradle to the grave. Organizational theorists Jim March and (Nobel Laureate) Herbert Simon state the following in their classic book *Organizations* (1958):

> But why are organizations important? A superficial answer is that organizations are important because people spend so much of their time in them. The working force—that is to say, the bulk of the adult population—spends more than a third of its waking hours in the organizations by which it is employed. The life of the child takes place to almost an equal extent in the environment of the school organization; and an uncountable host of other organizations, mostly voluntary, account for a large chunk of the leisure time of child and adult alike. In our society, preschool children and nonworking housewives are the only large groups of persons whose behavior is not substantially "organizational."
>
> (March & Simon, 1958, p. 2)

Organizations instrumentalize people. We are taught to be "valuable resources" to our employers. As tools we can be sacrificed. When a company makes a strategic choice and dismisses people in the name of shareholder value, the dark side of this tool perspective is revealed. People do not want to be game pieces whose fates are sealed simply for the pursuit of gain.

> I was the kind of manager that was both a teacher and a manager. I approached the matter like you would approach kids at summer camp. It's terrible to say, yet it's true—listen to what people really want and then make it clear what you are aiming for, what we have to try to do, and that we are going to do it together. And sometimes you just have to be hard on people . . .
>
> (Founder and manager of multimedia industry startup company)

The community perspective of organizations also highlights the inability of the tool perspective to explain the successful management of people; that is, leadership. People are not motivated to do their best if they are treated like tools. The idea of this kind of "people management" is not new. Management theorist Philip Selznick crystallized in his classic book

Leadership in Administration already in 1957 that an organization is not only a tool but an institution, a human community:

> The formal, technical system is never more than a part of the living enterprise we deal with in action. The persons and groups who make it up are not content to be treated as manipulable or expendable. As human beings and not mere tools they have their own needs for self-protection and self-fulfillment—needs that may either sustain the formal system or undermine it. These human relations are a great reservoir of energy. They may be directed in constructive ways toward desired ends or they may become recalcitrant sources of frustration. One objective of sound management practice is to direct and control these internal social pressures.
>
> (Selznick, 1957, p. 8)

The opposite approach of rational management is a humanist approach, which also has rather deep roots. Already in the early 1900s the management debate became a struggle between rational scientific business management on the one side and the school of human relations and its successors on the other.[4] With certain reservations it can be thought that the voice of rationalism has belonged to economic liberals, according to whom man makes his own luck, also in working life. Humanists in turn have promoted the communitarian idea that the community actively shapes the life of the individual. For liberals, the task of organizations is to create added value for investors—an organization is an investor's tool for transforming reasonable or unreasonable risks into reasonable or unreasonable profits. For communitarians, an organization is above all a workplace, a source of either well-being or ill feeling.

> My main role is to motivate and comfort. If we talk about everyday life, then it is to motivate and comfort. I have to genuinely motivate people to experience strategically important goals as being really important and so that they know what we're talking about. So that they can understand their own role in that wheel. That is my main role. Then I really have to make everything concrete for the bosses, so they know what it means. What are our goals? How are they connected to the goals of the entire chain and then support them and provide them the resources to move everything forward. I provide them with the manpower. I give them the means to do this, the advertising and everything. That's like my job. Then I am a comforter when we don't achieve something by taking into consideration the person behind it all. I remember to comfort them and sort things out. I also have to punish if we don't meet our goals, if we slip and people have been comforted. Then conclusions also have to be drawn. Maybe the

person is precisely wrong for the job, or they need training or other support. If everything has already been provided for that person, then we will stop wasting rations on that person.

(Department store manager)

When a particularly successful company dismisses employees, both the rationalist and humanist views are correct from their mutually opposite perspectives. The company's productivity and implementation of its strategy must be pursued. On the other hand, layoffs often lead to human tragedies and create ill feeling within the remaining work community.

For example, Finnish mobile-phone casings manufacturer Perlos announced in spring 2005 that it was increasing production in China. The company's motives were reported publicly. One of the factors behind the investments in China was seen as the price and flexibility of labor. In China the minimum wage of factory workers was around €60 to €90 a month. The workforce can thus be considered temporary. The number of personnel at factories is changed according to the current demand for their products. Workers are sourced through temporary labor recruitment agencies. Additional personnel can be recruited according to production peaks, even for just a week or two. The company's director for Asia emphasized how temporary labor "offers flexibility and cost efficiency. We are better able to maintain profitability. . . . of course we have a moral responsibility how we operate within our network of subcontractors" (*Helsingin Sanomat*, May 17, 2005).

When considering the strategy of the good company, the actions taken by Perlos attract interest. The rhetoric employed by Perlos in its human resource management strategy is in line with the instrumentalist conception of organizing. In the Perlos 2004 annual report it is stated quite plainly that the "focus areas of Human Resources in the years ahead will be to develop flexibility and the ability to change" (p. 15). Furthermore, "One of the key issues in the ability to change is the development of flexible working time solutions" (p. 15). Therefore the company's production operations in China are completely in line with the company's strategy.

Two gaping maws

On the one hand the humanist and rational positions are not easily reconcilable in terms of values and aims, yet neither of them alone is sufficient. The image that springs to mind is that of Ulysses sailing through the narrow straits between the sea monsters Scylla and Charybdis. An organization that is managed according to pure strategy is Scylla, whose bite means subjugating people into mere "human resources" with value only in the hands of the strategic manager. An organization that is managed according to pure humanistic values is Charybdis, in whose hands an organization is transformed into a rest home that eventually chokes on the ill feeling and uselessness of everyday experiences, drowning in the whirlpools of the humanistic monster.

The contest between humanists and rationalists does not look like it will have a pleasant ending. Both sound credible from their own perspectives. We do not want a world in which "faceless capital" controls the small person. On the other hand, few of us want to deny owners or their representatives the right to make decisions—it is sufficient to imagine ourselves establishing our own companies and employing people to work there. Fortunately, since the 1990s texts have begun to appear within the debate over strategy that integrate humanistic lessons about community and managing people with market analysis-led strategic thinking.

Strategy as communication: towards strategic management of the good

Regarding strategic management as a communal activity is an important step towards strategically managing the good. The concept of communal strategy rests on the interaction between an organization's members and other stakeholders, in other words on communications.

In our encounters with practitioners, our experience is that business leaders would like the researcher to evaluate the quality of their strategy work: "Are we handling strategy as well as other companies?" or "How is our strategy doing?" The researcher's job is to assure these people that everything is going well. Strategy practices tend to make sense only in context, and the task of comparing one to the other makes little sense in most situations.

Another typical cause of concern goes like this: "We've thought through our strategy with everyone on the executive team, but how can we make sure that our people will implement it?" This question reflects the idea that communication has been instrumentalized as part of the strategy. Managers consider it self-evident that communication is part of the strategic process, instead of strategy being a product of the communication process. Considering strategy as a part of communications would help develop the communal strategy concept. Furthermore, it would solve many problems that have traditionally complicated the implementation of corporate strategies, producing what can be conceptualized as the "formulation–implementation gap" (figure 6.1).

Strategy as analysis: Moses at the mountain

The causes of concern mentioned above illustrate the assumption that strategy is the analytical work of management. Strategy is discussed within tight and important groups. Strategic analysis typically tries to

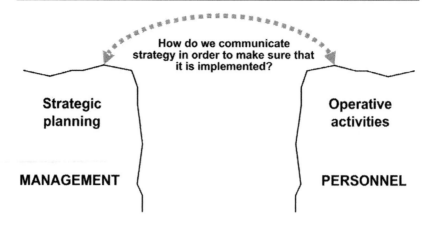

Figure 6.1 Strategy formulation–implementation gap (adapted from Aaltonen et al., 2001).

make an organization's intrinsic strengths compatible with the competitive situation. For example, forms of strategic analysis based on the compatibility between an organization and its environment include Kenneth Andrews's (1971) SWOT analysis and Michael Porter's (1980) so-called five-forces analysis. An essential trait of analysis is "starting from a clean sheet of paper" and "surpassing daily realities." A central element of strategy work is not to get stuck in old and familiar ways but instead to "look truth in the eyes" and make even tough decisions, if logic thus dictates (Andrews, 1971).

Once a strategy has been prepared, the strategist makes the strategy known to the people who will implement it, to the organization's bosses and to operative personnel. Symbolically speaking, the strategist steps out of his log cabin like Moses coming down from the mountain, with a pile of commandments intended to be realized by the organizational corpus, the body that will fulfill the orders of the mind. Critical management researcher Stewart Clegg and his colleagues (Clegg, Carter, & Cornberger, 2004) have ridiculed such strategy practice from the viewpoint of an implementer by paraphrasing James Brown: "Get up, I feel like being a strategy machine!" The purpose of this kind of communication is to convey information, not to distribute or build knowledge. Information about the strategy has been defined in advance and is unambiguous. There are only two ways to interpret the strategy: the right way and the wrong way—"my way or the highway."

According to this analytical concept of strategy, once the strategy message has been communicated, efforts are made to interpret it and understand what the message means. Interpreting alone is not enough, however. If the interpretation has nothing to do with learning new things or changing ways of working, the strategy message remains on the level of conditionals: "should do this, should do that."

> I'm sure I have to tell this thing in ten different ways. One person understands speech, another understands text, still another understands when it is demonstrated. But you have to be patient and keep repeating the message from every corner. And what is the right procedure, when it's good if you remember once to say to someone . . . When there is a good plan, how should the change be communicated so that at least everyone at least receives the message at the same time and in the same way, in the form of facts—that too helps already rather than having it spread by word of mouth with it changing along the way.
>
> (Marketing manager of a telecom company)

The analytical concept of strategy dominates, but it is problematic. From its own starting point, the perspective that organizations pursue their own benefit, the analytical concept of strategy is limited by its lack of historical depth. If an organization always begins thinking about the market situation with a clean sheet of paper, if strategy bubbles up from the minds of analysts and not from the expertise that has been nurtured by the organization with great effort, the strategy baby gets thrown out with the bathwater. Along the way organizations gather unique competencies that others find hard to imitate. These competencies create competitive ability as much as figuring out the market situation. Furthermore, since these competencies are spread out throughout the organization, the strategy debate should cover a large group of stakeholders to ensure that the strategy is based on expertise. Strategy concepts that rely on knowledge and competencies have emphasized continuity and utilizing the organization's experience instead of pure analysis.[5]

Even if analysis cannot wipe the slate clean, the idea that strategic management requires intense decision-making at the highest levels of the organization is alive and well. An organization is the body, while the strategy created by the executive team is its soul (Mantere & Vaara, forthcoming). Precisely the analytical concept of strategy creates the fear that someone else can perform a better analysis, figure out something that we cannot. This is why corporate executives have the need to ask researchers if their organization's strategy is in good shape. They do not remember that strategy comes from uniqueness, and not just from sharp minds.

Another problem with the analytical concept is its mechanistic view of implementing strategy. Once prepared, an analytical strategy should be implemented the way the analytical strategy has been conceived—the body should follow the soul's moves, resources deployed to follow strategy (Chandler, 1962). According to the analytical concept of strategy, the roles of different levels within an organization are clearly divided and differentiated. The task of upper management is to create strategy. The role of middle management is to interpret the word carried forward by Moses, to give orders and to monitor. It is left to operative personnel to obey.

> It is not enough to just nod your head, strategy has to be digested. I can't pinpoint any specific thing I do to make sure it happens. We go through it as specifically as we with our people can in the time we have, and then we see if anything happens. Measuring the implementation of strategy is an important part of the process.
>
> (Quality manager of a major technology company)

It is no coincidence that the symbol of roles is widely employed when discussing how strategy works in organizations. Roles require and adhere to ready-made scripts, and theater or movie directors represent interpretation authorities (Giddens, 1984). The analytical-strategy model can be read through the symbol of the theater: strategy is an organization's script that has been prepared by upper management. Middle management represents the director who interprets the practical implementation of the strategy. Operative personnel play the roles that have been assigned them. Another way of looking at this is that an organization's script is already written, as the external environment determines the correct strategic choices. In this case the play's director, upper management, has come down from the mountain and heard the higher voice, instead of having made the "strategic choice" themselves. The commandments have been written, and are then announced. As in the production of major motion pictures, the director does not have time to monitor all the scenes being shot. Instead, he has a team or trustworthy assistant directors, middle managers, who monitor the completion of these scenes.

The organizational theater, with its prepared scripts, can represent an agreeable way to perform work—an actor's work can be both pleasant and unpleasant. The key success factor, besides whether the director can interpret the script in a fruitful way, is whether the actors feel they can apply their skills and powers of expression to their roles. A lifeless performance can ruin a play just as much as a lousy director. Furthermore, it should be remembered that no troupe of actors can perform at their best in every single production. For this reason, three main management challenges can be found for the purely analytical-strategy concept from its original premises; that is, from the perspective of an organization's pursuit of success.

Challenge 1 motivation

The first challenge has to do with the motivation and commitment of the strategy's implementers, primarily operative personnel and middle management. The trained professionals who often constitute the workforce in organizations today are rather bad at taking orders. With the increase in experts, work has increasingly become a forum for self-realization. Ready-made strategy roles, with their explicit scripts and directions, poorly suit individualistic experts who want to realize themselves (Mantere, forthcoming).

The problem becomes even more serious if the strategy tries to find a mechanistic solution to the problem of commitment—hairs are bound to rise if the strategy announces that it is initiating "commitment and participation procedures." It is not rare to hear motivation mentioned ironically as a cover-up for coercion in today's business-speak. The problem that arises with the analytical perspective is that the performer of expert work rarely accepts the kind of strategy concept in which his role is seen as carrying out the thoughts of someone else in a planned way. Experts want to think, solve problems creatively, and express themselves.

What advice can be given to strategists to solve the motivation problem? They might try to hide the commitment procedures so well that the expert imagines he invented the strategy himself. In some organizational cultures more precise control is tolerated and some individuals appreciate the feeling of security created by explicit commands. Another alternative is to loosen the reins and keep the strategy open to interpretation. In principle, the first alternative involves lies and deceit and is in our experience rather common—it works when it works. The second alternative works best if the interpretation of the strategy involves challenging expert personnel to perform the same kind of thinking work that management has to do. Both alternatives are connected if, behind the thinking challenge, lies a hidden agenda; that is, if management has already decided the strategy and does not require new analyses. At their best, however, decentralized thought exercises help improve an organization's strategy.

> Discussing [strategies] is in my opinion how people learn them. Strategies can be distributed and duplicated, you can order people to read them and process them, but none of this helps. People discuss them in this way: does this mean something to us, how does this change our work. All kinds of things have to be discussed before they decide if they can accept this or not. For sure, a little criticism has to be included in these discussions.
>
> (Head of unit of major public organization)

Challenge 2 Know-how

Another challenge of the analytical strategy concept has to do with expert know-how. Actually, this is a kind of competence argument. An organization's experts have at their disposal information, ideas, experiences, and observations which have the potential to lead to a better strategy. Operative personnel are in fact often closer to the organization's environment than management—consider the customer interface, for example. Those serving customers continuously receive signals from the environment, and make observations and insights that would help management see the environment in a new way. Creating strategy with a "clean piece of paper" or in a "small group of good men," an expedition by the executive team to the holy mountain, is like the search for the Holy Grail. They would have the wisdom, but instead the executive team goes fishing over the seas.

> Everybody is promised everything, something is created as if you have had the chance to influence, there has been a representative. If we want a strong operating plan that is agreeable to strategists, it cannot be left up to everyone—instead we need the best boys and girls who are clearly seen within the organization to be prospects and resources for the future. These promising future leaders should be sought, conscientiously train them, take them into the inner circle, give them assignments that the old guys can't be bothered with or don't know how to do. I have a certain team that I train and provide opportunities for them, and I try to keep up with them which is not easy. I have decided that these guys have to be part of the process, but we are also beginning to have a spread of age groups that requires us to find new young people, new resources, who take this thing genuinely and enthusiastically as their own.
>
> (Top manager in a ministry)

From these kinds of premises we can present the analytical-strategy concept with a challenging demand to revise strategy. Instead of strategy work being a kind of two-part project in which the thinking part comes first and then the implementation part, strategy should be a continuous process in which the good ideas of operative experts revise the strategic direction.[6] Strategy scholar Robert Burgelman has made a number of revolutionary insights on strategy work based on the technology company Intel. In 1983 Burgelman published an article in which he analyzed Intel's radical change of direction in the late 1970s from a manufacturer of computer memory to the world's most successful manufacturer of processors. The initiative to change directions came from the lower middle management expert level and was implemented despite the systematic opposition of upper management, who continuously marketed Intel as a "memory company." Eventually they recognized that the strategy ideas bubbling up from below were in fact better (Burgelman, 1983).

Challenge 3 Application

> I wonder if anyone can get the true "big picture" by just seeing above. The forest looks just like a rug from a helicopter, and anyone who has taken a walk in the forest . . . knows that forests don't look much like that from the inside. Strategists do not understand much about forests if they stay in helicopters, nor much about organizations if they stay in head offices. . . . Thus, strategic thinking is also inductive thinking: seeing above must be supported by seeing below.
>
> (Mintzberg, 1991, pp. 22–23)

The third challenge has to do with the symbolic question of whether the prepared script is appropriate for the acting team to implement. Upper management may not be the best experts to assess what kind of strategy works in practice—this is where operational professionals are stronger. On the other hand, we know that daily realities can stop even the most necessary changes. The answer to the third challenge requires from above a bold decision on direction on the one hand and an understanding of the practical possibilities in everyday work on the other hand. Henry Mintzberg has described this interesting dynamic by stating that "structure follows strategy as the left foot follows the right" (Mintzberg, 1990).

> I guess it is the individual right of everyone to interpret strategy from their own perspective, and preferably so that not everyone has a yes-opinion—new ideas are also needed. Otherwise nothing develops. While we do have a yes-team here too, we also have active, constructive thinkers just like in all organizations, and that's how it should be, in my opinion. Alternatives should be found and new ideas should be formed, more radical ideas are welcome. This won't all collapse if we make a few experiments, but before we introduce these ideas for mass use, a little piloting is needed."
>
> (Managing director of telecom company)

Communication as strategy: like Real Madrid

While communication can be regarded as a tool for strategy implementation, another view of strategy has emerged, which treats strategy itself as communication. Strategy can be regarded as a practice of communication, where a community is seeking to understand itself better. This represents what Habermas (1985) has called "communicative action." This is an interesting development, as Habermas has also presented strategic action as representing instrumental rationality, exactly opposite to a communicative attitude. In this view, strategic management would always implicate an instrumentalist, rather than a communitarian, view on organization.

However, a discernible counterpoint to the instrumentalist view has emerged within strategic management, to challenge the instrumentalist notion of organizations, championing a more communitarian alternative (Barry & Elmes, 1997; Bartlett & Ghoshal, 1994; Crossan & Berdrow, 2003; Gioia & Chittipeddi, 1991; Hamel & Prahalad, 1994; Mantere & Vaara, forthcoming; Mintzberg, 1994; Weick, 2001). Strategy can be discerned as a discourse through which an organizational community finds collective purpose and meaning.

Juha Näsi has pointed out that strategy is the "red thread" of operations (Näsi & Aunola, 2001). Henry Mintzberg (1978) talks about strategy as a "pattern in a stream of actions." The aforementioned symbols refer on the one hand to coherence in operations, and on the other to collective future aspirations.

> Other events divert attention from the implementation of strategy . . . This is a bit like six-year-olds playing soccer: when something comes up, everyone piles up going after it . . . Not quite a zone defense . . . This is still not really a result-oriented organization.
>
> (Member of executive team of a major insurance company)

The difference between the communicative and analytical conceptions of strategy is very similar to the difference between organizational community and instrument perspectives. Where the analytical perspective emphasizes strategy as a tool of the owners to get the organizational instrument to realize desired objectives, the communication perspective in turn demonstrates the ability of strategy to make meaning out of work performed together. One of the characteristics of organizations is that their operations are in some way aspirational.

Strategy is a "fiction about the future" (Barry & Elmes, 1997), as it responds to the need of the human community formed by an organization to see its activities as being in some way significant—every one of us thinks from time to time, is there any sense to our work, and are we achieving anything useful? For many of us usefulness does not require earth-shattering achievements; it is sufficient that our activities fulfill certain objectives: for example, are we useful to our employers? In this sense strategy can offer the possibility to experience one's own work as important, since through our own small input we are implementing the organization's strategy. The experience of community maintains job satisfaction and is created in part precisely from experiencing and adopting common goals.

Where the instrumentalist metaphor was Moses, the communicational metaphor for strategy is the community in which all members participate organically in achieving a common goal: like a soccer team. Not a particularly novel conception, we know, but fitting. Even though the coaches analyze an opponent's playing style in advance and make all kinds of plans, in the actual match situation it is essential not only to actively pursue the goal and employ teamwork but also to react to the opponent's playing. Even though the players have different roles that are highlighted in different playing situations, any one of the players may have to kick the ball and in doing so make the decisive move in winning or losing the match. In most cases a single player does not decide the outcome of the match, however; what is important is how individual situations make the game.

We can use the example of the European soccer dream team Real Madrid, which spends countless millions on the world's best players. Although the individuals are the best, Real Madrid's real challenge is to play as a community, whose strategy arises out of a communicative and collective activity, building the game by listening to each other. The team's efforts will fail if any one of the star players creates his own ingenious strategies without following what the others are doing.

> It just has to be accepted that every member of our staff interprets strategy in their own way. This is definitely a fact. As long as something good comes of it, then it is good. But in no case can the strategy be realized as is. But there are still some things that we monitor.
>
> (Member of the executive team of a large governmental organization)

A contradiction arises between the communicational and analytical view, whether we like it or not (see table 6.1). The broad participation in strategy work emphasized by the communicational perspective gnaws at the sharpness of the analysis. In turn, the "small-team thinking" emphasized by the analytical view gnaws a branch from the united feeling of goals.

A claim that is rather widely accepted is that the turbulence in an organization's environment affects the balance between the analytical and communicational strategy process: In turbulent environments control is decentralized, as this allows an organization's members to react faster to changes. In a more stable environment, more official control mechanisms are formed, as this allows operating methods to be honed and standardized without fear of them becoming immediately outdated (Miles & Snow, 1978).

Table 6.1 Analytical and communicational conceptions of strategy.

	Analytical	*Communicative*
Metaphor	"Moses descending from the mountain"	"like Real Madrid"
Conception of organization	Instrument	Community
Participation in strategy formulation	Small group of "good men"	Wide-ranging participation
Focus of strategy	Environmental analysis	Collective purpose
Control	Tight and central, predefined implementation feedback and measurement	Distributed control, ideas move vertically and horizontally
Communication	Formal, planned	Informal, ad hoc, dialogical

Balancing between instrumental and collective

Strategic management for good companies is in many ways a problematic management doctrine. The militaristic history of strategy and its tendency to see life as a game or battle easily leads to instrumentalizing the whole world and to psychopathic operations. Strategy also easily instrumentalizes a company's personnel, making a company compete against its own employees (see, for example, Bartlett & Ghoshal, 1994; Ghoshal, 2005; Hamel & Prahalad, 1994). In this kind of relationship the commitment of personnel to good strategies, or overall to any strategies, is rather unlikely.

Strategic management is nevertheless the dominant management doctrine of our time. It does not appear that strategy will be discarded anytime soon. A better alternative is to transform the image of strategic management from within, to distance it from its militaristic roots and emphasize community and trends that promote natural goodness.

Strategic management has indeed changed, become more multidimensional, and it is still changing. In its 50-year history it has gone through two phases of complication. The first had to do with the observation that, in addition to creating strategies, implementing them is a real problem for companies. It was noticed that creating strategy certainly does not happen from a clean sheet of paper; instead, strategy is realized more easily if it relies on previous experiences, unique competencies that have been gathered over long periods of time, and a shared understanding of the direction of the common strategy.[7] A precise analysis of the competitive environment and actions based on this remain empty if the strategy is not realized. It can be considered that the first complication occurred after the observation was made that creating strategies is insufficient and that formulating and implementing strategy should be seen as aspects of the same process.[8] One of the essential observations of the strategic process concept is that strategy is created and implemented in a seesaw motion between the creators and implementers of the strategy. A successful statement of strategy confirms what has happened before, while also building a future; a successful strategic process contains the work efforts of both management and personnel.

An essential part of the strategic process debate is motivated by the observation that the instrumental perspective of organizations is not enough to explain why a strategy is realized or remains unrealized. A norm, created through analytical thinking about what an organization should do, does not make an organization's community work more efficiently or in a more goal-oriented way. Realizing a strategy means managing the organizational community, which is a communicative process. If the strategy is written in a way that corresponds with the questions about the future asked by the community, if strategy is a natural extension of the community's story, strategy at its best offers the community a common meaning—makes the community's work enjoyable and significant (Barry & Elmes, 1997). The fact that analytical talk inspires few people leads to a difficult situation. The well-known theoretician Karl Weick (2001) has demonstrated how credibility is a much more important success factor in strategy work than analytical precision: "any old map will do." In Weick's social-constructionist view, an organization is a key player in the creation of its own competitive environment, as a result of which it is more important to believe in the strategy than to hone its content.

The second period of complication occurred around the turn of the millennium, when networks became a relevant subject of the strategy debate (figure 6.2). As the core operations of organizations became integrated with various networks, the success of strategies became connected with how the organization's strategies were related to each other. Whereas we already know quite a lot about internal strategic dialogues, research into the network dialogue is in its early days, and compiled information is scattered. Two types of dialogue are thus ongoing within the strategic process: the dialogue between an organization's members (its management and other personnel), and the dialogue between an organization and its network.

The diversification of strategy has progressed towards a situation in which the possibilities to perform strategic analysis have become increasingly limited. Similarly, the number of key persons in the strategic process has increased. The original strategy authors thought that strategic analysis

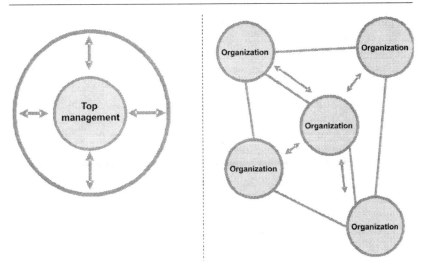

Figure 6.2 The two complicating factors of the strategic processes of organizations. The expansion of strategy into a dialogue between the creators and implementers of strategy (*left*), and the expansion of strategy into a dialogue between the organization and its network (*right*).

was the only significant strategic issue. What was important was to find the right strategy for the right environment. Strategy could be made by management alone. The problems of implementing strategy brought up the argument that strategic analysis means nothing if the strategy is not realized. Another crucial question was raised: how can an organization's members find a common strategy and remove the obstacles that prevent its implementation—often simultaneously. The number of key persons in the strategic process multiplied rapidly to include a large group of middle managers, in some cases all personnel. The network strategy brought up the problem of integrating the strategy with those of other members of the network. The group of people involved with strategies expanded to include those within other organizations (figure 6.3).

Summary: strategic management of the good

These days, a good company often makes its strategy within a kind of network. It is itself transected by various networks. A company has to integrate its own strategy with the network's strategy, as all stages of its production process begin to be infiltrated by different networks. How does this affect the way we think about strategy? In the networked world, which side is winning: the communicational or analytical concept of strategy?

There is no easy answer, because the contradiction between the communicational and analytical concepts that complicates strategy is amplified

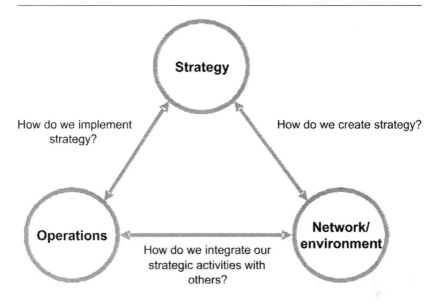

Figure 6.3 Three main strategy questions in a networked environment.

in various arguments related to networks. Networks do not make strategy more analytical or communal—it would seem that the network perspective deepens the chasm, simultaneously demanding more from both. On the one hand, the need for analysis in networked strategic work is further emphasized, as organizations perform best within a network by investing in it as astutely as possible. On the other hand, the challenge of maintaining a good reputation reveals the powerlessness of management to be responsible alone for the company's reputation or to control the interactive situations that form reputation—indeed as Davies et al. (2003) have demanded, there is a need for a reputational perspective on strategic management. The instrumental view of organizations also requires strategically controlling personnel, arguably a company's most immediate network. Strategic management that is dominated by economic thinking is obsessed with an organization's competitiveness, and this makes the organization ultimately turn against its employees. Indian-born strategy researcher Sumantra Ghoshal (2005) argues in his work "Bad management theories are destroying good management practice" that economic strategy doctrines encourage managers to compete with subcontractors, legislators, customers, and even their own employees. When managers of companies like Enron deceive customers, legislators, owners, and employees while paying themselves enormous options, it is time for business schools to take a look in the mirror.

On the other hand, if a network's interfaces, especially the staff members who are close to the customer interface, do not feel that they are standing behind a shared purpose, they identify with the interests of other networks than those within their organization. Especially when an organization's internal world turns into a battlefield, in which every individual seeks their own advantage, there is no room for growth for an organization's good operations. For this reason we claim that a purely analytical concept of strategy does not enable good strategic management, a strategy that leads to an organization's good deeds.

The strategic management of the good is a balance between the traditional analytical and instrumental concepts of strategy and the communality of the communicational concept. There are no all-encompassing rules for this balance; companies have to make choices in front of their publics: reveal the strategic beast that hides beneath the surface, or rely on the community. Good deeds are typically created from the organizational community's communicative strategy, as this kind of strategy is less limited by roots of the analytical strategy school that emphasize instrumental value.

Chapter 7

Communicating the good

They say thanks for the feedback, but between the lines they are saying don't contact us again. But that motivates me the most. That's when you should give feedback, even more so. There's something wrong if you ask for feedback yet still can't take criticism the way it is. What's that all about? Good question. Insecurity, I'd say.

(Telecom company's marketing professional)

In the previous chapter, we explored a second view to strategic management, which we called the communicative or the communitarian view. In this chapter, we explore what such a communicative view of an organization and strategy entails. We will not limit our discussion of communication within the organization, however; communication is also the key to reputation management from the perspective that good deeds can and should be actively communicated to external stakeholders. Indeed, this external communication aspect is likely to be the first association many people will get when faced with the notion of managing reputation.

The grand old man of Finnish organizational communications, Professor Emeritus Osmo A. Wiio, begins his 1968 book *Is Your Message Understood* (*Ymmärretäänkö sanomasi*) with the following story about the *Titanic*'s last minutes:

England's valiant giant, the world's largest passenger ship *Titanic* plies the Atlantic on its maiden voyage towards New York. It is the evening of April 14, 1912, and on board passengers are enjoying themselves. At the same time another vessel, the *Caledonia*, is sailing the same course ahead of the *Titanic*. An observation is made from the *Caledonia*: drifting ice ahead. A quick order is made from the bridge to the engine room, and the screws begin spinning in reverse. The captain is aware that the *Titanic* is coming behind and orders the telegraph operator to notify the *Titanic*. The *Caledonia* avoids the ice and continues on its way. The radio message is sent from the

Caledonia and reaches the *Titanic*'s radio room. But at the same time the luxury liner receives a large number of other important radio messages for important passengers. The *Caledonia*'s message about the iceberg is buried under a pile of other messages on the telegraph operator's desk. The message is not forwarded to the captain of the *Titanic*.

The *Titanic* collides with the iceberg. The *Titanic* radios the *Caledonia* for help. The *Caledonia* is so close that its lights can be seen from the deck of the *Titanic*. The telegraph operator calls the *Caledonia*, but nothing happens. The ship's only telegraph operator has already gone to bed. The ship's mate happens to pass the radio room and hears the signals. He puts on the headphones but then shakes his head and leaves. He cannot understand the message. When the call for help fails, the captain of the *Titanic* gives the order to shoot off flares. Red flares cannot be found, so white fireworks are used instead. The crew aboard the *Caledonia* see these and smile. More partying aboard the *Titanic*. The message is misinterpreted. *Caledonia* continues on its way. The *Titanic* sinks in the Atlantic, taking with it 1,635 passengers.

(Wiio, 1968, pp. 7–8)

This story is indeed a classic example of the importance of communications, about how essential it is for communications to work and for messages to be understood. And not just in this one story, but everywhere. Wiio (1968, p. 9) points out that "all human life is a constant exchange of information, giving and taking information, understanding and being made understood." Later, for example in his 1997 book, he clarifies how communication is a prerequisite for all ordered communal life and a way of helping realize the aspirations of communities. In other words, human societies, and thus organizations, simply could not exist without communication.

Reputation management is a communicational activity. However, communication is more than just a tool for companies. The majority of the operations of any organization are communications. In fact we can consider that an organization is communications, individual thought, and a few material issues on top, such as equipment and buildings.

The relationship between reputation and an organization's communications can be clarified through the concept of reputation as stories, discussed in the previous chapter. According to Smythe, Dorward, and Reback (1992, p. 19) reputation is the sum of stories told about an organization. This is significant in terms of communications, as behind this definition lies a fundamental assumption: human communication is a vital process in our society; we do not just communicate, we live in communication. Reputation is a question of what is mentioned, spoken, told, or presented about something. In this way reputation has traditionally been linked to talking and listening, to presenting messages and understanding them. Reputation is thus more or less a matter for a good company's communications. The latest definitions of corporate communications consider the connection between communications and reputation, as well as management, to be a matter of fact. For example, Joep Cornelissen's book *Corporate Communications: Theory and Practice* employs the following definition:

> Corporate communication is a management function that offers a framework and vocabulary for the effective coordination of all means of communications with the overall purpose of establishing and maintaining favorable reputations with stakeholder groups upon which the organization is dependent.
>
> (Cornelissen, 2004, p. 23)

To manage is to communicate

> When I was a little boy I wanted to grow up to become the ring-master of a circus. In a sense this company is a circus, as we have all kinds of different artists. We have very few so-called assembly-line workers. Some people say that it's a good thing we have such different tasks, but our biggest challenge is to continuously provide new challenges for all these people. There is a conflict with client companies, who want specific individuals to be responsible for them—forever. But for our people, this situation is an impediment to their own creativity and development—telling them to do just one thing. Some of our clients recognize that we have to take care of several things at the same time, but not with them. We have to constantly renew these processes.
>
> (IT growth company pioneer)

Towards the end of the 1990s, at the threshold of the so-called "new economy," company leaders were turned into heroes. A pile of expectations came with the territory. It was fashionable to list the skills of these leaders. When these heroes fell, and the new economy collapsed, a healthy dose of sarcasm was added to these lists. Future leaders were expected to have all kinds of super-qualifications. This kind of sarcastic description of the new leader was given by *Fortune* magazine (October 11, 1999):

> "You Must Know Everything" is the title of a story by Russian writer Isaac Babel. Maybe the phrase ought to be inscribed over business school entrance gates as a challenge to entering students. Tomorrow's

captains of industry must be e-commerce adept and old-economy tested; must have powerful analytical skills and superb instincts, including perfect pitch when it comes to hiring people; must know EPS, TCP-IP, ROE, HTTP, EVA, and WAP; must be innovators, visionaries, and change agents; must know the difference between a thin client and a lean supply chain; must be able to say no in a way that doesn't demoralize and to inspire people to exceed their own expectations; must be coaches and team players; must have spent several years working on another continent; must be able to work harder, longer, than most people, while keeping their personal lives in balance; must be young at heart but mature in judgment; and must have good teeth and look great in a suit—and on Friday in trousers and a sweater.

(Stewart, 1999)

Amidst the dizzying heights of the new economy a model of the ideal manager–leader was created. Andersen Consulting carried out a major study in 1999 entitled *The Evolving Role of Executive Leadership*. Corporate leaders and future leaders around the world were interviewed and asked to assess leadership in the past, the present, and the future. On the basis of the study, 14 dimensions of leadership were outlined that together create the portrait of the ideal leader. Accordingly, the ideal leader thinks globally, anticipates opportunities, creates a common vision, develops and further develops people, values cultural diversity, promotes teamwork and partnership, accepts changes, demonstrates technological intelligence, encourages people to face new challenges, guarantees customer satisfaction, creates competitive advantages, shares power, and lives according to his values.

Many of the definitions of management and leadership from that time today seem comical, to say the least. In fact, they fit quite well with the Moses-caricature of the strategic analyst, presented in the previous chapter. However, one important factor survived from those years. According to Gemini Consulting's 1999 study of future leadership, all leaders share one thing: at the heart of management and leadership skills is communication. Only open and interactive organizations succeed, and corporate leaders must be able to attract the right employees, to motivate them, and to develop their expertise. In order for this to succeed, corporate leaders have to be communicatively talented.

I have asked my subordinates to list our customer promises on the spot and explain what they mean. The one who has been first to give me the correct answer has been rewarded with a gift certificate of €20.

(Department store manager)

The role of communicative understanding as the basis for communicative skills is an important observation. What are the assumptions, the implicit mental models, which determine the communicative behavior of leaders? This relationship between understanding and acting is emphasized when considering the role and importance of communications in leadership. Leaders can see communications simply from the perspective of informing, and of transferring information, and can be extremely talented within this framework. The most important role of communications really is seen as disseminating information. According to this view it is enough to tell things the right way. A company's communications systems play a key role, and multifaceted communications channels maintain good communication processes.

The terminology typical of this dissemination view swarms with communications derivatives: leadership communications, foreman communications, internal communications, strategic communications, vision communications, work communications, and so on. As with internal communications in general, managerial communications have also focused on various information derivatives. Communications activities and systems have been built to prevent undesirable information from leaking within, and out of, the organization. Corporate communications are controlled through communications channels; the concern is whether too much or too little information is received, whether the communications tools work, who receives what, and why don't I get it? Corporate communications are carried out on technology's terms. Information and communications systems are optimized so that information will spread throughout the organization in the best possible way (Aula & Heinonen, 2002).

> In principle, in theory, a lot of information was distributed. In theory this information flowed, yet in practice it didn't.
>
> (Director, IT growth company)

Until this point, the definition of communication has been rather straightforward. Communication is something that is separated from management and leadership. First we are bosses and then communicators; first there is a strategy and then the strategy is communicated. The most important criterion for success is that the message gets across. Communication is evaluated according to whether the message was received by the intended audience. Communication is successful if we shout loud, talk a lot and repeat ourselves sufficiently. The process is promoted through pretty packages, and the success of communication becomes a question of buying and selling whatever is being communicated. We speak about "internal marketing" or "selling to the staff." Another way of handling communications is to communicate nothing. If we are quiet enough and don't say anything, no one will be able to ask any questions. For example, Lippitt (1982) describes three ways of approaching communications: through decibels, sales, and minimal information.

The relationship between management and communications has special significance in terms of a good company's reputation. All too often the relations between an organization and its audiences are managed from the perspective of communications, which are based on a company's desire to control and dictate its reputation. The basic idea behind this perspective is that the main purpose of stakeholder communications is to communicate and transfer contents that are determined by the organization itself. As a result the desire to control the content of communications is always present within the interaction. The purpose is to have the desired message transferred unchanged from the sender to the receiver, for example from a company to its stakeholders. If this does not happen, communication, and thus the interaction, has failed.

This kind of stakeholder communications approach contains within it not only the criteria for success but also a basic explanation for why the interaction has failed. In other words, this model liberates the sender from responsibility. It is easy for him to be guilty and for him to blame the receiver for incorrect opinions or faulty views. These wrongs result from "wrong," faulty communications. You can even go further and see the mistakes at the receiver's end. They do not understand what we are saying. Increasing the amount of communication is considered to be the best way of remedying this wrong. This kind of communications concept reminds us of the old stereotypical tourist who tries to make himself understood by the hotel receptionist by shouting louder in his native language. Thought about in this way, the concept of communications returns to the information transfer model of human communications: sending and receiving is how we think and act.

Reputational communication: from *communicatio* to *communicare*

The Finnish Sports Federation (SLU) believes in the strong link between reputation and communications. The SLU website states that

> reputational communications are one of SLU's main duties. SLU's goal is to diversify the images that citizens and decision-makers have about sports and exercise. The positive image of sports and exercise is built in millions of interactions every day, whether wanted or not. The formula for reputation is clear: good reputation = good operations + good communications.

> (www.slu.fi, read May 31, 2005)

The same observation is reinforced elsewhere on the Internet. Google provides 15,400,000 hits (as of January 16, 2007) for the combined search words "communication" and "reputation."

The Finnish Sports Federation's message is descriptive. There is indeed a clear connection between reputation and communications, but reputation management is more than just communications. For example, the popular claim that reputation management is the same as "integrated communications" is too narrow and misleading. However, since the connection is there, it is necessary in order to understand and apply good reputation management to study what lies at the core of communications: what ultimately do we mean by communications?

There are, broadly speaking, two genres of paradigm of human communication. These can be illustrated by looking at the root of the English word "communication." The word comes from the Latin word *communicare*, which means doing things together, sharing, and participating. On the one hand it means belonging, a connection, socializing, and brotherhood (*communis*: "community"). On the other hand, the Latin word for "communication," *communicatio*, denotes sending or distributing. Traditionally the communications of organizations have been seen primarily as an exchange of information and as a framework supporting this, and not as a form of organizational operations or community. Similarly, in views connected with reputation management, communication is taken as a given. It is often just information about issues related to reputational deeds.

We can make a clear distinction between the two views. The *communicatio* view sees human communication as a mechanistic process and the *communicare* view sees communication as a negotiation and exchange of meaning (see Fiske, 1990; O'Sullivan et al., 1994). The *communicatio* view is closely connected to the traditional organizational communication process models, which, in turn, have their roots in traditional information theory. *The Mathematical Theory of Communication* of Shannon and Weaver (1949) is an early attempt to extend the applicability of information theory into human communication and it has been one of the most important and authoritative in the development of later communication process models and theories. It models communication on a process in which a source encodes and then transmits a message along a channel. The message is received and decoded at its destination, upon which it produces an effect. Regardless of the model's omissions and deficiencies in relation to human communication, it has remained as perhaps the longest-lasting description of the communication process (Bowman and Targowski, 1987).

Information theory has made notable contributions to the study of communications, including the measurement of the quantity of information in bits and the understanding of entropy as applied to communication. However, the model is, by nature, a reductionistic sender-centered model and a straight derivative of the so-called linear main paradigm of human communication: A → B = X, or, in other words, A communicates something to B, with X resulting. Thayer stated already in 1978 that this paradigm can be found behind most western communication models and theories:

> No matter what type of communication we talk about, this model directs—whether in its appearance or by its support—a large part of research and literature. It also determines how we relate to everyday communication—the model is linear, mechanical, atomic, reminiscent of algebraic formulas, and appears official.
>
> (Thayer, 1978, p. 18)

Furthermore, Shannon and Weaver's theory is associated with the balancing and strengthening of a system's structure. Only one direction is possible, which is towards balance. Similarly, new information is also in the first place centered on the strengthening of already existing information structures. The amount of information is taken as given; due to inevitable disturbances it can only diminish (Jantsch, 1980). Communication process models are linear and predictable, are more rational than a human being, and can be considered to be part of the framework of positivistic thinking. Residual values, stochastic errors, or human factors are abstract explanations of deviations from the linear model and most often they seem to be the receiver's mistake. The visual presentations of the communication process models define the matter. They are more often than not on the box and arrow level, and cannot be used to quantify the processes they portray. Causality appears in the order of the boxes and in the direction of the arrows; nonlinear factors are framed within the disturbance or noise box.

The *communicare* view of human communication concentrates on the relationship between fundamental components necessary for meaning to emerge (see Fiske, 1990; O'Sullivan et al., 1994). Messages, people as members of cultures, and reality interact so that the meaning is able to be produced. Accordingly, human communication can be defined as a process through which people, acting together, create, sustain, and manage meanings through the use of verbal and nonverbal signs and symbols within a particular context. After communality and connectivity, the *communicare* definition of corporate communications is based on the assumption that communication is a prerequisite for all social life, and that human socialness is a prerequisite for communications. No one can be without communicating (Watzlawick, 1967; Williams, 1984).

When communication takes place in a company the definition has to be modified a little. A company is an organization, yet it differs from many other organizations, such as clubs or sports teams. Organizations are always goal-oriented. Companies have to produce a profit in order to stay alive. In this way corporate and organizational communications are largely determined from the perspective of attaining goals. For example, community communications can be comprehended as exchanges of messages between parts of the work community that make it possible for the work community and its members to realize goals in various situations. Communications is thus a tool, a coupling, used by the work community to join its different parts together and the entire work community to its environment (Åberg, 1993). This definition is a good attempt to combine both the transfer and conveyance of information with communications.

> The information dissemination practices were shamefully bad and disconnected. Sometimes terrible bombs were thrown right at your face, and then complete silence for a whole month.
>
> (Systems expert, IT growth company)

Organizational communication differs from general notions of communication in terms of the complexity of the context and people dimensions. Organizational relationships are both like and unlike any other interpersonal relationships. We communicate with people at work because we like them and because our tasks require us to do so. Thus our relationships at work have both an interpersonal and an organizational dimension (Conrad, 1994). From this perspective, corporate communication is an interactive process that occurs in certain organizational conditions and in which people create, maintain, process, and transform meanings (Aula, 1999). This definition follows the interpretive view of human communication (Carey, 1975) and is based on the fundamentals of the social construction of reality (Berger & Luckmann, 1966), according to which an organization and even its environment (Weick, 1979) is socially constructed among its members and this construction takes place not just with, but also within, communication (Deetz, 1986). Meaning factors of organizational communication need to be considered to be able to understand organization as a human community (Weick, 1995). Communication is used to create shared realities about an organization that reflect its members' interpretations of the organization itself and its environment. For example, an organization's culture reflects the organization's shared realities and how these realities create and transform the organization's events. Communication essentially includes the subjective and appraising reactions of an organization's members to the organization's communicational events (Aula, 2000). Thus, in terms of reputation, communication provides the building blocks for an organization's good internal and external relations.

According to this view, an organization's members interact with messages and realities that are constantly being interpreted in such a way

as to enable the production of meanings and thus common understanding. An organization's conditions can include official and unofficial
encounters and formal or informal texts. This concept of communications emphasizes how communication is a question of relations between
people. What is essential is that the form of the message is as important
as its content—and that communication strengthens cultural unity. Communication is unity and community; what is central is maintaining this
community over time and renewing shared beliefs. Communication is
a symbolic process that produces, maintains, repairs, and transforms
reality (Carey, 1975). It should be noted that, in addition to strengthening community, communications can also destroy it.

As we can see, the *communicare* definition borrows elements from
the *communicatio* view. *Communicare* accepts that communication is a
process, yet the "outcome" is not the transmission of messages but the
production of meaning. In general people communicate in order to share
information and experiences. "Sharing" implies that we want to convey something that we know or think we know to others. We strive to
convey information. In addition, our communications strive to make
information and its experience something communal, something that is
shared. In addition to conveying information we build knowledge. To
be precise, no kind of sense can be made of anything without sufficiently
shared meanings. The general forms taken by human communication
are language, speech, writing, gestures, and expressions. According to
its definition, communication can be interactive, purposeful, or purpose-
less. It can also be verbal or nonverbal, bilateral or multilateral. Sharing
information and experiences within organizations can also be a reason to
communicate.

> One lesson we've learnt is that this kind of communication and
> exchange of thoughts between people and everything related to this
> is one of the most important success factors in a company. If commu-
> nication is just banging on drums and gossiping in the corridors, it is
> not particularly healthy. And ultimately that's where our communi-
> cation went, and with it all credibility and trust—no doubt on both
> sides. What we learned is that people should talk to each other.
> (Director, IT growth company)

Communication has always had a double meaning in terms of both its
definition and its activities. It produces community spirit, interpretations, and meanings, while also conveying information, the raw material
of interpretations and meanings.

Organization is based on human communication

Organizations require organizing. According to Åberg (1997), organizing is an event in which people come together to achieve something that could not be done individually. This results in an organization, a community. Put simply, people organize in order to get things done (Daniels, Spiker, & Papa, 1997). Organizing is thus a prerequisite for all organizations. They need to have the goals, vision, or mission of their founder, for example, the attainment of which provides the starting point for working together. Structures of power and divisions of duty and communications are soon formed within the new organization, and these change as the organization develops.

Organizations exist through human interaction. Structures and systems result from the information that people produce and react to. In this way the processes of organizing, delegating, and decision-making, for example, can be seen ultimately as communicational processes—in the end they are similar processes. Karl Weick (1979) points out that organizations do not exist in and of themselves, but that they receive their form through continuous human interaction. Instead of organizations, it would be more interesting to look at organizing, the continuous process of arranging relations between people. According to Weick (1979: 88), many of what we consider "things" in organizational life are in fact relationships, variables that are systematically related to each other. In other words, an organization is a continuous and limitless flow of human interactions that continuously creates and transforms events. And as we pointed out, human interaction is ultimately a communicational process.

The question arises, how can an organization be nothing but interactive processes? What about buildings, machinery, equipment, logos, ads, press releases, management groups, organizational charts? Of course, they too are an "organization." Organizations leave footprints, such as mission statements, ads, logos, and countless other marks. Organizations are discussed, and their plans and goals are talked about in many different contexts. Organizations are bought and sold, and people act in their name or communicate for them or against them. Yet organizations themselves have no material existence. In practice everything that we know about organizations is based on some kind of symbolic expression and thus on secondhand information. Organizations are not things, objects, or goods. They are always the product of human thought (Taylor, 1993).

Reputation management as *communicare*

I don't believe that this organization will collapse simply because its communications don't work, but that it is something we have to remember to develop all the time. And above all this means that we have to carry out communications. That things have to be discussed between people.

(IT growth company pioneer)

Many things depend on how we think about organizations. This is specifically a question of views, various interpretations of what we refer to by "organization." There is no single right organization. Each stakeholder member, including management, employees, and others, has his own opinion about the organization, and no two opinions can ever be totally identical. This is also the basis of one of the basic assumptions of a good company's reputation management. Since there is no single good company, it or its image cannot be transferred as it is to the minds of stakeholders.

Therefore opinions about good companies are always negotiable, and sometimes even in direct conflict. On the general level this means that managing an organization means ensuring that the views and interpretations of the organization are sufficiently uniform for cooperation and successful operations. And since interpretations are made within the interactive networks of organizations, and because these networks are constructed in communications, managing an organization is to a large extent a "communicative action." The idea of communicative management borrows from the classic sociological concepts of Jürgen Habermas. Put basically, Habermas's (1985) communicative action means action that is realized in and through communication, and that communicative action is always social in nature. An important task of management is to create conditions that support and promote interaction throughout the organization. This is not, however, a question of building a single unified organization. An organization cannot and should not be a single unified organizational culture. Organizations require also rebellious cultures. In order to succeed an organization has to accept mistakes, errors, unfortunate circumstances, stupid questions, and dissenting opinions. Moreover, simply accepting these is not enough. In order to be creative an organization has to be a "dork" in a good way compared to being just "sensible" (Aula, 2000).

Mintzberg and Van der Heyden describe the state of organizational definitions with the following poignant example:

Walk into any organization—factory, design studio, sales department—and look around you. In one corner a group of people are busily solving a troublesome logistics problem. In another corner someone is negotiating loudly with a customer. In another corner someone is having Internet problems. Everywhere you look, people and things are in motion, gliding back and forth . . . Next, request a description of the place. Most likely you will be shown the company's organizational chart, in which tidy squares have been arranged in relation to each other. The chart may tell you the names and titles of managers, but not much else. Indeed, using an organizational chart to describe an organization is like trying to navigate your way through a strange town by looking at the membership list of the town council. The truth is that organizational charts only tell us how fascinated we are with management. It is no wonder that these charts are practically of no importance in our contemporary organizational world.

(Mintzberg & Van der Heyden, 1999, p. 87)

The different kinds of charts, processes, and systems are an organization's descriptions of how it does things and how it talks about how it does things. And these descriptions are always susceptible to different interpretations. Therefore an organization's communications are not just a part of resources but the creators, maintainers, and destroyers of the organization itself. Organizations are created and exist due to the plans and actions of their members.

From the perspective of reputation, the relationship between management and communications can be seen in two ways: a company's stakeholder communications are a tool for managing reputation, and the efficacy of reputation management is in the skillful use of different communications tools. What, then, is reputation management in terms of *communicare*? We can follow some footprints if we believe that what is important in management on the whole is a unified view of what the company is, where it is coming from, and where it is going. We can get even closer if we consider that a company's strategy is something that gets its meaning and effectiveness only when it is understood. If we believe further that understanding (comprehension) is something that cannot be transferred from one head to another but instead is something that is created in dialogue, we find ourselves at the heart of reputation management.

One of the key tasks of leadership is to organize or create organization, which means arranging operations, reducing chance, and creating security. However, leaders cannot forge an organization the way a smith forges a horseshoe. As we have shown, an organization is not a concrete "thing." More important than physical organizing systems or computer-based security systems is the feeling of security or the interpretation that everything is all right. This feeling and interpretation is created through communications, communications between people. Communications are therefore not just a leadership issue; instead leadership is always a communicative act. From a slightly more theoretical perspective, it is a question of creating organizational reality. At the heart of good operations is an organization that is created together. We create a common reality, a common interpretation about what we are. In the best case, the reality is sufficiently unified for the company and its stakeholders, and effective enough for long-term cooperation. This creative process of reality cannot be directed by increasing the amount of information or communicating simplicities or self-evident facts. It is better to try and improve the quality of communications.

Of course it is important that information flows within companies and that information is available to all. A separate role must be demonstrated for each channel of leadership. Intranet, e-mail, question-and-answer sessions, road shows, committee meetings, press conferences, employee magazines and bulletins, employee financial publications, employee guidelines, corporate and customer magazines, notice boards, internal TV, phone news—all are necessary. Even more important, however, is that alongside this kind of information-channel thinking is a constant awareness of the deep meaning of communications within the comprehensive process in which a company is created over and over again every day. For example, strategies can be and have to be communicated. However, it is essential to understand that writing up what has to be communicated about the strategy is just a starting point. The task of leadership is to create the conditions in which its strategies are made unified and understood. The *communicatio* model of reputation management would work if reputation were something concrete. However, reputation is a company's immaterial capital created from the interpretations made about the organization.

Summary: communication of the good

Good communication that builds reputation demands a lot, and there is no single right way to create reputation. Several prerequisites for good communication can nevertheless be stated:

- Good communication is seamlessly connected to a company's strategies and leadership practices. A clean connection is necessary for good communication, yet it does not yet guarantee the excellence of communication processes. A company's reputation should be a uniform value for all throughout the organization. Reputation management is interaction and cooperation among all parts of the organization. Only in this way can communication be built into the structures and operations supporting a good company's reputation, into good deeds.
- Good communication serves many different audiences simultaneously. A good company's communicative connections to both internal and external stakeholder groups are interactive relationships, and

communication means taking care of these relationships. This is the challenge of reputation management: to work in multiple environments with diverse audiences, each member of which demands its own kind of relationship.

- A good company comprehensively builds, takes care of, and maintains reputation. Becoming good entails that for a company to take care of one relationship successfully, it has to take care of all relationships just as well. In an increasingly complex and networked operating environment, an organization has to communicate good deeds continuously in all directions. It is a question of prioritizing relationships in the flow of time. Public opinion about an organization is susceptible to change. The key to successful reputation management lies in understanding when a specific public relationship should be taken care of and how.

- Good communication, and thus also reputation management, belongs to each member of the organization. Within a good company it is clear that each contact between management and employee, employee and customer, and organization and environment is a potential reputation-influencing factor. For this reason it must be made clear within the organization that each member of the organization is worthy of the reputation and each member has to do his/her own share to maintain and strengthen that reputation. Ultimately, all forms of communication serve a unified purpose in a good company.

- Good reputation cannot be forced. Ideally, each person should have the opportunity to influence their own organization's events. This influence should be real and it should be encouraged, but it should also be voluntary. No one can be forced to participate. For some silence is more important than having a voice.

In good interactive relationships built through communications, a company and its stakeholders create a common vision, a shared reality of what the organization and its operations are. In this sense communicating the good means building communities (see Aula, 2000). If stakeholders are more satisfied in this relationship than in other relationships with other organizations, it offers the organization the chance to become the first choice (Fombrun, 1996) among stakeholders. Reputation becomes an organization's magnet (Fombrun & van Riel, 2004), attracting the choices of stakeholders towards itself.

For these reasons it is apparent that good communications should be built more upon the idea of community (*communicare*) than on the transfer of information (*communicatio*). In addition to the contents of communications, an organization should offer and produce the conditions in which communications are interpreted. This interpretation is always ultimately a subjective process, whereby influencing by means of the contents of communications alone is always uncertain. Therefore influencing conditions can be more important than contents or communication channels.

Good communication alone does not, however, make a good company. Good communication is a necessary but insufficient precondition for a good company. Good communication requires content; good communication requires deeds.

Chapter 8

Managing good relationships

In concluding the previous chapter, we noted that communications in a good company are sensitive to various stakeholders. We discussed differences in stakeholder groups in our chapter on reputation strategies (chapter 5). Now it is time to focus on the relations aspect in detail.

An organization's reputation is built on what it does in relation to its stakeholders and how it communicates what it does. Yet the business environment is not a monolith, and the stakeholders do not represent a unified "wall," against which the organization's actions and messages echo back as its reputation. Organizations act within networks where different kinds of relations exist between stakeholders of different kinds. Moreover, organizations themselves are networks. Indeed, the issue of where to draw the border of an organization—that is, where the internal network ends and the external network begins—is a research topic itself, one which is becoming more and more complicated (Santos & Eisenhardt, 2005).

The network view puts in the foreground the important notion that some relations are more valuable than others. Whether the managers of reputation manage to make sense and predict which relations they should focus on is another issue.

Indeed, herein lies a tension in relations management: being sensitive to specific stakeholder needs, and preparing for the surprise emergence of new stakeholders by maintaining a coherent enough policy of good action and communication. As we discussed in chapter 5, the two foci emerging out of this tension are a personal and an institutional orientation to reputation strategy.

The relations aspect to managing a good company is based on the notion that while the good deeds that the company conducts are the basis of reputation and need to be communicated outside the organization, the organization's audiences are far from uniform. They are more relevantly perceived as a network in which the organization is a member.

Good companies in networks

> She's a grandmother, she lives in a big house in Chicago, and you've never heard of her. Does she run the world?
>
> (The *New Yorker*, January 11, 1999, on Lois Weisberg, the commissioner of cultural affairs in the City of Chicago)

The concept of networks has become a prerequisite for thinking about contemporary societies: it has become a core element in what is called the "network society" (Castells, 1996). It would seem to be an intuitive idea that societies and social networks are diverse and complex—and big. For example, the world is an enormous network in which I am basically far from my other associates and even further from theirs. The same basic idea applies on the business level. A small company from the north is far from everything in this world. The world is basically a "big world." It could be otherwise, however. The phenomenon of "small worlds" refers to the idea that every person in the world is separated by just a few handshakes.

In the 1960s Milgram published a famous communications experiment under the undated title "Results of Communication Project." In the study Milgram tried to prove that any two random people in the world are separated by no more than "six degrees of separation" (Granovetter, 1973). This suggestion is based on the idea that some people have friends that do not live next door. Through these distant contacts the local community creates short paths to people who live very far away. These people who are connected with the community generally do not know each other. Just a few of these distant links shorten the distances between networks dramatically.

Milgram also identifies the so-called "funneling" effect, according to which the six-degrees phenomenon in social systems is dependent on a few special people ("connectors") whose contact network is enormous and who serve as bridges between less networked individuals by connecting them with each other.

A networked environment that emphasizes meanings increases the importance of good reputation as a strategic resource. It is clear that experiences about products and services are passed on as stories, tales, anecdotes, and symbols among customers and potential customers. The products of a good company do not disappear in the hands of customers but instead are willingly shown to friends and associates. The subject of good work while getting your car serviced might arise over lunch at work when a colleague mentions his car needs repairing. A stylish hairdo will excite inquiries into the name and address of the hair salon. Someone afraid of getting their teeth checked will ask members of his network about their experiences with reliable and compassionate dentists. Someone looking for cleaning services will ask his friends about a reputable cleaning company—who wants an unreliable person sniffing around their property?

Similarly, terrible experiences with services and products are eagerly passed on—in fact, they are much more often relayed than positive experiences. Unfriendly service and lousy products are easy subjects to discuss. When a car dealer or travel agent treats a customer like dirt, the prerequisites for a rapidly spreading story are in place.

Strategic thinking these days is characterized by an emphasis on short-term profits. By contrast, reputation is characterized by its long-term nature. Reputation is built through practical deeds from which stake-holders gradually form meanings about the company's nature and operations. According to traditional wisdom, one should take care not to lose one's reputation, as getting it back is ten times harder. It might be hard to cash in on reputation immediately, but losing it through short-term operations is easy. Reputation can be thought of as social capital that is accumulated through interactions with stakeholders.

It's not how you look, it's what they say: network as a small world

> Fred Jones of Peoria, sitting in a sidewalk cafe in Tunisia, and needing a light for his cigarette, asks the man at the next table for a match. They fall into conversation; the stranger is an Englishman who, it turns out, spent several months in Detroit. "I know it's a foolish question," says Jones, "but do you by any chance know a fellow named Ben Arkadian? He's an old friend of mine, manages a chain of supermarkets in Detroit . . ."
>
> "Arkadian . . . Arkadian . . ." the Englishman mutters. "Why, upon my soul, I believe I do! Small chap, very energetic, raised merry hell with the factory over a shipment of defective bottle caps." "No kidding!" Jones exclaims, amazed.
>
> "Good lord, it's a small world, isn't it?"
>
> (Milgram, 1967)

The story above reflects what today's network thinkers call the "phenomenon of small worlds." Small worlds and the contemporary ideas about networks can offer an explanation for why what is spoken is important, which is why reputation is important.

As we noted in chapter 3, where we discussed linkages between reputation and related concepts such as image and brand, reputation is mistakenly used as a synonym for a company's public image. This would mean that in terms of reputation what is most important is how companies look. While image no doubt is important in terms of reputation, it is by no means the same thing as reputation. In terms of reputation what is most important is what is said about a company. Reputation is established through stories that are told about an organization, and these stories value the organization. An organization becomes either good or bad in these stories. Stories originate, strengthen, or change when an organization interacts with its interpreter, for example a stakeholder.

In these interactions an interpretation is made about what the organization is, where it is coming from, where it is going, and so on. Thus what lies at the core of reputation is the good experiences created through interactions. These interactions are therefore essential in terms of an organization's reputation. They are also situations in which an organization can genuinely affect its stories and in this way its reputation. What is essential in terms of reputation management is that the experience is transformed into a story that is spread rapidly and widely through various networks. In this case, too, badness is more powerful than goodness. It is claimed that a good experience is voluntarily communicated onwards to three people, whereas a bad experience is told to seven people.

Reputation is thus narrative. Stories move within networks. The basic essence of networks, their structure and operation, ensures that a good company's stories move rapidly over time and place. Three network concepts are particularly relevant for our understanding of how reputation is spread and built in networks: (1) weak and strong ties, (2) reputation as social capital, and (3) the advantage created by managing structural holes.

The secret of reputation lies in weak ties

Networks are formed from parts and the factors connecting them, which are referred to in network theory as bridges. The parts of a network are connected to each through either weak ties or strong ties. Strong ties are long-term and bilateral, and they are not directed by short-term pursuit of individual advantage. Strong ties are built on firm confidence and the feeling of emotional proximity (Granovetter, 1993). Strong ties are relied upon when an ethical problem or a personal dilemma arises. Weak ties are typically considered to be the opposite of strong ties. They are described as superficial or temporary, and they are not considered particularly binding. Weak ties are considered to be less reliable than strong ties. We shake hands with weak ties, but we can never be sure if the handshake implies an agreement, trust, or long-term commitment.

Ronald Burt, one of the key contemporary social network theorists (2005, p. 100), defines reputation as "behavior expected of you." In Burt's theory, reputation is a control mechanism, which ensures conformance to group interests in networks where closure is encountered. Closed networks are parts of larger networks where the density of relations within the network exceeds the density of extra-network relations. Within

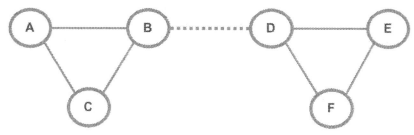

Figure 8.1 This diagram shows a weak tie between B and D. Through them
information that is essential to the organization spreads to the world
as reputational stories.

closed networks, members identify strongly with network members. It also means that the risk of getting caught in illegitimate behavior is increased as network members are much more aware of each other. When network members misbehave, they are punished and ultimately ejected from the closed network as they lose reputation. Reputation is thus conceived as a disciplinary mechanism within closed networks.

As open structures, networks can expand without limits. At the same time new ties are integrated with them if they "are able to communicate within networks, in other words, if they have the same communication codes" (Castells, 1996, p. 501). A firm, for instance, is a network in which employees are often strongly connected to each other. The stronger the culture and the more communication there is, the stronger also are the organization's networks and so also the organization itself. From the perspective of social systems, within organizations people have a tendency to rely on strong ties when asking advice and requesting help or support in many different types of issues related not only to their work but also their broader lives (figure 8.1).

For organizations, reputation is not just relevant in closed networks portraying strong ties. For instance, many organizations are not in close relations with their end customers. Sociologist Mark Granovetter (1973; 1983) has developed a theory about the "strength of weak ties." Before Granovetter, the accepted wisdom was that strong ties were the ones that mattered. It was assumed that people receive a more significant portion of information that is important to them specifically through strong ties, for example from family members, friends, and close work colleagues. In the late 1960s Granovetter studied how people found new jobs in a working district of Boston. It turned out that the decisive information about workplaces was usually given by a friend of a friend and not a friend as such. Granovetter was intrigued by the fact that friends of friends played a more important role than friends. It had previously appeared that strong ties are more important than weak ties for an individual's success. However, it turns out that a community of strong ties is often only as wise (or stupid) as an individual person. Friends do not know about things, such as new jobs, any better than other members of that group of friends. More distant and indirect contacts are members of their own communities, as a result of which their information or their perspective on information is different. The weak link that connects these two communities could be a key to new information, fresh thoughts, and new people.

The traditional division between strong and weak links gives the impression that in the organizational world strong ties are somehow more significant than weak ties and those weak ties are just tools for a short-term opportunistic pursuit of gain. The network concept formed by Granovetter's theory does not support the view that weak ties are less important. Similar evidence was produced by Onnela et al. (2007) in a groundbreaking study of seven million cell phone users over the period of 18 weeks. The findings suggest that weak ties are responsible for the integrity of a global network. Removing the weakest ties (i.e. individuals who only spoke to each other for the shortest time) caused the network to collapse. On the other hand, removing the strongest ties caused the network to gradually shrink, but not break apart. According to the study, strong ties exist in small communities and their removal only collapses the community without doing much harm to the network.

Strong ties are, naturally, important in networks. However, weak ties would seem to be even more important. Who you know is important, but who these people know is even more important. Noshir Contractor and Peter Monge (2002) have argued that it is no longer important "who knows who," or even "who knows what." What is essential is "who knows who knows who," and above all "who knows who knows what" (p. 249).

Communities are built from both the inner circle of strong ties and the strong ties of members within this inner circle to their own circles, as well as from weak ties to other communities. These weak ties play a decisive role in the communicational structures between communities and are essential for the operations of the community. It has also been suggested that weak ties play an important role in creating social capital within organizations and societies (see e.g. Buchanan, 2002). The same applies also to regions. Buchanan (2002) tells two examples. In the 1970s two US regions were competing with each other, one of which would become a hub for new technology: Silicon Valley in California and Route 128 in Boston. Silicon Valley's success story has been explained by arguing that, contrary to business life in general, there was a lot of interaction right from the start between people and ideas among the region's different companies. By contrast, the Boston region operated along more traditional lines. Companies kept to themselves, and communication between companies, perhaps for cultural or competitive reasons, did not develop anywhere close to the level in Silicon Valley. The Californian openness was a cultural strength for the region's growth companies. In Boston companies did not communicate with each other, so ideas could not feed off each other.

Another example of the influence of weak ties can be found in the Italian car industry in the 1970s and 1980s. Fiat and Alfa Romeo, which were competitors at the time, faced the same organizational challenges regarding the need to improve efficiency and the cost structure. Fiat's factory in Turin tried to achieve flexibility by fighting against the power of local unions, which created a serious conflict between the employer and its employees. Alfa Romeo in Milan acted differently. It chose the path of negotiations and teamwork and achieved success. Why? The difference in approaches has been explained by the difference between the interactive structures of the region's social networks. In Turin the conflict was exacerbated by the severe political climate in the region, and employee and employer groups had hardly any contact with each other. Fiat based its strategy on this network of opposition. For Alfa Romeo, too, the region's network structure had a major impact. Their success was based on the region's social networks, in this case the atmosphere of local politics that was used to open dialogue. The network has significant weak links between business, unions, and other organizations, which affected the foundation of trust that had been established at the factory (Buchanan, 2002).

Reputation as social capital

The network world is not democratic, or at least no more democratic than the societies that have preceded it. All people are not equal within the network, nor are all people at the core of the communicational structure, or even close to it.

People who are more networked than others can always be found in social systems. These social connectors have a huge contact network, as well as the communicational skills to build and maintain this network. Social connectors are the key people within a social network. They determine the topics of conversation and trends, what to buy or not to buy, where to go or not to go. As the subtitle of Berry and Keller's (2003) book tells us, "One in ten Americans tells the other nine how to vote, where to eat, and what to buy."

It is easy to recognize the special importance of connectors for building, spreading, and managing reputation. When a "reputation connector" has a positive opinion about an organization, it is likely that he will convey this opinion forwards, perhaps to a connector in another network, and so on. In this way reputation's story network demonstrates its strength.

If we think of reputation in terms of economics, reputation represents a kind of social capital for organizations. Social capital becomes interesting when we recognize that, in fact, nowhere near all the resources available for use by an organization are economic.

In a networked society consisting of a number of interdependent, yet non-equal, members, the network position of an individual person, group, or organization may be conceptualized with the use of the concept of social capital. The first and still extremely influential account of social capital, as well as other forms of non-economic capital, can be found in the writings of French sociologist Pierre Bourdieu. He defines social capital as

> the aggregate of the actual or potential resources which are linked to possession of a durable network of more or less institutionalized relationships of mutual acquaintance and recognition—or in other words, to membership in a group—which provides each of its members with the backing of the collectivity-owned capital, a "credential" which entitles them to credit, in the various senses of the word.
> (Bourdieu, 1986, 248–249)

Social capital resides in groups and collectivities of various kinds, and individuals gain access to it through membership relations. This is easily seen if we think about what kinds of things are valuable in the social competition between individuals. A good example is the many different forms of capital offered by education. Even if more money can be earned with a good education, the mechanism creating the value of education includes many different forms of capital: cultural, social, intellectual, symbolic, and economic (Bourdieu, 1986).

It is often said that money does not buy everything. The social status created by education, which is related in part to furthering one's career, is a good example of this. If this status could be bought with money, why do we not buy university degrees from all the offers that we receive as spam mail? The titles awarded with degrees can be regarded as a kind of cultural capital that we can use to demonstrate our expertise. Higher education provides people also with symbolic capital, as nearly all forms of education introduce students to new systems of meanings, for example the fundamentals of how the human body works for medical students, or the fundamentals of engineering for technical students. This kind of symbolic capital can be utilized alongside regular work to emphasize the unity of members within a profession. Symbolic capital is closely related to intellectual capital, which is particularly relevant to organizations competing in knowledge-intensive environments.

Cultural capital and symbolic capital are thus connected to each other. A professional degree offers an individual additional cultural capital, although entry into a profession through a degree requires that the individual demonstrate that he has sufficient symbolic capital to master the trade's specialized fundamentals. In addition, individuals receive social capital through their education as they get to know students of the same age within their field. A social network is formed that can be utilized in many ways later on in life: when looking for a job, in demanding cooperation projects, and so on. It is no wonder, therefore, that students entering university are often reminded that it is as important to participate actively in student life as it is to attend lectures (Bourdieu, 1986).

A good salary is considered a basic feature of a good job. The road to a good job involves symbolic (or cultural) capital obtained through studying, cultural capital connected with the status derived from degrees, and the social capital connected with new contacts. Looking at this critically, it can be noted that financial capital makes it easier to achieve other forms of capital; why else do the children of wealthy parents so often have degrees from top universities? Also, the improvement of one's social position, connected with increasing non-financial capital, also requires an increasing amount of financial capital—playing golf is expensive, as is drinking wines and cognacs (see Bourdieu, 1986). We remember fondly our own early years as students when we tasted expensive cognac even if we barely had the money to buy the basic things in life. This was partly connected with cultivating ourselves, or in this case cultivating the expensive hobbies of the cultural elite.

MBA programs provide an excellent example of how financial and non-financial capitals are intertwined in relation to organizations. MBA programs are by nature so expensive that entering one requires either a lot of personal financial risk or a favorable financing decision by a high-level representative of an organization. MBA programs often provide access to the executive ladder, and they are administered by universities, the gatekeepers of cultural and symbolic capital. Their curricula essentially represent symbolic capital—theoretical questions related to organizations, management, and strategy. Often, however, it is said that the actual added value of these programs comes from somewhere else altogether. One promising future executive who invested a large sum of borrowed money in an MBA program is quoted as saying that "it's not the daytime lectures that are important, it's the evening cocktail events." The high price of education makes students an elite, as a result of which the contacts formed during one's education have special value as social capital. In addition, an MBA degree earned from a good school is a culturally valuable resource for the individual, as the degree often demonstrates that some organization has believed in the individual enough to invest a large sum of money in him.

This examination of non-financial capital on the individual level is easy to extend to organizations and their reputations. Organizational scholars often use the concept of social capital to denote many of Bourdieu's (1986) forms of non-financial capital. For instance, Nahapiet and Ghoshal (1998) propose that an organization's social capital has structural, relational, and cognitive dimensions. The structural dimension has to do with an organization's social network. This refers to either an organization's official PR activities or the personal relationships of its employees, generally those of its management. In other words, structural social capital refers to the scale of the network and the organization's own position within the network: is it a central or marginal part of the network?

Relational social capital does not involve the structure of a network but rather the quality of an organization's relationship with other members of the network. We could in fact refer to this as relationship or trust capital. If an organization is in control of its relational capital, then the organization is trusted. In addition to trust, other important factors include a unified identity, norms, mutual agreements, and other social phenomena that determine the network's key relationships.

In Bourdieu's terms, the cognitive dimension in turn has to do not only with social capital, but also with cultural and symbolic capital. It involves the language and shared stories and meanings of the actors belonging to the network. It would be sensible to think that simply existing in a network, having warm relations with other members of the network, is insufficient. The ability to communicate effectively within the network is also needed.

An organization's reputation plays a role in all three forms of social capital mentioned above. The reputation of a good company exists among an organization's stakeholders as stories and other shared meanings. In this way, it is a key aspect of an organization's social-cognitive capital.

Trust and other aspects of relational capital are also connected with reputation; it is not enough for good reputation that an organization is known—"all publicity is good publicity." Good reputation means that an organization is trusted and identified with.

Identification is a process where stakeholders build a small part of their identity by finding resonance with a perceived organizational identity, as interpreted based on the organization's reputation. The inverse process to identification is disidentification, which is also significant in reputational and relational terms. Elsbach and Bhattacharya (2001) have studied the phenomenon of identifying with organizations and demonstrated how the reputation of the National Rifle Association (NRA) was used as a tool for disidentification—"they certainly don't represent my values." The NRA is an organization that is connected with the political extreme right in the USA and supports the right of individuals to carry arms, as they did back in the days of the Wild West. In this case the NRA had a clear position within the network of meanings of the target group

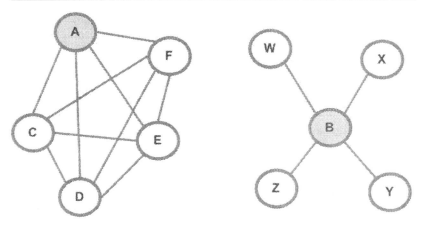

Figure 8.2 Both A and B are connected to four others. B is its communication
network's connector and thus manages structural holes. A is simply
"one among others" within its own network.

being studied, i.e. its structural capital was under control, but its relational capital was zero or even negative.

Reputation and structural holes

There are people also within organizations who have broad contact networks and lots of acquaintances. However, organizations also always
have people who are separated from the rest, either of their own free
will or of the will of others, and who communicate with few (figure 8.2).
This has been recognized by Ronald Burt, who has described "structural holes" that break communications within a network. If one is in a
position to act as a mediator between two unconnected people within a
network, one can usually benefit from this role of mediator. Managing
structural holes is thus an individual's social capital (Burt, 1997).

It is no wonder, therefore, that social networks consisting of human
relations have become key concepts for people aiming at success and
influence. It is important to know people and to exchange contacts,
making sure at the same time not to give away contacts free of charge.
One of the most recent products of this phenomenon is Internet databases
designed to maintain and build social networks, such as www.linkedin.
com, which has attracted hundreds of thousands of users. This database
reveals to anyone interested job and residence information about another
person, as well as the number of other users who are directly connected
to that person's network. There is also a reputation-building tool within
linkedin.com. One may recommend the work of network members and
receive recommendation from others.

Linkedin also serves as a clear example of a number of important concepts that help to make sense of the relation between structural holes and reputation. To openly recommend somebody in Linkedin is to offer to act as a broker in a relationship. To broker a relationship between two parties who do not know each other is to span a structural hole (Burt, 2005).

To recommend another person involves reputation risk. If a colleague of yours hires an acquaintance of yours, based on your recommendation, and the acquaintance fails in his or her job, your reputation is also at risk. The colleague, acting on trust placed in you, may lose some of that trust because of the harm your recommendation has caused him or her. Your unwise recommendation, if it is a cause of much unrest, might even lead to the colleague telling of your betrayal of trust to your shared acquaintances, leading to you losing social capital, not only in the sense of losing relational capital in a single relationship but losing reputation in a larger network (Burt, 2005).

Companies have become increasingly aware of reputation risk and the need to manage it. Indeed, well-known cases such as Nestlé, Shell, H&M, and others, and their costly efforts in rebuilding their reputations after scandals, have put the concept on the map. For a consultant specializing in reputation, offering tools to manage reputation risk may be the best sales pitch. In the risk society which we inhabit, where control of the consequences of one's actions is often impossible, managers are looking for ways to avoid unexpected reputational catastrophes.

Foundations for good relations

If we look at the concept of reputation as capital within networks, we can see several phenomena existing between an organization and its network that create and maintain reputation capital, as well as facilitate reputational exchanges. When trust exists between an organization and its network, it is easier to build and maintain reputation. In addition, reputation accumulates trust and vice versa. When respect exists between an organization and its network, all members of the network—regardless of rank, whether they are managers or staff, or subcontractors or important clients—recognize the importance of each other's roles in joint projects. Respect is based on recognition of the fact that all kinds of actors are needed and that no partner can succeed without the others.

Yet in our age, when strategic thinking urges us to discern the organizational environment as a chessboard or a battlefield, the building of trust and respect—indeed the very notion of cooperation between organizations and other actors, is problematic. Trust and respect are central phenomena that are specifically dependent on belief; they are based on the idea that both parties believe in the goodness of the other to some extent, even if they are not ultimately convinced that this virtue will be demonstrated when push comes to shove. It is not certain that the other will act honorably or trustworthily in future challenges. In conditions of trust, members of networks rely on each other and believe that this mutual support will continue.

Organizations and the paradox of cooperation

> Sure you don't trust some people—because of what they do. If there is a big discrepancy between words and deeds, then it is wise to use a very long fork and knife when eating at the same table.
>
> (Founder and president of multimedia company)

In terms of economics, the problem of cooperation is often regarded from the perspective of game theory. One of the basic tenets of game theory is the so-called prisoner's dilemma, which can be presented through the following metaphor: two criminals are caught and encouraged to confess, as there is no conclusive evidence against either. If both prisoners confess, both will receive a ten-year sentence. In this case, each prisoner has decided not to cooperate with the other. The price to be paid for not cooperating is therefore high. If they decide to cooperate and not confess, each prisoner will receive a five-year sentence, making cooperation worthwhile. The most dangerous option in the prisoner's dilemma, however, is to choose to cooperate, when the other prisoner chooses not to play along. If one confesses and the other does not, the one who did not will be hanged while the other will receive a one-year sentence. The most favorable option for each prisoner, therefore, is to betray the confidence of the other (cf. Frank, 2004).

The challenge in this dilemma is that the criminals cannot agree on a joint strategy in advance, as they have been separated by the police, so the decision has to made from the perspective of the individual. From a purely rational standpoint, the best option for each prisoner would be for his accomplice to trust him while he himself betrays the other, thus minimizing his sentence. The second-best option would be for neither prisoner to confess, i.e. for the prisoners to cooperate. However, refusing to confess entails the risk of losing your life should the other prisoner confess anyway (Frank, 2004).

The more the prisoners think about their dilemma, the more cooperation begins to look like the worse solution. Confessing would save either prisoner from the death that would result from the betrayal of the other, while also offering the possibility of getting away easy if the other can be conned. Cooperation would reduce the sentence from ten years to five without fear of death. The problem is how to contact the other prisoner and to convince him that cooperation is possible?

Very few people have betrayed my confidence, but those who have know who they are. I'm a completely non-collective person . . . At this moment I'm thinking only of my company's interests in the things I do. And if someone is in my way, then that person is the one who has to move . . . Then again, I think that [my division] is one of the best however you choose to measure it.

(Founder-shareholder and managing director of IT company)

The prisoner's dilemma can be considered a symbol of our times. In the economic reality permeated by strategic thinking, it is natural to think of social interaction as a game in which the other guy could always stab you in the back.

Milton Friedman famously claimed that the only morally justified interest of corporate executives is to ensure a financial return on the shareholder's investment. Seeking social, environmental, or other non-fiscal advantage is only justified if it creates economic advantage over a certain time period.[1] Socially responsible activities would thus be immoral if no connection could be found between social responsibility and the company's financial result.

Friedman's view can be criticized for being cynical, although it can also be defended in terms of the overall functionality of business and the resulting growth in the collective benefit. If corporate management and other business interests can be seen as accepting Friedman's moral principle, then in the communal life of organizations no "prisoner" would have the natural need to cooperate. Instead, the expectation would be that the other guy would not shed a tear over your execution if this meant a shorter prison sentence for him. It is a dog-eat-dog world.

According to the Roman proverb, senators are good men, but the senate is a beast. In other words, a wise statesman should not blindly trust the decisions made by a democratic body, as the collective will can and will distort goodwill. We can believe that many shareholders, such as those investing in their retirement, are good people. However, their advantage is being pursued with disregard for other considerations. Moral thinking based on the pursuit of one's own advantage sits uncomfortably with most ethical systems. A lack of empathy and using others as tools is considered reprehensible on the individual level and even sick. A company managed purely strategically is very much a psychopath—or sociopath (Bakan, 2004; Daneke, 1985; Mantere, Pajunen, & Lamberg, forthcoming).

It is possible to think, therefore, that the "Roman way" in business life instrumentalizes others and is considerably infertile ground for co-operation. Operating in networks nevertheless increases the importance of cooperation as a success factor, which should arouse the interest of even Friedman's disciples. For companies in a network it is rational to co-operate with partners who can be expected to function in a cooperative way. This is because in a network interdependence among organizations means that an organization has to be able to build its own operations by relying on relationships of trust.

How does a company that is interdependent and benefits from co-operation, then, solve the prisoner's dilemma? One rather familiar strategy is the so-called tit-for-tat principle, in which you never trust someone who has already deceived you. Then there is the story of the boy who cried wolf. In this case an organization assumes that it will not lose its head if cooperation fails, so cooperation can be tested. If the opposite partner proves to be worthy of trust, cooperation is continued—if not, you count your losses and look for another partner.

In a tit-for-tat situation, a good reputation opens doors to new partnerships. If the principle is expanded to cover the transfer of relationships of trust within a network—"vouching for a friend"—reputation can spread to others with whom cooperation has not been previously carried out.

But is this so? What if all actors have become aware of the "name of the game" and there is silent acceptance of deceit as a form of strategic thinking? Management researcher David Hawk has emphasized that deceit is an essential basis for strategy in the battlefield.[2] Henry Mintzberg (1987), too, has demonstrated this, pointing out that strategy can be seen as a ploy. A certain managing director, whom we know, responded to the claim that an honest reputation would be a competitive advantage by saying: "Listen, everyone in business knows that money and not honesty determines the decisions that are made."

The value of reputation among other resources determines the name of the game at any given time. It can be typical in a partnership network for everyone to be expected to maximize their own advantage and, when needed, at the expense of others. On the other hand, celebratory toasts among partners often emphasize how in a good relationship everyone looks in the same direction and stands shoulder to shoulder. A good partnership is always a so-called win–win situation. In the arenas that are outside the immediate business environment, pursuing one's own advantage as defined by pure strategic thinking is not looked upon kindly. Companies are expected to be good citizens, or at least to have a good public image. Nevertheless, the social debate of the 1990s has been described as even more managerial than ever and as highlighting the dominance of the markets.

A popular solution for the prisoner's dilemma in an organization's partnerships—both internal and external—is to build trust. When partners trust each other, continuous assurances and demonstrations of the durability of cooperation are not needed. What, then, is trust, and how can it be built? Trust can be thought of as risk-taking towards another, or rather the readiness to surrender to the actions of another in some issue and to a certain degree. More precisely, trust can be defined as the "Willingness of a party to be vulnerable to the actions of another party based on the expectation that the other will perform a particular action imposed to the trustor, irrespective of the ability to monitor or control that party" (Mayer, Davis, & Schoorman, 1995, p. 712). In addition, trust often involves the belief that the intentions of another towards oneself are benevolent. Sometimes we can, of course, claim that "I will trust that you will treat me as you would yourself," in which case "trust" and "belief" are thought of as one and the same.

Building trust is one of the big questions of all communality. It is always as relevant in terms of entire nations as it is between individuals and organizations. If an individual cannot trust anyone, his life will be a tragedy, as a good life means functioning in an interdependent community (cf. MacIntyre, 1985; Sennett, 2003).

Reputation is built on trust

In terms of entire nations, trust plays a key role in the debate over the legitimacy of state power. A social contract in which the benefits received by an individual outweigh the drawbacks is possible if a certain basic trust exists between individuals. We can also consider how trust is focused on social institutions: judiciary institutions, the police, and so on. Where there is rule of law an individual dares to walk down the street unarmed without fear of a physically stronger person coming the other way taking his money or his life. Although the stronger party should subdue the weaker in a disorganized state, legislators and law enforcers maintain an order in which subduing others is not worthwhile—at least in theory. I can thus trust a complete stranger, as I know that the same social contract applies to us both.

Social-contract theoreticians believe that the coercion employed by nations under the rule of law creates the basis for civilized and constructive interaction between people—a kind of basic social trust. The classical example of this is the philosophy of Thomas Hobbes: the authority of the social contract comes from the fact that even if the legitimate state power limits an individual's freedom, it also increases freedom even more. If this order is not controlled, people are by nature savage. Individuals therefore agree to give up some of their freedom in order to receive even more in return in the form of basic trust. In a certain way we can consider how the prisoners can trust each other, as both rely on the social contract.

However, legislation provides only the basis for basic trust. Trust in human relations is built on a variety of more or less open systems of norms and meanings by which we expect others to act. With the professional specialization that succeeded industrialization, it began to be considered how people are part of an interdependent system in which they act in different roles. According to French sociologist Émile Durkheim, the solidarity that kept the agrarian society together was built on tight commitment to the same kind of unified culture, as the success of the community was based on very similar roles (Durkheim, 1997). Industrialization and urbanization in turn led to a more complex system of roles. At the same time difference began to be tolerated as the importance of different roles became apparent.

Trust in society is a very similar phenomenon to solidarity: a force that keeps society together and enables fruitful interaction. We can consider how solidarity is a kind of "basic trust" in society and in other citizens. In this sense solidarity is a social phenomenon, whereas trust is often considered to be between individuals.

The network society is at least in part replacing Durkheim's system of interdependency as the industrial society transforms into a postindustrial society. Postmodernism, which flowered as part of the postindustrial social sciences, challenges the concept of society as an interdependent system and offers in its place an image of society as a garish collage in which the common advantage of all cannot be presented in the name of the functionality of the system, as the system operates to the advantage of whoever is strongest at any given moment. The time of "great stories" is over, and what we are left with is a competition between small stories (Lyotard, 1984). Basic trust appears in different forms at most among small subcultures in which the relationships between individuals can also be interpreted from many different perspectives.

Trust within organizations

> We had a principle that the guys that we hired, we trusted them completely, so right from the start, without really asking anything, we gave them big responsibilities and areas. I noticed then these three-month phases. Always when we hired a new person, for three months you felt like canceling everything because nothing worked. But then, after three months it in fact worked better than it had before. So it always takes a while before people grow into their roles. My principle has been to always give a little too much responsibility to people so that they grow to take care of it.
>
> (Director, IT growth company)

The disappearance of great stories and the postindustrial period also affect our concepts of organizations and the solidarity within them. Trust is not created by itself clearly from solidarity in an interdependent organizational system, as the different parts of the system do not automatically have the feeling that they belong to a single entity. For example, in an organization where executives have been recruited using stock options, it is easy for them to view the organization as a tool for producing profit, whereas the regular staff who do not have options recognize primarily a work community in the organization. The resulting different types of behavior are detrimental to solidarity.

Trust within an organization should not be examined solely from the point of view of instrumental roles, nor should we define solidarity within organizations solely through the functions performed by individuals. A member of an organization does of course feel solidarity towards another, partly because he understands that the other is doing his part to promote the good of the organization. However, organizations are also communities whose solidarity is based on social interaction. Furthermore, the common good of an organization's members is very hard to define in today's world. Communal phenomena are indeed more important than the instrumental perspective in terms of forming trust. An organization's members' experiential assessments of the ability, goodwill, and value basis of others impact on their predisposition to trust the decisions made by others. Trust that has been established in turn leads to a readiness to take calculated risks that, it is assumed, will lead to improved operations (Mayer, Davis, & Schoorman, 1995) and even to the development of an organization's intellectual capital (Nahapiet & Ghoshal, 1998). Assessments of the trustworthiness of other members of an organization are built over time and they exist in time. It can also be claimed that negative experiences are remembered much more easily and for longer than positive experiences. Like reputation, trust can also collapse quickly, and rebuilding it is slow work—within an organization's internal network also a bad experience is related more easily and more often than a good experience.

Trust can thus be viewed as risk-taking in an individual's activities and is built as relationships of trust between individuals. Trust can also be examined as a part of an organization's culture, its system of meanings. Not only do individuals trust or not trust each other, we can consider also how a habit exists within organizations of either trusting or not trusting. Trust or distrust is embedded as part of shared meanings, stories, jokes, rituals, and other expressive forms of organizational culture. Indeed, we sometimes speak about relational and institutional trust (Rousseau, Sitkin, Burt, & Camerer, 1998). An essential aspect in the creation of this kind of cultural trust is organizational justice. If the methods practiced within an organization are considered to be just, then the organization is also considered to be worthy of trust (cf. Korsgaard, Schweiger, & Sapienza, 1995).

Some researchers have suggested that the need for trust varies within an organization as a function of the reigning interdependency. It is claimed that within bureaucratic organizations, in which the roles of members are precisely defined and differentiated, less trust is needed (Wicks, Berman,

& Jones, 1999). If an organization is thought of as an instrument, this could well be in order for precisely defined role behavior to be easier to measure and monitor, in which case trust is not a direct condition for success. In terms of a community, however, it is rather dubious to claim that trust is not needed in bureaucratic organizations and that it would not have an impact on results in terms of work satisfaction.

Organizational culture: relations within the organization

One of the professors in a management course I took said in his presentation that nerds can't be ordered about. For me that summarizes pretty well the problem of management: nerds can't be ordered about. If you give them orders, they leave or still don't do what you want them to do. They have a dozen other takers. Managing an expert organization is terribly hard. All the reward systems and management systems are different. I'm no expert in this area, but to me it is very clear. When it comes to other aspects of corporate culture, it is maybe a bit difficult to separate different factors, as usually in these new industry companies the personnel is very young. And that has maybe even a bigger effect. Even we have around 200 employees, and the average age is 28. This is a completely different place than other traditional companies. I was chatting at a bank event last week, and I was told that you couldn't be fun in a bank. That's how it really is.

(Middle manager in a telecom company)

An organization is a network of networks in itself, and it is always a part of other networks. In fact, separating a modern organization from its environment is hard. For the sake of clarity, however, it makes sense to talk about an organization's internal and external networks, as well as networks existing between organizations.

The networking that permeates organizations cannot be seen only in the blurring of the lines between organizational tools or its core processes, but also in the organizational community. An organization is a culture, a community of meaning. As the big social stories, such as the united meaning of national states or religions, lose their position, the community of meaning becomes splintered (Lyotard, 1984). This splintering does not leave the organization unchanged—an organization's internal community of meaning is a network whose borders with external communities of meaning are blurred. As a phenomenon this blurring between conceptual borders is nothing new, as even organizations that employ traditional professionals, such as schools, hospitals, and law offices, have been permeated by professional identities. A hospital's community of meaning is infiltrated by the identities of nurses, doctors, and administrators and is thus networked with blurred borders. Teachers always make decisions based more on their professional identity than on their schools' strategies.

Nevertheless, the networking of meaning has increased in importance with the development of the network society. The unified cultures within organizations decay or are not even considered achievable.

A classical way of thinking is the model of a single unified internal environment of meaning, a single organizational culture. Here an organizational culture is buried in people's beliefs, but in practice the organization's management has a key position in forming the culture. For example, organizational culture guru Edgar H. Schein represents this view. According to Schein (1997), it is precisely an organization's management that creates, changes, and administers cultures. The only way to interpret and explain culture is to work with management: what they do and how they do it, what they value and want, and what the basic thinking is that directs these.

From a managerial perspective, Schein's view of culture is attractive as it demotes culture beneath management control and gives the impression that management or individual managers play the key role in the success of the organization. Culture is built and maintained primarily through managers: what they focus on; how they assess and control; how they react to critical events and crises; how they distribute resources, serve as role models, teachers, and trainers; how they reward and punish; and what kind of people they recruit, select, recommend, encourage to retire, and kick out. If an organization's subcultures differ too much from the common culture, the task of managers is to bring them back into line by establishing common goals, creating common communications and common operating models. In brief, according to this view an organization's management is in charge of organization's culture.

The view of a unified culture makes a strong organizational culture an important prerequisite for success: a strong unified culture has a positive correlation with the company's success. This concept also contains the view according to which both main cultures and subcultures can be controlled in the same way as other resources by managing from the top down.

According to the common wisdom of organizational research, broadly distributed strong cultural norms are an essential prerequisite for co-operation occurring within an organization. It is believed that this strong distribution creates the conditions for trust by integrating people into the organization and thus ensuring their commitment to the organization's goals. A strong cultural unity creates a feeling of acceptance in which key benefits and efforts are seen in relation to achieving the organization's goals together. It is often emphasized that an organization needs a strong commonly shared culture specifically for achieving success in the future.

Organizations are often consulted to develop a strong unified culture. Recruiting and initiation communications, for example, are used to help the organization's new members identify and blend in with existing practices and meanings. However, success sometimes requires creating several parallel or overlapping cultures, favoring difference and diversity. Cultures create interaction, diversity, and questioning within an organization, which allows disagreements, conflicts, and dilemmas to be transformed into something that can be utilized by the organization. To constructively destroy the dominating consensus, a diversity of opinions, approaches, and cultures is needed.

According to Canadian organizational researcher Gareth Morgan, organizations can be seen as miniature models of societies with their own unique cultures and subcultures (Morgan, 1986). Cultures are historic. They emerge and develop over time by adjusting to their members, tasks, problems, and purposes, and to the changes occurring within these. The heritage of past events, people, and forms of communication influences how people interpret and react to their organizations. Expectations about the future and the endurance of the culture influence how people act and communicate with each other.

According to Morgan (1986), shared meanings, a shared understanding, and a shared speculation are all ways of describing a culture. When we talk about culture, in fact we are talking about processes of building reality that allow people to see and understand certain events, activities, objects, opinions, and situations in a clear-cut way. These structures of understanding also offer a basis for understanding one's own behavior.

Culture is a collection of values and symbols that can be different and contradictory to others or in relation to how people operate in their everyday work. Diversified organizations are more a team of different and separate subcultures than a single homogeneous and unified culture that is managed from the top down.

An organization's culture can even be seen as a form of "organized anarchy," in which the organization's subcultures are not only different but also in conflict and in nonconformity with each other in terms of values, methods, and attitudes. In organized anarchy conformity, nonconformity, and a mixture of the two are always present. Unlike a unified culture in which planned change is possible, or a culture in which change can be somewhat controlled, in organized anarchy managing change is impossible.

One culture or many? Neither view is right or wrong. Both offer alternative ways of looking at the relationships between organizations and cultures (Martin, 1992). A unified view of organizational culture can be compartmentalized alongside the other properties and resources of the organization. Just like an organization's machinery or capital, culture can be managed and changed. Culture is a part of the organization that builds the organization into a concrete organizational chart. Organizations with diverse cultures are less easy to define or compartmentalize and do not fit formal structural descriptions. Different views of cultures can be simultaneously present within an organization (Martin, 1992). These perspectives are important, as they not only create cultural interpretations, but they also, through the activities of an organization's members, direct the organization's behavior and form the structures of the organization (Aula, 2000).

Culture is created, maintained, and transferred as a result of social interaction by modeling, continuous learning, negotiating, telling stories and myths. In this way communication and culture are in continuous contact with each other, and they continuously transform each other. In a strongly unified culture, consensus is maintained and conflicts are avoided. In organizations with diverse cultures, people do not share strong similar cultural norms. Their organizations contain different and varying norms, and there is little unconscious cultural uniformity.

An organization's internal world unavoidably has multiple meanings, as its members are permeated by various institutions in the organization's environment. For many the workplace is no longer the kind of permanent foundation of life that was comparable to the traditional ideal of marriage. Instead, contemporary employment relationships, just like contemporary marriages, represent an agreement between two parties that both parties continuously reassess. Employees do not feel the same sense of duty to conform their own value structures to those of their companies; instead, the possibility for individuality is presented as an advantage when competing for capable employees. Nokia, whose values are eagerly mimicked by other Finnish companies, has crystallized this view in its statement "Respect for the individual," which was one of Nokia's five core values (as of May 2007).

Reputation necessitates mutual respect

A long-term approach and tenacity, and the ability to listen to others and interpret how they express themselves and perform their work. More attention should be paid to realizing that people do things in different ways. When these things are learned and accepted, the final result will turn out positive.

(Telecom company's product trainer describing the development of its service processes)

In addition to trust, the social sciences also highlight the force that binds communities together. This aspect has been examined especially by American sociologist Richard Sennett (2003), who argues that respect is created through recognition of interdependency within a society in which everyone is not equal. The importance of respect is felt especially when it is lacking. Sennett describes the social support systems of Western democracies, whose purpose is to balance inequality. In terms of pure economics this certainly happens—the rich pay a higher percentage of taxes, which promotes the transfer of wealth via social support systems. Why, then, does picking up a welfare check increase the sense of inequality rather than promote equality?

Sennett's answer is that social support systems attempt to instill the values of society's stronger members into its weaker members. Support systems attempt to "reform" the recipients of support, and receiving support means accepting the monitoring of a system based on the values of society's stronger members. This challenges the self-respect of weaker members, as the system is basically communicating that the community does not need the input of weaker members unless they first accept the values of the stronger members. It is no coincidence, in other words, that those in a weaker position form their own subcultures in which individuals have the possibility to be recognized as valuable members of the community. It is no coincidence that "respect" plays such a strong role in the rap music, for example, of American gang culture (Sennett, 2003).

Respect is relevant within both an organization's internal network and its external network. Actors within networks are certainly not all equal to each other. The feeling of interdependency is the basis for respect both within organizations and between cooperation partners.

A typical arena in which respect is put to the test is when management and staff are pitted against each other. In Finland, the home of tripartite cooperation, employees often end up as the weaker party, defending the communal perspective of the organization, whereas management sees the organization as an instrument (see chapter 6). We can nevertheless argue, however, that both parties have their own interests and that neither has the sole right to speak for the entire community. It is perfectly clear that workers on the factory floor have nowhere near the same possibilities to affect the fate of the managing director than vice versa. A feature of the basic nature of organizations is the unequal distribution of authority and control among individuals. There is nothing essentially good or bad about this; organizations do not work without some kind of hierarchy. The feeling of interdependency is endangered when it is forgotten that both parties need each other. When an organization succeeds, it is not self-evident that management alone deserves the praise.

Respect is maintained in part through various types of rituals. Central to these is the demonstration that participants in the ritual cannot succeed without each other. Sennett examines many of these rituals, such as the ritual of exchanging gifts among aboriginal tribes in which both parties have to downplay their own gift to the best of their abilities. This is despite the fact, or rather precisely due to the fact, that often one of the gift-givers is considerably wealthier than the other. In the language of capitalism, this is a question of aiding the poor, except here the experience of society's interdependency is emphasized above financial value. If the giver of the more expensive gift did not downplay his own gift, he would at the same time be communicating that he did not really need the less expensive gift given by the other.

Similar rituals emphasizing and building interdependency can be found almost anywhere, including within families. It is not uncommon to see a couple in which both man and woman actively support the views of the other in conversations, even without actually understanding what the other is talking about. Immaterial rewards are given to the other without thinking whether he or she deserves them. Common understanding is placed above honesty. We often find ourselves in situations where it is more important to build a social connection with another than it is to think whether he or she deserves to be rewarded.

Situations can also be seen within organizations in which the feeling of belonging is put before the pursuit of truth. For example, there are situations in which decisions are rationalized even without anyone understanding the arguments. American sociologists John Meyer and Brian Rowan (1977) have talked about rational myths that are used to explain decisions whose rational reasons cannot be found. The purpose of rational myths is to ensure the feeling that decisions are justified. If justifications cannot be found, the community creates a myth of rationality.

The feeling of interdependency that respect demands in these rituals is created from reciprocity. During the ritual, participants subject themselves to the harm that can be caused by the others, which communicates their trust in them and their need for them. Team spirit is sometimes built in exercises in which each member of the team has to fall backwards into the arms of the others. Another famous example is the monkey dance performed by Microsoft boss Steve Ballmer at a staff event. Seeing a middle-aged, slightly balding, and overweight man making a fool of himself by jumping around the stage shouting "I love this company" could have caused the audience to feel ashamed and embarrassed, in which case the boss would have humiliated himself publicly. Instead, the audience encouraged their boss by shouting and applauding. They participated in a ritual in which the boss gave his subordinates the opportunity to humiliate him, and this courage was rewarded.

It might be hard to imagine how Ballmer could have improved mutual respect through his unique performance. However, the boss of one of the world's biggest companies was held in such high esteem that most bosses would have had a hard time throwing this prestige away. Prestige is a form of immaterial capital, permission to look better than other members of the organization. By endangering his own prestige by performing his ridiculous dance, Ballmer demonstrated that he was prepared to sacrifice his prestige at least for a moment and to be judged by his staff, who in turn rewarded this brave gesture with new credibility. It was as if a new "rational myth" had been created, and everyone agreed to see the emperor's new clothes. This created a feeling of belonging and interdependency, which in turn created mutual respect.

Rituals like Ballmer's performance are complicated by measuring how genuine they are. If Nokia's present CEO Olli-Pekka Kallasvuo, a subdued lawyer type, had performed the same dance, his staff would probably have thought it too radical, as Finnish culture is more reserved. The rituals of interdependency require a truly genuine experience, and objectively predicting this is hard. It is easy to view the traditional "we're all in the same boat" speech favored by bosses as superficial and insincere. A partial solution is a long-term approach to decisions affecting employees and applying rhetoric honestly to decisions that have been made. It is hard to talk sincerely about management and staff being in the same boat if one party has just been paid millions in stock options and the other party has not.

Can respect appear in networks between organizations? In principle there are no obstacles to creating rituals between organizations that highlight codependence. However, this requires that one party subject itself to the potential harm that can be caused by the other party. This requires trust.

Good reputation is thus for companies the immaterial capital of networks. Companies both form networks and operate within various networks—in fact, companies are permeated by networks. Good reputation is capital in networks between companies and within networks. Reputation can be seen as social capital that a company can use to establish a favorable position within its networks. Reputation is connected with phenomena that promote the mutual functioning of networks, such as trust, solidarity, and respect.

We began this chapter by pointing out that organizational audiences are not uniform. They are organized into complex networks. We have demonstrated that reputation finds its way among myriad configurations of stakeholders, traveling on weak ties at unexpected speed. As organizations by their very nature are not prone to collaborate, care must be taken to build relations of trust and respect, both internal and external to the organization.

Part IV

Conclusion

Our journey is nearing its end. In our search for the source for good companies, we have crossed the terrain of reputation from extra-organizational arenas into the realm of managing the company itself. Now it is time to reflect upon what we have learned.

We began by problematizing the notion of a good company. We argued that a good company is in many ways a paradox. Contemporary organizations have to be good, look good, and perform good deeds. Yet, at the same time, truly ethical business can be seen as unethical. An ethical company easily betrays its promise of profit-making to the shareholders, while ethical actions fail to be authentic if the only underlying objective is to make profit. Despite this, most companies and other organizations strive to be "good companies"—to be an organization with a good reputation.

Companies are by their very nature geared towards instrumental good, whereas audiences want to see them as capable of having intrinsically good characteristics.

In the first part of the book, we portrayed reputation as the external component of goodness in a company. Reputation does not reside within a company but in the communicational interaction between the company and its stakeholders (figure IV.1).

Our notions can be summarized in three principles of reputation. On the one hand, reputation is something talked and told about (Smythe, Dorward, & Reback, 1992). From this perspective, reputation is produced and reformed through storytelling or in other kinds of culturally bound representations (Geertz, 1973). Reputation is thus always linked to a communicational dimension, which can be called the communication principle of reputation. On the other hand, reputation is related to an assessment of its object, which can be summarized as the evaluation principle of reputation. In addition, reputation has something that makes a difference between one object and another; this can be called the distinction principle of reputation. Through these principles, good organizational reputation necessitates functional communication networks both inside an organization and between it and its cooperation

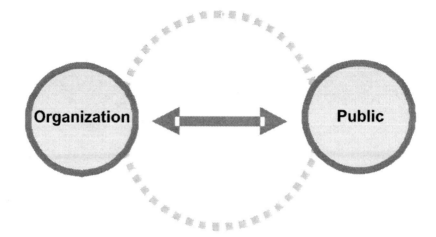

Figure IV.1 The encounter model of reputation.

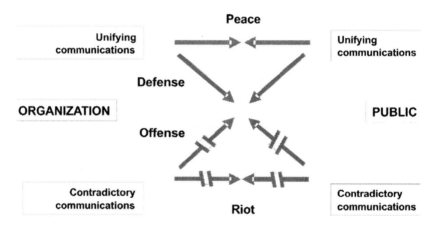

Figure IV.2 The reputational conflicts between an organization and its public.

partners. Organizations must endeavor to manage their reputation and thus affect the evaluations made of it. Moreover, an organization must develop something unique, which distinguishes it from other organizations (see Aula & Harmaakorpi, forthcoming).

We have tried to show how a company can analyze its surrounding environment of meanings and thus consciously construct a relationship with its publics in various reputation arenas; that is, how it can build reputation strategies (figure IV.2).

The reputations strategies are not necessarily solo endeavors for the

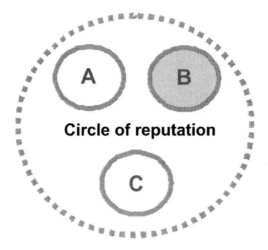

Figure IV.3 The circle of reputation.

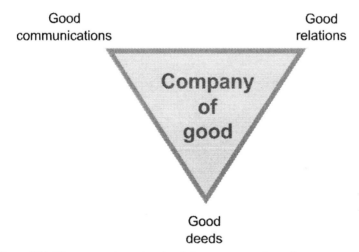

Figure IV.4 The reputation triangle of the company of good.

company of good. They can also be collective activities of fitting strategies together within networks, as we have demonstrated in chapter 5. Reputation can be shared within a "circle of reputation" (figure IV.3). This enclosing of reputation and exchanges through the circle show that reputation, while it exists primarily between organizations, also has an intraorganizational aspect, as it can be exchanged among companies and networks of companies.

As communicating is acting, reputation management cannot be galvanized as a specific organizational function or activity. To understand what creates good reputation over the long term is to understand the company of good. Thus, we have looked at the management of a company of good from an internal perspective in part III. We have presented strategic management as an activity with an intricate and paradoxical relation to what the organization does, as it reflects both the instrumental and collective aspects of organizing. We have seen the same dichotomy emerge in communication. We have looked at the networking that penetrates the core of society and organizations and considered the importance of reputation as social capital within various networks. We have analyzed the relationship of reputation to trust and respect: reputation both creates trust and respect and is created by them. From these three aspects, we have built the "triangle of good" as a sketch of the management of the company of good (figure IV.4).

Our journey is nearing its end. It is to time reflect upon the steps ahead.

Chapter 9

The company of good

Get yourself a bad reputation and no one will ever ask you for anything.

(Paul Theroux, American author)

A company cannot have values—people have values. And when you have a group of people who think alike, that appreciate the same things, it creates for the company a certain way of operating. And if the key personnel in a company are jackasses, then of course they will lead the company in a jackass direction. And if somewhere down the line someone realizes what this jackass is doing, the ethical values of this leader will gain a greater significance in the future.

(Founder and director of multimedia startup company)

The business environment of today has many names. For example, much is written these days about the information, knowledge, network, image, story, experience, attention, brand, creative and emotion society or economy. Similarly, management and leadership these days are characterized using such terms as quality, information, emotion, collectivity, intelligence, possibility, and meaning. No doubt dozens more names can also be found to describe the business environment and management. Many of these definitions disappear when we scratch their surface, or change into something that we realize was discovered a long time ago. There are as many interpretations that are received and sought as there are people to define these concepts and use them. Many have political motives.

According to our view, however, all the ways of describing the "new economy" or "new management" have in common two basic and essential assumptions. Firstly, they all emphasize and try to account for the increasingly important role of the communicative actions of companies. In other words, they all stress the distribution and production of collective meaning structures within networks that exist within and between companies. The expansion and increasing complexity of these networks mean that the hierarchies of communicational relationships are easily broken and managing the content of communications is harder. In fact, the development of communicativeness means that control is more difficult in all types of organizing.

Secondly, practically all the notions mentioned above share the idea of responsibility and good operations. This pursuit of goodness even applies to quality management and emotional management, two concepts that at first seem remote from each other. Quality is based on good operations, just like successful emotion management. Quality operations involve responsibility to customers, the promise not to instrumentalize customers into mere payers. Similarly, an emotion-manager will not instrumentalize those under him but instead relate to them as individuals who have feelings propelling them.

The emphasis on the value of communicative action is revealed in every chapter of this book—when we talk about reputation, strategy, networks, and arenas of meaning. What, then, is the "good company" that we set out to find at the start of this book? The answer is straightforward: a good company does good deeds, knows how to tell about these, and, above all, takes care of people. In other words, a good company has a good reputation. In practice this essentially means responsible business operations, professional communications, and excellent skills to handle stakeholder relations.

The strategic reputation management of the company of good

Good companies depend on their reputation. Reputation is therefore *conditio sine qua non* ("without which it could not be") for good companies. According to its definition, reputation is built on the experiences and opinions of publics. To a great extent, it is the publics that build reputation, not organizations themselves. This observation challenges the idea of reputation management as the control of public opinions and repairing experiences.

Reputation management is nevertheless at the heart of becoming good. It is essential to understand what in fact is sought to be "managed," however. Influencing opinions is always indirect and therefore problematic, albeit possible, for companies. Reputation, the stories that live in arenas about organizations, opinions, tales, anecdotes, rumors, and countless other verbal creatures cannot be shepherded.

In fact, perhaps it is misleading to talk about reputation management. The growing emphasis on communicativeness and expanding networks make control—influencing things in such a way that a predicted result is achieved—difficult or impossible. Companies can nevertheless influence all three of the basic pillars of goodness that we have described: good deeds, good communications, and good relations. Reputation management is doing good, communicating good, and "treating well" or good relations. These three aspects are tightly bound together and transform organically into each other.

This book has been about building and promoting an interpretive view of reputation management, reputation-as-*communicare*, if you will. Our intent has not been to trivialize a financial discourse on reputation, however, but to expand and extend it, as well as to provide a number of constructive observations.

Reputation management is about influencing good deeds. In many instances, the challenges of building relationships and doing good deeds are very similar, as indeed managing good deeds is essentially a question of an organization's relationship with its own personnel. An organization's most essential goodness-maker is close to the customer interface, close to the public. It cannot be emphasized enough that the most important stakeholder of any organization is its own personnel. It is even absurd to name one's own personnel as stakeholders. A good company is not much more than its people. If the people are taken away, little remains.

Managing good deeds is at the core of reputation strategies. The strategic management of goodness nevertheless differs essentially from mainstream ideas of strategic management that emphasize economic and instrumental value. The strategic management of goodness is created from communication between an organization's members and arises out of their expertise and desire to do good.

Good companies constantly have to work hard to ensure that stakeholders are satisfied and thus favorable. And good relations are built, or rather they are formed, in the communications between a company and its publics. In terms of reputation management it is essential to recognize the interactions between a company and its publics, the reputation arenas, and to be aware that different arenas require different reputation-management strategies. In terms of management this means having the wisdom to make the right decisions at the right time. The deeds and words of companies have a direct impact on the interactions within reputation arenas (figure 9.1).

The good company is not a fad

We began this book somewhat provocatively by stating that a psychopathic seed has been sown in each company already through legislation. The broad range of source material that we have used in this book—company examples, personal interviews, theories—hopefully demonstrated that companies and the people working within them are able to do good as well as bad.

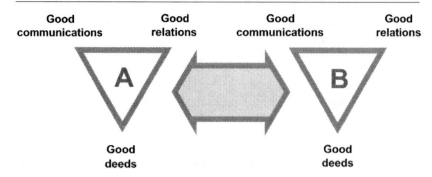

Figure 9.1 The encounter model of strategic reputation management.

A company of good is not a psychopath, even if a psychopathic company can be good in what it does. The potential for psychopathic behavior is built into all companies, especially companies that take strategic thinking seriously. A good company is nevertheless able to find its own balance between pursuing instrumental value and being a good corporate citizen.

Becoming good and being good are extremely challenging. Company operations are continuously influenced by paradoxes that are always changing. The border between good and bad is in continual movement, and nothing or no one can be absolutely good. Becoming good and staying good is by and large a relative project in multi-value societies: what is good to one person may appear differently to someone else. It is possible to create bad results with good intent. For example, the mantra about socially responsible activities contains a potential bubble. If a company's socially responsible activities and its communications do not meet the expectations of its publics (such as partners, the media, and competitors) over the long term and do not lead to a change or even strengthening in the behavior of its publics, the socially responsible dollars are basically thrown out of the window. They will certainly be wasted if the words do not correspond with the company's activities. Illusion-building, while sometimes inevitable, is always risk-inducing.

A company of good is considered to be intrinsically good, to have a good nature. Building a reputational story is ultimately about creating a human face for a company. This kind of view of intrinsic goodness is achieved in the long term when the public learns to trust that the company will continue to operate in a way that is appropriate to its good nature. There are no simple strings for a company's "good life," however. Often living a good life amidst stakeholders who want different things is a profoundly complicated project. Sometimes the world does not treat the company fairly. Nevertheless, we want to believe that each story can have a happy ending, and that goodwill and good deeds will receive their just rewards.

For the good audience

At the beginning of our book we stated our intent to present a critical look at the reputation and reputation strategies of the good company. However, we used the fifth chapter to present a new model for a company's strategic reputation management. Have we ourselves succumbed to malevolent behavior by creating tools for the needs of corporate management and communications, regardless of whether they are used to look good or to behave well?

Yes and no. A researcher should feel responsibility for how his results are used. We would like corporate executives to use our conclusions to analyze their own reputation strategies and to create new ones. Hopefully our model will be regarded as interesting and be used to provide answers to the knotty problems affecting companies today. We strongly believe that through good reputation management a company can become a good company and that being good is an essential condition for long-term success.

We do not have the possibility to control how our ideas are applied, however. We therefore wish especially that our model will be used by the public who inhabit reputational arenas: the media, citizens' groups, activists, and troublemakers. We believe that the world will become a better place through dialogue, struggle, and negotiation. We would also wish that our model will be useful to groups that are challenging managerialist corporate behavior, the blind side of market determinism, and the spread of strategic value thinking to all spheres of life.

Above all we wish that our book will be used by organizations that want to be companies of good.

Notes

1 The question concerning the good company

1. The diagnosis of a psychopathic personality is defined precisely in medical terms. See Robert Hare's *The Revised Psychopathy Checklist* (1991).

5 Reputational arenas within markets of meaning

1. "A tale of two CEOs: How public perception shapes reputations," Alan Murray, *Wall Street Journal* (Eastern edition), New York, July 12, 2006: A1.
2. "Behind Nardelli's abrupt exit; executive's fatal flaw: Failing to understand new demands on CEOs," Alan Murray, *Wall Street Journal* (Eastern edition), New York, January 4, 2007: A.
3. We got the lead for the Igglo case from a paper written by a student group at the Helsinki University, consisting of Eevi Hannula, Salla Laaksonen, Helena Mustonen, Reetta Mäkinen, and Hanna Walinen.
4. Camping it up, Emily Blick, *Contemporary Magazine*, issue 60, FOCUS: IAVNAhelsinki (*sic*).
5. Swedish newspaper *Aftonbladet* after the 2001 Lahti doping scandal.
6. We got the lead for the Paulig case from a paper written by a student group at the Helsinki University, consisting of Iivari Airaksinen, Tarja Chydenius, Minna Hyytiäinen, Leena-Mari Tanskanen, and Tarja Vilén.

6 Doing good deeds

1. Our division into instrumental goodness and goodness by nature is undeniably crude from the perspective of ethics, yet we believe it serves as a useful comparison for studying what is meant when we talk about a good company. For those interested in ethical theory, we highly recommend *Varieties of Goodness* by Von Wright (1963).
2. We owe this remark to Professor Eero Vaara.
3. *Yrityksen yhteiskuntavastuu: Mistä on kysymys (Corporate social responsibility: What is it all about?)* Confederation of Finnish Industry and Employers, Helsinki, 2001.
4. Strategic management can be considered to be the most significant successor to the tradition of scientific management—at least with regard to human nature. The school of human relations, on the other hand, was succeeded at least by the human resources school, organizational culture, and

organizational learning. See, for example, Barley & Kunda (1992); Perrow (1973).

5.   A good introduction to the scientific basis of competence literature is Barney (1991), and the most famous presentation of practical-managerial competence has to be Hamel and Prahalad (1994). A special edition of the *Strategic Management Journal* in 1996 focused on the scientific organizational concept and represents a kind of platform for the scientific strategy perspective.

6.   The amount of literature about renewal is expanding all the time, and a recommended assessment of its current state can be found in *Building Strategy from the Middle* (Floyd & Wooldridge, 2000).

7.   The most famous book about the competence perspective would be Hamel and Prahalad (1994), *Competing for the Future*, which argues in favor of "strategic intent." The basic assumptions of this book were published in 1989 in two classic articles in the *Harvard Business Review* (Hamel & Prahalad, 1989; Prahalad & Hamel, 1990). A good academic overview of the scientific strategy concept, to which the competence perspective belongs, is Floyd and Wooldridge (2000), *Building Strategy from the Middle*.

8.   One of the best-known rallying calls for the process perspective to strategic management was published in the *Strategic Management Journal*, special issue on the strategy process in 1992. Henry Mintzberg's impressive corpus of work is often cited as one of the cornerstones of the process perspective. A good introduction to his view of strategy is provided by Mintzberg & Waters (1985). Other process classics include the work of British organizational researcher Andrew Pettigrew, who has studied in particular the influence of an organization's internal politics in the strategic process. See, for example, Pettigrew (1992).

8 Managing good relationships

1.   Friedman's claim can be found in an article of his published in the *New York Times* entitled "The social responsibility of business is to increase its profits," *New York Times*, September 13, 1970.

2.   Lecture by David Hawk as visiting professor at Helsinki University of Technology in 2002.

References

Aaltonen, P., Ikävalko, H., Mantere, S., Teikari, V., Ventä, M. & Währn, H. (2001). *Tiellä strategiasta toimintaan*. Espoo: Helsinki University of Technology Research Report.

Abbott, H. P. (2002). *The Cambridge Introduction to Narrative*. Cambridge: Cambridge University Press.

Ainamo, A. & Tienari, J. (2002). The rise and fall of a local version of management consulting in Finland. In Matthias Kipping and Lars Engwall (eds), *Management Consulting: Emergence and Dynamics of a Knowledge Industry*, pp. 70–87. Oxford: Oxford University Press.

Albert, S. & Whetten, D. (1985). Organizational identity. *Research in Organizational Behavior*, 7: 263–295.

Alsop, R. (2004). *The 18 Immutable Laws of Corporate Reputation: Creating, Protecting, and Repairing Your Most Valuable Asset*. London: Kogan Page Limited.

Alvesson, M. (1990). Organization: From substance to image? *Organization Studies*, 11: 373–394.

Alvesson, M. (2000). Social identity and the problem of loyalty in knowledge intensive companies. *Journal of Management Studies* 37(8): 1101–1123.

Andrews, K. R. (1971). *The Concept of Corporate Strategy*. Homewood, IL: Irwin.

Aula, P. (1996). Chaos and the Double Function of Communication. In W. Sulis & A. Combs (eds), *Nonlinear Dynamics in Human Behaviour*, 191–206. London: World Scientific Publishing.

Aula, P. (1999). *Organisaation kaaos vai kaaoksen organisaatio: Dynaamisen organisaatioviestinnän teoria*. Helsinki: Loki-kirjat.

Aula, P. (2000). *Johtamisen kaaos vai kaaoksen johtaminen*, Helsinki: WSOY.

Aula, P. & Harmaakorpi, V. (forthcoming). An innovative milieu: A view on regional reputation building. Article accepted for publication in *Regional Studies*.

Aula, P. & Heinonen, J. (2002). *Maine: menestystekijä*, Helsinki: WSOY.

Aula, P. & Mantere, S. (2005). *Hyvä yritys: strateginen maineenhallinta*. Helsinki: WSOY.

Aula, P. & Oksanen, A. (2002). *Eepos: suomalainen Internet-unelma*. Helsinki: WSOY.

Aula, P. & Rapo, H-M. (2001). Negotiating reputations: Organizational communication and the arenas of reputation representations. Unpublished paper presented at the 5th Global Conference on Corporate Reputation, Identity and Competitiveness. Paris, May 17–19, 2001.

Aula, P. & Siira, K. (2007). Towards social complexity view on conflict, communication and leadership. In J. K. Hazy, J. A. Goldstein, & B. B. Lichtenstein (eds), *Complex Systems Leadership Theory: New Perspectives from Complexity Science on Social and Organizational Effectiveness*, pp. 367–386,]. Mansfield, MA: ISCE Publishers.

Bakan, J. (2004). *The Corporation: The Pathological Pursuit of Profit and Power*. New York: Free Press.

Balmer, J. M. T. (1998). Corporate identity and the advent of corporate marketing. *Journal of Marketing Management*, 14: 963–996.

Barley, S. R. & Kunda, G. (1992). Design and devotion: Surges of rational and normative ideologies of control in managerial discourse. *Administrative Science Quarterly*, 37: 363–399.

Barney, J. (1991). Firm resources and sustained competitive advantage. *Journal of Management*, 17: 99–120.

Barney, J. B. & Stewart, A. (2002). Organizational identity as moral philosophy: Competitive implications for diversified corporations. In M. Schultz, M. Hatch, & M. Larsen (eds), *The Expressive Organization: Linking Identity, Image and the Corporate Brand*, pp. 36–50. Oxford: Oxford University Press.

Barry, D. & Elmes, M. (1997). Strategy retold: Toward a narrative view of strategic discourse. *Academy of Management Review*, 22(2): 429–452.

Bartlett, C. A. & Ghoshal, S. (1994). Changing the role of top management: Beyond strategy to purpose. *Harvard Business Review*, 72(6): 79–88.

Beer, M. & Eisenstat, R. A. (1996). Developing an organization capable of implementing strategy and learning. *Human Relations*. 49(5): 597–619.

Bennett, R. & Kottasz, R. (2000). Practitioner perceptions of corporate reputation: An empirical investigation. *Corporate Communications*, 5(4): 224–235.

Berger, P. L. & Luckmann, T. (1966). *The Social Construction of Reality*. New York: Anchor.

Bernstein, D. (1986). *Company Image and Reality: A Critique of Corporate Communications*. London: Cassell.

Berry, J. & Keller, E. (2003). *The Influentials: One American in Ten Tells the Other Nine How to Vote, Where to Eat, and What to Buy*. New York: Free Press.

Boje, D. (1991). Organizations as storytelling networks: A study of story performance in an office-supply firm. *Administrative Science Quarterly*, 36: 106–126.

Boje, D. (1995). Stories of the storytelling organization: A postmodern analysis of Disney as Tamara-land. *Academy of Management Journal*, 38(4): 997–1035.

Boorstin, D. J. (1962). *The Image: Or What Happened to the American Dream*. New York: Atheneum.

Boulding, K. (1956). *The Image: Knowledge in Life and Society*. Ann Arbor: University of Michigan Press.

Bourdieu, P. (1986). The forms of capital. In J. G. Richardson (ed.), *Handbook for Theory and Research for the Sociology of Education*, pp. 241–258. New York: Greenwood.

Bowman, J. & Targowski, A. (1987). Modeling the communication process: The map is not the territory, *Journal of Business Communication* (fall): 21–34.

Boyce, M. E. (1995). Collective centering and collective sense-making in the stories and storytelling of one organization, *Organization Studies*, 16(1): 107–137.

Bromley, D. P. (1993). *Reputation, Image and Impression Management*. Chichester: John Wiley.

Broms, H. & Gahmberg, H. (1983). Communication to self in organizations and cultures. *Administrative Science Quarterly*, 28: 482–495.

Brown, S. P. (1995). The moderating effects of insuppliers/outsuppliers status on organizational buyer attitudes. *Journal of the Academy of Marketing Science*, 23(3): 170–181.

Bruner, J. (1996). *Actual Minds, Possible Worlds*. Cambridge, MA: Harvard University Press.

Buchanan, M. (2002). *Nexus: Small Worlds and the Groundbreaking Science of Networks*. New York: W. W. Norton.

Budd, J. Jr. (1994). How to manage corporate reputations. *Public Relations Quarterly*, 39(4): 11–15.

Burgelman, R. A. (1983). A process model of internal corporate venturing in the diversified major firm. *Administrative Science Quarterly*, 28: 223–244.

Burt, R. S. (1997). The contingent value of social capital. *Administrative Science Quarterly*, 42(2): 339–365.

Burt, R. S. (2005). *Brokerage and Closure: An Introduction to Social Capital*. Oxford: Oxford University Press.

Cappella, J. N. (1981). Mutual influence in expressive behaviour: Adult–adult and infant–adult dyadic interaction. *Psychological Bulletin*, 89: 101–132.

Carey, J. (1975). A cultural approach to communication. In J. Carey, *Communication*, vol. 2: 1–22. New York and London: Routledge.

Carey, J. (1985). *Communication as Culture: Essays on Media and Society*. Boston: Unwin Hyman, p. 18.

Carow, K. A. (1999). Underwriting spreads and reputational capital: An analysis of new corporate securities. *Journal of Financial Research*, (spring): 15–28.

Caruana, Albert (1997). Corporate reputation: concept and measurement. *Journal of Product & Brand Management*, 6(2): 109–118.

Caruana, A., Pitt, L., & Berthon, P. (1995). The organizational reputation concept: Its role and measurement. Working Paper Series. Greenlands: Henley Management College.

Cassidy, J. (2002). *dot.con: The Greatest Story Ever Sold*. New York: Harper Collins.

Castells, M. (1996). *The Rise of the Network Age*. Oxford: Blackwell.

Chandler, A. D. (1962). *Strategy and Structure: Chapters in the History of the American Enterprise*. Cambridge, MA: MIT Press.

Clegg, S., Carter, C., & Cornberger, M. (2004). Get up, I feel like being a strategy machine. *European Management Review*, 1: 29–34.

Coleman, J. (1988). Social capital in the creation of human capital. *American Journal of Sociology*, 94, 95–120.

Conrad, C. (1994). *Strategic Organizational Communication: Toward the Twenty-First Century*. New York: Harcourt Brace College Publisher.

Contractor, N. & Monge, P. R. (2002). Managing knowledge networks. *Management Communication Quarterly*, 16: 249–258.

Cornelissen, J. (2004). *Corporate Communications: Theory and Practice*. London: Sage.

Cornelissen, J. & Thorpe, R. (2002). Measuring a business school's reputation: Perspectives, problems and prospects. *Europea/n Management Journal*, 20(2): 172–178.

Crossan, M. M. & Berdrow, I. (2003). Organizational learning and strategic renewal. *Strategic Management Journal*, 24: 1087–1105.

Cruver, B. (2002). *Anatomy of Greed: The Unshredded Truth from an Enron Insider*. New York: Carroll & Graf Publishers.

Daneke, G. A. (1985). Regulation and the sociopathic firm. *Academy of Management Review*, 10: 15–20.

Daniels, T., Spiker, B., & Papa, M. (1997). *Perspectives on Organizational Communication*, 4th edition. Dubuque, IA: Brown & Benchmark.

Davies, G. (2003). *Corporate Reputation and Competitiveness*. London: Routledge.

Davies, G., Chun, R., Da Silva, R., & Roper, S. (2003). *Corporate Reputation and Competitiveness*. London: Routledge.

Courtés, J. (1991). *Analyse sémiotique du discours. De l'énoncé à l'énonciation*. Paris: Hachette.

Deetz, S. (1986). Metaphors and the discursive production and reproduction of organization. In L. Thayer (ed.), *Organizations-Communication: Emerging Perspectives*, pp. 168–182. Norwood, NJ: Ablex Publishing Co.

Dewey, J. (1997). *Democracy and Education*, p. 4. New York: The Free Press.

DiMaggio, P. J. & Powell, W. W. (1983). The iron cage revisited: Institutional isomorphism and collective rationality in organizational fields. *American Sociological Review*, 48: 147–160.

Dolphin, R. (2004). Corporate reputation: A value creating strategy. *Corporate Governance*, 4(3): 77–92.

Doorley, J. & Carcia, H. F. (2007). *Reputation Management: The Key to Successful Public Relations and Corporate Communication*. New York: Routledge.

Dowling, Grahame (2001). *Creating Corporate Reputations: Identity, Image, and Performance*. Oxford: Oxford University Press.

Dowling, Grahame R. (2006). Communicating Corporate Reputation through Stories. *California Management Review* vol. 49, no. 1, 82–100.

du Gay, P. (2000). Markets and meanings: Re-imagining organizational life. In M. Schultz, M. Hatch, & M. Larsen (eds), *The Expressive Organization: Linking Identity, Image and the Corporate Brand*, pp. 66–76. Oxford: Oxford University Press.

Durkheim, E. (1997). *Division of Labor in Society*. New York: Free Press.

Dutton, J. E. & Dukerich, J. M. (1991). Keeping an eye on the mirror: Image and identity in organizational adaptation. *Academy of Management Journal*, 34: 517–554.

Dutton, J. E., Dukerich, J. M., & Harquail, C. V. (1994). Organizational images and member identification. *Administrative Science Quarterly*, 39(2): 239–263.

Eccles, R., Newquist, S., & Schatz, R. (2007). Reputation and its risks. *Harvard Business Review*, 85(2): 104–114.

Elsbach, K. & Bhattacharya, C. B. (2001). Defining who you are by what you are not: Organizational disidentification and the National Rifle Association. *Organization Science*, 12: 393–413.

Fisher, W. R. (1987). *Human Communication as Narration: Toward a Philosophy of Reason, Value, and Action*. Columbia: University of South Carolina Press.

Fiske, J. (1990). *Introduction to Communication Studies*. London: Routledge.

Floyd, S. & Wooldridge, B. (2000). *Building Strategy from the Middle: Reconceptualizing Strategy Process*. Thousand Oaks, CA: Sage.

Fombrun, C. (1996). *Reputation: Realizing Value from the Corporate Image*. Boston, MA: Harvard Business School Press.

Fombrun, C. & Shanley, M. (1990). What's in a name? Reputation building and corporate strategy. *Academy of Management Journal*, 33: 233–258.

Fombrun, C. & Van Riel, C. (1997). The reputational landscape. *Corporate Reputation Review*, 1(1/2): 5–13.

Fombrun, C. & Van Riel, C. (2004). *Fame and Fortune*. Upper Saddle River, NJ: Prentice Hall.

Fornäs, J. (1995). *Cultural Theory and Late Modernity*. London: Sage.

Frank, R. H. (2004). *What Price for the Moral High Ground? Ethical Dilemmas in Competitive Environments*. Princeton, NJ: Princeton University Press.

Freeman, R. (1984). *Strategic Management: A Stakeholder Approach*. Boston: Pitman Publishing.

Friedman, M. (1970). The Social Responsibility of Business Is to Increase Its Profits, *New York Times*, September 13, 1970.

Fryxell, G. E. & Wang, J. (1994). The *Fortune* corporate "reputation" index: Reputation for what?, *Journal of Management*, 20(1): 1–14.

Gahmberg, H. (1986). Symbols and values of strategic managers: A semiotic approach. *Acta Academiae Oeconomicae Helsingiensis*, A:47.

Garbett, T. (1988). *How to Build a Corporation's Identity and Project its Image*. Lexington, MA: Lexington Books.

Geertz, G. (1973). *The Interpretation of Cultures: Selected Essays*. New York: Basic Books.

Gentzkow, M., & Shapiro, J. (2006). Media bias and reputation. *Journal of Political Economy*, 114: 280–316.

Gephart, R. P. (1991). Succession, sensemaking, and organizational change: A story of a deviant college president. *Journal of Organizational Change Management*, 4: 35–44.

Getz, K. A. (1997). Research in corporate political action: Integration and assessment. *Business and Society*, 36(1): 32–72.

Ghoshal, S. (2005). Bad management theories are destroying good management practices. *Academy of Management Learning and Education*, 4(1): 75–91.

Giddens, A. (1984). *Constitution of Society*. Berkeley: University of California Press.

Gilmore, J. & Pine, B. (1999). *The Experience Economy: Work Is Theatre and Every Business a Stage*. Boston, MA: Harvard Business School Press.

Gioia, D. A. & Chittipeddi, K. (1991). Sensemaking and sensegiving in strategic change initiation. *Strategic Management Journal*, 12: 433–448.

Gioia, D. A., Schultz, M., & Corley K. G. (2000). Organizational identity: Image and adaptive instability. *Academy of Management Review*, 25(1): 63–81.

Gioia, D. A. & Thomas, J. B. (1996). Identity, image, and issue interpretation: sensemaking during strategic change in academia. *Administrative Science Quarterly*, 41(3): 370–403.

Goffman, E. (1974). *Frame Analysis: An Essay on the Organization of Experience*. New York: Harper and Row.

Goffman, E. (1983). The interaction order. *American Sociological Review*, 8(1): 1–17.

Granovetter, M. S. (1973). The strength of weak ties. *American Journal of Sociology*, 78: 1360–1380.

Granovetter, M. S. (1983). The strength of weak ties: A network theory revisited. *Sociological Theory*, 1: 201–233.

Granovetter, M. S. (1985). Economic action and social structure: the problem of embeddedness. *American Journal of Sociology*, 91: 481–510.

Granovetter, M. S. (1993). The nature of economic relationships. In Richard Swedberg (ed.), *Explorations in Economic Sociology*, pp. 3–41. New York: Russell Sage Foundation.

Gray, E. R. & Balmer, J. M. (1998). Managing corporate image and corporate reputation. *Long Range Planning*, 31(5): 695–702.

Greimas, A. J. (ed.) (1987). *On Meaning: Selected Writings in Semiotic Theory*. London: Frances Pinter.

Greimas, A. J. (1991). *Narrative Semiotics and Cognitive Discourses*. London: Pinter.

Greimas, A. J. & Courtés, J. (1982). *Semiotics and Language: An Analytical Dictionary*. Bloomington: Indiana University Press.

Grunig, J. (ed.) (1992). *Excellence in Public Relations and Communication Management*. Mahwah, NJ: Lawrence Erlbaum Associates.

Grunig, J. (2002). The value of public relations can be found in relationships, only secondarily in reputation. *Maine-magazine*, February, pp. 18–22.

Grunig, J. E. & Hung, C. J. F. (2002). The effect of relationships on reputation and reputation on relationships: A cognitive, behavioral study. Paper presented at the PRSA Educator's Academy 5th Annual International, Interdisciplinary Public Relations Research Conference, Miami, FL.

Grunig, J. E. & Hunt, T. (1984). *Managing Public Relations*. New York: Holt, Rinehart and Winston.

Grunig, J. E. & Repper, F. C. (1992). Strategic management, publics and issues, in J. E. Grunig, (ed.), *Excellence in Public Relations and Communication Management*, pp. 117–157. Mahwah, NJ: Lawrence Erlbaum Associates.

Habermas, J. (1985). *Theory of Communicative Action*, Vols 1–2. Boston: Beacon Press.

Hall, S. (1973). *Encoding and Decoding in the Television Discourse*. Occasional Paper 7, University of Birmingham, Centre for Contemporary Cultural Studies. Birmingham: University of Birmingham.

Hall, S. (1980). Cultural Studies: Two paradigms. *Media, Culture and Society*, 2: 57–72.

Hall, S. (1992). *Kulttuurin ja politiikan murroksia*. Tampere: Vastapaino.

Hall, S. (ed.) (1997). *Representation: Cultural Representations and Signifying Practices*. Glasgow: Sage Publications and the Open University.

Hamel, G. & Prahalad, C. K. (1989). Strategic intent. *Harvard Business Review* (May–June): 63–76.

Hamel, G. & Prahalad, C. K. (1994). *Competing for the Future*. Boston, MA: Harvard Business School Press.

Hardy, C. & Clegg, S. R. (1996). Some dare call it power. In S. R. Clegg, C. Hardy, & W. R. Nord (eds), *Handbook of Organization Studies*, pp. 622–641. London: Sage.

Hare, R. D. (1991). *The Revised Psychopathy Checklist*. North Tonawanda, Canada: Multi-Health Systems, Inc.

Hart, S. L. (1992). An integrative framework for strategy-making processes. *Academy of Management Review* 17: 327–351.

Hatch, M. & Schultz, M. (2000). Scaling the Tower of Babel: Relational differences between identity, image, and culture in organizations. In M. Schultz, M. Hatch, & M. Larsen (eds), *The Expressive Organization: Linking Identity, Image and the Corporate Brand*, pp. 11–35. Oxford: Oxford University Press.

Haywood, R. (2005). *Corporate Reputation, the Brand & the Bottom Line: Powerful, Proven Communications Strategies for Maximizing Value*. Sterling, VA: Kogan Page.

Hazen, M.A. (1993). Towards polyphonic organization, *Journal of Organizational Change Management*, 6(5): 15–26.

Hébert, L. (2006). The veridictory square. In Louis Hébert (dir.), Signo [on-line], Rimouski (Quebec), http://www.signosemio.com.

Herbig, P. & Milewicz, J. (1995). To be or not to be . . . credible that is: A model of credibility among competing firms. *Marketing Intelligence & Planning*, 13(6): 24–33.

Jamieson, K. & Campbell, K. (1997). *The Interplay of Influence: News, Advertising, Politics, and the Mass Media*. Belmont, CA: Wadsworth Publishing Company.

Jantsch, E. (1980). *The Self-Organizing Universe: Scientific and Human Implications of the Emerging Paradigm of Evolution*, New York: Pergamon Press.

Johnson, G., Melin, L. & Whittington, R. (2003). Micro strategy and strategizing: towards an activity-based view. *Journal of Management Studies* 40: 1–22.

Kambara, K. (2000). Corporate reputation and firm performance. Unpublished article presented at the Fourth International Conference on Corporate Reputation, Identity and Competitiveness, Copenhagen, Denmark.

Kantola, A. (2002). *Markkinakuri ja managerivalta: Poliittinen hallinta Suomen 1990-luvun talouskriisissä*. Helsinki: Loki-kirjat.

Kapferer, J.-N. (1997). *Strategic Brand Management*. New York: The Free Press.

Karvonen, E. (1999). *Elämää mielikuvayhteiskunnassa. Imago ja maine menestystekijöinä myöhäismodernissa maailmassa*. Helsinki: Gaudeamus.

Karvonen, E. (2000). Imagon rakennusta vai maineenhallintaa? In P. Aula & S. Hakala (eds), *Kolmet kasvot*, pp. 51–76. Helsinki: Loki-Kirjat.

Kitchen, P. & Laurence, A. (2003). Corporate reputation: An eight-country analysis. *Corporate Reputation Review*, 6: 103–117.

Knights, D. & Morgan, G. (1991). Corporate strategy, organizations, and subjectivity: A critique. *Organization Studies*, 12: 251–273.

Korsgaard, M. A., Schweiger, D. M., & Sapienza, H. J. (1995). Building commitment, attachment, and trust in strategic decisions, *Academy of Management Journal*, 38: 60–85.

Kovačić, B. (1994). New perspectives on organizational communication. In B. Kovačić (ed.), *New Approaches to Organizational Communication*, pp. 1–39. Albany: State University of New York Press.

Larkin, J. (2002). *Strategic Reputation Risk Management*. Basingstoke: Palgrave Macmillan.

Lehtonen, M. (1996). *Merkitysten maailma*. Tampere: Vastapaino.

Leifer, R. (1989). Understanding organizational transformation using a dissipative structure model. *Human Relations*, 42: 899–916.

Levitt, T. (1965). *Industrial Purchasing Behavior: A Study of Communications Effects, Division of Research*, Boston, MA: Harvard Business School Press.

Lippitt, G. (1982). *Organization Renewal: A Holistic Approach to Organization Development*. Englewood Cliffs, NJ: Prentice-Hall.

Lyotard, J.-F. (1984). *The Postmodern Condition. A Report on Knowledge*. Minneapolis: University of Minnesota Press.

MacIntyre, A. (1985). *After Virtue*, 2nd edition. London: Duckworth.

McQuail, D. (1983). *Mass Communication Theory: An Introduction*. London: Sage.

Mantere, S. (2005). Strategic practices as enablers and disablers of championing activity. *Strategic Organization*, 3: 157–184.

Mantere, S. (forthcoming). Role expectations and middle manager strategic agency. Article accepted for publication in the *Journal of Management Studies*.

Mantere, S. & Vaara, E. (forthcoming). On the problem of participation in strategy: A critical discursive perspective. Article accepted for publication in *Organization Science*.

Mantere, S., Pajunen, K., & Lamberg, J. (forthcoming): Vices and virtues of corporate political activity. Article accepted for publication in *Business and Society*.

March, J. G. & Simon, H. A. (1958). *Organizations*. New York: John Wiley.

Marimekko Stock exchange release, August 24, 2000, www.marimekko.fi, read June 6, 2005.

Martin, J. (1992). *Cultures in Organizations: Three Perspectives*. Oxford: Oxford University Press.

Mayer, R., Davis, J., & Schoorman, F. (1995). An integrative model of organizational trust. *Academy of Management Review*, 20: 709–730.

Meyer, J. & Rowan, B. (1977). Institutionalized organizations: Formal structure as myth and ceremony. *American Journal of Sociology*, 83: 340–363.

Miles, R. E. & Snow, C. C. (1978). *Organizational Strategy, Structure, and Process*. New York: McGraw-Hill.

Milgram, S. (1967). The small-world problem. *Psychology Today*, 1: 61–67.

The Ministry of Trade and Industry (2002) Bakery industry sector report, Toimiala Media.

Mintzberg, H. (1978). Patterns in strategy formation. *Management Science*, 24: 934–948.

Mintzberg, H. (1987). The strategy concept I: Five Ps for strategy. *California Management Review*, 30(1): 11–24.

Mintzberg, H. (1990). The design school: Reconsidering the basic premises of strategic management. *Strategic Management Journal*, 11: 171–195.

Mintzberg, H. (1991). Strategic thinking as 'seeing', in J. Näsi (ed.), *Arenas of Strategic Thinking*, Foundation for Economic Education, Helsinki.

Mintzberg, H. (1994). *The Rise and Fall of Strategic Planning*. New York: Free Press.

Mintzberg, H. & Van der Heyden, L. (1999). Organigraphs: Drawing how companies really work, *Harvard Business Review* (Sept.–Oct.): 87–94

Mintzberg, H. & Waters, J. A. (1985). Of strategies, deliberate and emergent. *Strategic Management Journal*, 6: 257–272.

Mitchell, M. L., (1989). The impact of external parties on brand name capital: The 1982 Tylenol poisonings and subsequent cases. *Economic Inquiry*, 27(4): 601–618.

Morgan, G. (1986). *Images of Organization*. Newbury Park, CA: Sage.

Morley, M. (1998). *How to Manage your Global Reputation. A Guide to the Dynamics of International Public Relations*. London: Macmillan Press.

Nahapiet, J. & Ghoshal, S. (1998). Social capital and intellectual capital, and the organizational advantage. *Academy of Management Review*, 23(2): 242–266.

Näsi, J. & Aunola, M. (2001). *Yritysten strategiaprosessit: Yleinen teoria ja suomalainen käytäntö*. Helsinki: MET-kustannus.

Oakes, L. S., Townley, B., & Cooper, D. J. (1998). Business planning as pedagogy: Language and control in a changing institutional field. *Administrative Science Quarterly*, 43: 257–292.

Onnela, J.-P., Saramäki, J., Hyvönen, J., Szabó, G., Lazer, D., Kaski, K., et al. (2007). Structure and tie strengths in mobile communication networks. *Proceedings of the National Academy of Sciences*, 104(18): 7332–7336.

O'Sullivan, T., Hartley, J., Saunders, D., Montgomery, M., & Fiske, J. (1994). *Key Concepts in Communication and Cultural Studies*. London: Routledge.

Perelman, C. (1971). *The New Rhetoric: A Treatise on Argumentation*. Notre Dame, IN: University of Notre Dame Press.

Perrow, C. (1973). The short and glorious history of organization theory. *Organization Dynamics* (Summer): 2(1): 2–15.

Peters, J. (2000). *Speaking into the Air: A History of the Idea of Communication*. Chicago, IL: University of Chicago Press.

Petrick, J. A., Scherer, R. F., Brodzinski, J. D., Quinn, J. F., & Ainina, M. F. (1999). Global leadership skills and reputational capital: Intangible resources for sustainable competitive advantage. *Academy of Management Executive*, 13(1): 58–69.

Pettigrew, A. M. (1992). The character and significance of strategy process research. *Strategic Management Journal*, 13: 5–16.

Podolny, J. M. (1993). A status-based model of market competition. *American Journal of Sociology*, 98: 829–872.

Porter, M. (1980). *Competitive Strategy: Techniques for Analyzing Industries and Competitors*. New York: Free Press.

Porter, M. (1985). *Competitive Advantage: Creating and Sustaining Superior Performance*. New York: Free Press.

Porter, M. (1990). *The Competitive Advantage of Nations*. New York: Free Press.

Prahalad, C. K. & Hamel, G. (1990). The core competence of the corporation. *Harvard Business Review* (May–June): 79–91.

Pratt, M. G. & Foreman, P. O. (2000). Classifying managerial responses to multiple organizational identities. *Academy of Management Review*, 25(1): 18–42.

Prigogine, I. (1976). Order through fluctuations: Self-organization and social system. In E. Jantsch & C. H. Waddington (eds), *Evolution and Consciousness: Human Systems in Transition*, pp. 95–133. Reading, MA: Addison-Wesley.

Prigogine, I. & Stengers, I. (1984). *Order Out of Chaos*. New York: Bantam Books.

Rao, H. (1994). The social construction of reputation: certification contests, legitimation and the survival of organizations in the American automobile industry 1895–1912. *Strategic Management Journal*, 15: 29–44.

Ravasi, D. & van Rekom, J. (2003). Key issues in organizational identity and identification theory, *Corporate Reputation Review*, 6(2): 118–132.

Reinikainen, J. (2002). *Brandien brandit: kaikkien aikojen suomalaiset tuotemerkit*, pp. 131–138. Loviisa: Interpress.

Rindova, V., Petkova, A., & Kotha, S. (2007). Standing out: How new firms in emerging markets build reputation. *Strategic Organization*, 5(1): 31–70.

Rindova, V., Pollock, T., & Hayward, M. (2006). Celebrity firms: The social construction of market popularity. *Academy of Management Review*, 31(1): 50–71.

Rindova, V., Williamson, I., Petkova, A., & Sever, J. (forthcoming). Being good or being known: An empirical examination of the dimensions, antecedents, and consequences of organizational reputation. *Academy of Management Journal*.

Rousseau, D. M., Sitkin, S. B., Burt, R. S., & Camerer, C. (1998). Not so different after all: A cross-discipline view of trust. *Academy of Management Review*, 23: 393–404.

Santos, F. M. & Eisenhardt, K. M. (2005). Organizational boundaries and theories of organization. *Organization Science*, 16: 491–508.

Schein, E. (1997). *Organizational Culture and Leadership*, 2nd revised edition. San Fransisco: Jossey-Bass.

Schultz, M., Hatch, M., & Larsen, M. (eds) (2000). *The Expressive Organization: Linking Identity, Image and the Corporate Brand*. Oxford: Oxford University Press.

Sedley, D. (1998). Aretē. In E. Craig (ed.), *Routledge Encyclopedia of Philosophy*, 1: 373–374. London: Routledge.

Selznick, P. (1957). *Leadership in Administration: A Sociological Interpretation*. Berkeley: University of California Press.

Sennett, R. (2003). *Respect*. London: Penguin.

Shannon, C. & Weaver, W. (1949). *The Mathematical Theory of Communication*. Urbana: University of Illinois Press.

Shrivastava, P. (1986). Is strategic management ideological? *Journal of Management*, 12: 363–377.

Smythe, J., Dorward C., & Reback, J. (1992). *Corporate Reputation: Managing the New Strategic Asset*. London: Century Business.

Spence, A. M. (1974). *Market Signalling: Informational Transfer in Hiring and Related Screening Procedures*, Cambridge, MA: Harvard University Press.

Stacey, R. (1991). *The Chaos Frontier: Creative Strategic Control for Business*. Oxford: Butterworth-Heinemann.

Stewart, T. A. (1999). Have you got what it takes? *Fortune* (October 11), 318–320.

Tarantino, Q. (1994). *Pulp Fiction: A Quentin Tarantino Screenplay*. Los Angeles, CA]: Miramax Books.

Taylor, J. R. (1993). *Rethinking the Theory of Organizational Communication: How to Read an Organization*. Norwood, NJ: Ablex Publishing.

Thachankary, T. (1992). Organizations as texts: Hermeneutics as a model for understanding organizational change. In W. A. Passmore & R. W. Woodman (eds), *Research in Organizational Change and Development*, 6: 197–233. Greenwich, CT: JAI Press.

Thayer, L. (1978). Viestinnän tutkimus: kritiikki ja kehitysnäkymät, In E. Erholm & L. Åberg (eds), *Viestinnän virtauksia*, pp. 15–43. Keuruu: Otava.

Trompenaars, F. & Hampden-Turner, C. (1998). *Riding the Waves of Culture: Understanding Diversity in Global Business*. New York: McGraw-Hill.

Vaara, E. (2002). On the discursive construction of success/failure in narratives of post-merger integration. *Organization Studies*, 23(2): 213–250.

Van Riel, C. & Balmer, J. (1997). Corporate identity: The concept, its measurement and management. *European Journal of Marketing*, 31(5/6): 340–355.

Van Riel, C. & Fombrun, C. (2007). *Essentials of Corporate Communication: Implementing Practices for Effective Reputation Management*. New York: Routledge.

Von Wright, G. H. (1963). *Varieties of Goodness*. Oxford: Routledge & Kegan Paul.

Watzlawick, P. (1967). *Pragmatics of Human Communication: A Study of Interactional Patterns, Pathologies, and Paradoxes*. New York: W. W. Norton.

Weick, K. (1979). *The Social Psychology of Organizing*. 2nd edition. Reading, MA: Addison-Wesley.

Weick, K. (1995). *Sensemaking in Organizations*. London: Sage.

Weick, K. (2001). Substitutes of strategy. In K. Weick, *Making Sense of the Organization*, pp. 345–355. Oxford: Blackwell.

Weigelt, K. & Camerer, C. (1998). Reputation and corporate strategy: A review of recent theory and application. *Strategic Management Journal*, 9: 443–454.

Wenger, E. (1998). *Communities of Practice*. Cambridge: Cambridge University Press.

Wicks, A., Berman, S. L., & Jones, T. M. (1999). The structure of optimal trust: Moral and strategic implications. *Academy of Management Review*, 24: 99–116.

Wiio, O. A. (1968). *Ymmärretäänkö sanomasi*. Helsinki: Weilin+Göös.

Wiio, O. A. (1997). *Viestinnän perusteet*, 6–7 edition. Juva: WSOY.

Williams, F. (1984). *The New Communications*. Belmont, CA: Wadsworth.

Wittgenstein, L. (1951). *Philosophical Investigations*. Oxford: Basil Blackwell.

Yoon, E., Guffey, H. J., & Kijewski, V. (1993). The effects of information and company reputation on intentions to buy a business service. *Journal of Business Research*, 27(3): 215–228.

Zadek, S., Hojensgard, N., & Raynard, P. (2001). *Perspectives on the New Economy of Corporate Citizenship*. Copenhagen: The Copenhagen Centre.

Åberg, L. (1993). *Viestintä—tuloksen tekijä*. Helsinki: Tietopaketti.

Åberg, L. (1997). *Viestinnän strategiat*. Helsinki: Inforviestintä.

Åberg, L. (2000). *Viestinnän johtaminen*. Keuruu: Inforviestintä.

Index

Note: page numbers in *italic* indicate figures and tables.

Related titles from Routledge

PUBLIC RELATIONS THEORY II
Edited by Carl H. Botan and Vincent Hazleton

The public relations landscape has changed dramatically from what it was in 1989, when the original *Public Relations Theory* volume was published. Reflecting the substantial shifts in the intervening years, *Public Relations Theory II,* while related to the first volume, is more a new work than a revision. Editors Carl H. Botan and Vincent Hazleton have brought together key theorists and scholars in public relations to articulate the current state of public relations theory, chronicling the ongoing evolution of public relations as a field of study. The contributors to this volume represent the key figures in the discipline, and their chapters articulate the significant advances in public relations theory and research.

Like its predecessor, *Public Relations Theory II* will be influential in the future development of public relations theory. Taken as a whole, the chapters in this book will help readers develop their own sense of direction for public relations theory. *Public Relations Theory II* is an essential addition to the library of every public relations scholar, and is appropriate for use in advanced public relations theory coursework as well as for study and reference.

HB 978–0–8058–3384–3
PB 978–0–8058–3385–0

For ordering and further information please visit:
www.routledge.com

Related titles from Routledge

PUBLIC RELATIONS METRICS
Edited by Betteke van Ruler, Ana Tkalac Verčič, and Dejan Verčič

The core question for every public relations researcher is how public relations works: what it does in, to and for organizations, publics, or in the public arena. The answer to this question varies according to the methodologies the researcher uses. To address this circumstance, and to contribute toward establishing a solid research foundation, *Public Relations Metrics* goes beyond the "how to" of public relations research methods to think formally about research itself.

Chapters in this volume explore the issue of metrics in public relations from a theoretical angle—taking into account epistemology and conceptualization—and consider questions of definitions and measurement tools. Examples of actual research projects demonstrate a variety of metrics in implementation.

Responding to the basic truth that increasing knowledge requires study anchored in solid research programs, this volume makes a major step toward promoting relevant, timely, and well-considered research. It is certain to change how public relations research is conducted in the coming years, and as such it is required reading for scholars, researchers, and practitioners working in the public relations arena.

HB 978–0–8058–6272–0
PB 978–0–8058–6273–7

For ordering and further information please visit:
www.routledge.com